Novels, Readers, and Reviewers

The Shape of Hawthorne's Career

Woman's Fiction: A Guide to Novels by and about Women in America, 1820–1870

NOVELS, READERS, AND REVIEWERS

Responses to Fiction in Antebellum America

NINA BAYM

Cornell University Press

ITHACA AND LONDON

Copyright © 1984 by Cornell University

First published 1984 by Cornell University Press.
First printing, Cornell Paperbacks, 1987.

International Standard Book Number 0-8014-1709-0 (cloth)
International Standard Book Number 0-8014-9466-4 (paper)
Library of Congress Catalog Card Number 84-5033
Printed in the United States of America
Librarians: Library of Congress cataloging information
appears on the last page of the book.

The paper in this book is acid free and meets the guidelines
for permanence and durability of the Committee on Production
Guidelines for Book Longevity of the Council on Library Resources.

Contents

Preface

In this book I attempt to describe and analyze the repertory of ideas about the novel that were generally circulating in the United States before the Civil War. I have used as my sources original reviews of novels—any and all novels—appearing in the most widely read periodicals of the antebellum period. The bulk of the material comes from the years 1840–1860, for in these decades magazines, novels, and novel reviews all proliferated. Reviews were almost always anonymous, and since I am interested in a body of critical opinion rather than in individual personalities, I have usually left them so.

Studies of American attitudes toward fiction commonly use general pronouncements on literature as their sources—theoretical and pan-generic rather than practical criticism. This book, in contrast, taking the novel as its field, uses only material about novels, and usually about specific novels. In Chapter 1, I talk about the journals and reviews I use and describe my method. In Chapter 2, I show that "the novel" was itself, long before 1840, a cultural concept thought to refer meaningfully to a large number of specific literary works. In the remaining chapters I work with those aspects of the novel most frequently defined and discussed in reviews. I do not discuss the correctness of reviewer evaluations, for I am not interested in their judgments so much as in the criteria on which judgments were allegedly based.

So far as I know, no work like this exists for any genre in America (or England, for that matter). Where the United States is concerned, reviews have figured importantly in two kinds of research: reception studies and investigations of the phenomenon of literary nationalism. Both kinds tend to disregard genre, and hence to render it invisible. My assumption is that ideas about the genre of the work at hand enter into that work at every phase of its history: into its creation by the writer, its presentation by the publisher, its reception by readers, and its assessment and transmission by critics. The cultural concept of the novel, then, is an influential historical reality. I hope that the scope of my coverage will provide for some comprehensiveness in the assertions I make about the state of novel discourse in antebellum America.

Although my focus is not on major authors, my work may suggest how our current view of their historical situation might be in error. Many antebellum writers and reviewers whose names today are forgotten were, in their time, among the most immediate influences on the literary thinking and output of their contemporaries who have since achieved "major" status, and correctly understanding the impetus and intentions behind the work of a major literary figure frequently requires some familiarity with issues that only briefly animated the literary world. From the vantage point of a large number of novel reviews one can perceive the commentary of a particular author—Hawthorne, say, on romance; or Poe on unity of effect—as intended to persuade rather than to describe; or, more precisely, to persuade by pretending to describe. Again, taking the reviews of Melville's *Pierre* at face value we can only conclude that the book's immorality killed its sales. But when we note how very many novels were faulted for their immorality and how many of these were thought by reviewers to be popular *on account of* that immorality, and as we read review after review lamenting the critic's inability to affect the sales of "vicious" novels, we may have to revise this opinion.

I am grateful to the University of Illinois for a sabbatical leave and to the National Endowment for the Humanities for a fellowship, which together gave me the time to carry through this work. The library of the University of Illinois at Urbana-Champaign, which has complete holdings of most of the periodicals I used, was a wonderful place to work, and a helpful staff greatly expedited my research. A portion of Chapter 11, in different form, has appeared in *Nineteenth-Century Fiction*, and I am grateful to the editor for permission to republish it here. Lawrence Buell gave me good advice at various stages of this work; other literary historians whose publications have been most helpful to me are cited in the bibliography.

NINA BAYM

Urbana, Illinois

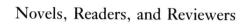

Novels, Readers, and Reviewers

I

Introduction

Our literary historians tell two stories about the novel in America before the Civil War. First, our Puritan tradition, enhanced by Scottish common sense philosophy, created an atmosphere hostile to fiction. Second, the sparseness of American social life made conventional novels difficult, even impossible, to write. Together these narrative strands conduce to a single denouement. The would-be American novelist before the Civil War was drawn or forced toward a quasi-novelistic form better suited to American imaginative space—the "romance," created in an ambience of isolation, alienation, defiance, and apology that left its traces in the work. The antebellum romances established an American tradition that persists to this day.

This powerful critical myth, which at least since the 1950s has controlled our understanding of the novel in America, does not hold up well under empirical investigation of prevailing historical conditions. For one thing, expressed hostility to fiction was no less strong in England than in America; much of what Americans wrote and said about novels was derived from English sources. Scottish common sense philosophy should not be described as an American phenomenon. Second, the "conventional" novel at that time was only in the process of becoming conventional. Third, a great many novels were written and published in America at this time of supposed hostility to fiction, and a great many more were being read. In the American reviews of novels that form the basis of this study, about eight hundred separate titles received individual attention and about half of these were American in origin. Nor were American works received adversely by the reviewers.

On the contrary, those on the magazine staffs who set themselves up as guardians of critical integrity complained about indiscriminate puffery among reviewers rather than the opposite. The America into which Hawthorne launched *The Scarlet Letter* and Melville launched *Moby-Dick* was a nation of novel readers. The essential premise on which our history of the American novel is based, that the nation was hostile to fiction, is demonstrably incorrect.

This book attempts to chronicle actual American thinking about novels. It is based on reviews of individual novels—any novels—that appeared in major American periodicals, chiefly between 1840 and 1860. The 1840s in America were the time when the periodical press came into its own. Whereas, according to Frank Luther Mott's *History of American Magazines*, there were fewer than 125 American magazines in 1825, by 1850 there were about 600, with most of the expansion occurring in the 1840s. Many of these magazines were local or specialized in their appeal, but a few dozen, by virtue of their circulation, influence, or national scope, are properly called "major." Some journals passed the 100,000 subscriber mark in the 1850s (a number that would extrapolate to over a million today), including *Harper's*, *Godey's*, *Peterson's*, and the *Ledger*, while Horace Greeley's *Tribune* in the aggregate of daily and weekly editions surpassed 200,000 in 1858. None of the journals I have used fell below 5,000 paid subscriptions during their strong years, which would bring them into the contemporary range of *The New Yorker* and the *New York Review*. Not all of the national magazines carried novel reviews, or even book reviews, but most did. My sources are the more than two thousand novel reviews I found that make some attempt, occasionally in only a sentence but often much more, at description and evaluation. By 1850 the vocabulary available for writing about novels was extensive, flexible, and sophisticated, a sign that the novel had entered the world of intellectual discourse.

The periodicals on which I draw, ordered according to the number (not necessarily the complexity or richness) of reviews from most to least include:

1. *Godey's Lady's Book* (hereafter *Godey's*). Issued monthly in Philadelphia between 1830 and 1898; published by Louis A. Godey and edited chiefly by Godey and Sarah J. Hale. It avoid-

ed politics and current events, containing mostly stories, poems, and sketches, and had numerous engravings, colored fashion plates, patterns, recipes, and household hints. A woman's magazine with a national circulation, early issues were about thirty-two pages long, but by the 1850s a number usually ran to ninety-six pages or more. (Growth in the size of individual issues is characteristic of other journals of the period as well and is evidence, along with the increasing number of periodicals, of their success.)

2. *Peterson's Magazine* (hereafter *Peterson's*). Issued monthly in Philadelphia between 1842 and 1898, at first under other names. Published by Charles J. Peterson and edited chiefly by Peterson, but also by the popular writer Ann Sophia Stephens between 1842 and 1853. It was a woman's magazine similar in scope and appearance to *Godey's*. It made a greater point, however, of publishing work by women as well as work of interest to them, boasting from time to time that contributions in a given issue were entirely from women.

3. *Harper's New Monthly Magazine* (hereafter *Harper's*). Published monthly in New York City by Harper and Brothers publishing house from 1850 on. It began as an "eclectic" journal, that is, a magazine reprinting material published elsewhere, especially in British journals, and it popularized the serialization of fiction in America. It soon modulated to a magazine of general interest using original American contributions along with its foreign borrowings, and it featured monthly narratives of current events, foreign affairs, and literary intelligence as well as a variety of editorial features: the Editor's Table, a serious monthly editorial; the Editor's Chair, a more genial and informal editorial; and the Editor's Drawer, a potpourri of reader contributions. It was lavishly illustrated but had no women's features as such. Its issues often ran over a hundred pages; it was the most ambitious and successful journal of the decade. It led to format alterations in several of its competitors and forced some others out of business.

4. *The Literary World*. Issued weekly in New York City between February 1847 and December 1853. Published and edited chiefly by E. A. and G. L. Duyckinck, it was a successor to their literary nationalist *Arcturus* but was much less stridently nationalist in tone. It was a large-format journal of sixteen to twenty-four pages per issue, featuring a great deal of book advertising

(almost none of the other journals carried advertising), literary gossip, and numerous reviews.

5. *The Knickerbocker Magazine* (hereafter *Knickerbocker*). Published monthly in New York City from 1833 to 1865. It had many publishers and editors, most prominently Lewis Gaylord Clark from 1834 to 1860 with his brother, Willis Gaylord Clark, as associate from 1834 to 1841. A magazine of general interest for and about New Yorkers, featuring opinion, literature, and reviews; its opinions and essays were reprinted around the nation in other journals.

6. *The North American Review* (hereafter the *North American*). Published quarterly in Boston from 1815 to the twentieth century. The most "serious" American magazine, determined to establish an American intellectual presence and to lead educated public opinion. It was made up chiefly of long review essays, though in time it added a section of briefer reviews as well; its tone was scholarly (many of its contributors were academics) and its influence immense, since the editors of many other journals read it.

7. *Graham's Magazine* (hereafter *Graham's*). Published monthly in Philadelphia from 1826 to 1858. A beautifully illustrated magazine of general interest directed toward women, though with a broader scope than *Godey's* or *Peterson's*. It had many editors, most importantly George R. Graham.

8. *Putnam's Monthly Magazine* (hereafter *Putnam's*). Published monthly in New York City from 1853 to 1857 as an alternative to *Harper's* for the more highly educated. Its initial readership was based on the subscription list of the defunct Whig *American Review* (see below). The journal was discontinued in 1857, a victim of the Panic of that year, and did not resume publication until 1868.

9. *The New York Tribune* (hereafter the *Tribune*). Published daily in New York City from 1841 into the twentieth century; edited from its inception until after the Civil War by Horace Greeley. It began as a large-format four-page publication, expanding to eight and then twelve pages in the 1850s. A weekly edition, designed for the nation, carried its opinions throughout the country.

10. *The Southern Literary Messenger*. Published monthly in Richmond from 1834 to 1864 with various editors and publishers, it

attempted to speak for the educated South, addressing the North and the South.

11. *The Christian Examiner*. Published bimonthly in Boston between 1824 and 1869; a Unitarian journal, written by clergy-man contributors and specializing in lengthy reviews of theological works but containing more general review essays as well. It had various publishers and editors including William Ware (1839–1844), George Putnam (1849–1857), and Frederick Henry Hedge and Edward Everett (1857–1861).

12. *The Ladies' Repository*. Published monthly in Cincinnati between 1841 and 1876, it was the leading Methodist journal and was directed toward women. It eschewed the frivolous; its illustrations were not fashion plates or domestic scenes but landscapes and portraits of leading Methodist ministers.

13. *The New York Mirror* (hereafter the *Mirror*). Published weekly from 1823 to 1842; a lively New York City magazine widely read by editors of other journals, though its general tone and approach became dated in the 1840s.

14. *The American Review, a Whig Journal* (hereafter the *American Review*). Published monthly in New York City between 1845 and 1852, when it went down with its party. A journal of politics and current events including literary essays and some imaginative literature as well.

15. *The Home Journal*. Published weekly in New York City from 1846 to the twentieth century; between 1846 and 1864 edited chiefly by the popular magazine writer Nathaniel P. Willis. An eight- or twelve-page, large-format family-centered journal.

16. *The United States Magazine and Democratic Review* (hereafter the *Democratic Review*). Published monthly, at first in Washington and then in New York City, from 1837 to 1859. It had various editors, chiefly John Louis O'Sullivan, a friend and booster of Hawthorne's, and was a political magazine of opinion and current events. Although it published much of Hawthorne's work in the 1840s, it contained little other imaginative writing.

17. *Sartain's Union Magazine* (hereafter *Sartain's*). Published monthly in New York between 1847 and 1852. Its chief publisher was John Sartain, an engraver, and it contained more essays and features about art than any other journal of the time. It was edited chiefly by Sartain, by the popular writer Caroline

Kirkland, and by John S. Hart, a professor and compiler of anthologies. In format it resembled *Godey's* and *Peterson's*, and like them it defined its audience as mainly women. It was unable to survive the competition of these magazines and *Harper's*.

18. *The New York Review*. Published quarterly in New York City from 1837 to 1842, it was meant to attain the quality of the *North American* from a more conservative stance and had a loose Episcopalian association. It had various editors and publishers.

19. *Arthur's Home Magazine* (hereafter *Arthur's*). Published monthly in Philadelphia between 1852 and 1898, at first by Timothy Shay Arthur, a didactic writer.

20. *The Atlantic Monthly* (hereafter the *Atlantic*). Published monthly in Boston from 1857 to the twentieth century and intended as Boston's answer to *Harper's*. It had various publishers and editors, including James Russell Lowell from 1857 to 1861. Its late inaugural date explains the small number of reviews I use from this source, but from the 1860s on it was an important vehicle of critical opinion on literary works and other cultural matters.

21. *The New York Ledger* (hereafter the *Ledger*). Published weekly from 1847 to 1898, its chief editor from 1851 to 1887 was Robert Bonner. It was the nation's most popular fiction weekly, attaining a circulation of 400,000 by 1860, and featured exciting serialized novels, lively columnists, and entertaining fillers. It had a large format, running about twelve pages an issue. Book reviews appeared only occasionally, usually touting a *Ledger* contributor; Bonner explained that the periodical reviewed few books because few were worth reviewing. Little essays on fiction, however, were frequent fillers.

Taken together, these journals represent a diversity of opinions and interests. They share the characteristics, important for my study, of being general rather than specialized publications and of aiming for and achieving a wide circulation. The opinions they expressed were directed toward, but also responsive to, the views and interests of their supposed readers. Of course a review does not necessarily represent the notions of anybody except its author, and even numbers of congruent reviews may express only the opinions of a particular group of interested people. This caveat, with respect to accepting reviewer opinion as representative of public opinion more generally, was articulated by William Charvat some time ago. But novel reviewing, I have found, was directed toward readers, was conducted in constant awareness of what people were reading, and was always trying to understand the reasons for public preferences. The reviews offer guidance and correction in a way that enables us to see what they thought they were guiding and correcting.

Reviewing, like magazines themselves, began in America because it had begun in England. In the early years of the nineteenth century, reviews tended to be long and to include lengthy extracts from the books being considered. In the context of few and expensive books, these reviews served many as substitutes for reading the book itself. Between 1830 and 1840 in the United States the publishing scene changed dramatically: improvements in papermaking, typesetting, and printing machinery, along with the railroad and the steamboat, put books within the physical and financial reach of a vast segment of an increasingly literate population. The 1840s in particular were the decade of "cheap books," when, for example, a reprint of Bulwer's *Zanoni* was available for only six cents. The nature of reviewing changed: long extracts were not necessary, and reviews became more essaylike. But the very large number of reviewable books called for concision; the essay became something like a brief report.

Although a few of the journals—the *North American* and the *Christian Examiner* in particular—were from the first made up of long review essays, most journals put their reviews in a special section a few pages long at the back of each issue, along with other editorial columns. (In the 1850s such special sections were added to the *North American* and *Christian Examiner* as well.) A particularly notable book might call out an entire article or inspire an essay on the author, and occasional essays on the novel as a form also appeared in leading journals; but the preponderance of reviews were no more than a few paragraphs of commentary and assessment, and many were even briefer—a few sentences. Happily for my project, despite their brevity, many of these reviews were careful to articulate the general principles according to which they were faulting or praising a particular work.

Review sections, often set in smaller type than the rest of the journal, were arranged with the longest reviews first, descending in length to the mere notices of books received. The number of books reviewed in one issue or another of the same journal varied considerably. Novels were by no means the only kind of book reviewed; histories, biographies, memoirs, collections of letters, and books of poetry were regularly noted along with an occasional philosophic or scientific work. The resulting section of the periodical was flexible and informal, the only apparent rule being that reviewers considered only works issued by American publishers.

Because they were brief, reviews tended to be written by staff rather than occasional contributors and to be anonymous. In many instances the reviews appear to have been written by the chief editor or editors; in others one editor had particular responsibility for reviews. The editors were often engagingly frank in admitting that they had been too busy in a given month to read more than a fraction of the books on their table, or in promising a review for the next issue that never materialized, or in copying a review from a brother or sister journal. These conditions parallel those in the British journals, but a comparative study of the journals of the two nations was beyond my scope at this point, though I think it would be very rewarding to carry out. It is important to remember that the leading British journals were available in American reprints throughout this period; the *Revue des Deux Mondes* was also accessible from its inception in the early 1850s. The American reviews were not so much derivative as contributory to an ongoing discussion, for with their orientation toward American authors and readers they naturally take on a different emphasis in a transatlantic dialogue. Overall, the reviews were both less severe in their judgments and much less savage and lofty in their rhetoric than their British counterparts.

Because they were so often staff people, the reviewers are most usefully thought of as members of the group that Frank Luther Mott has called "magazinists," that is, people who were professionally engaged in producing magazines. As such they were literary people of a certain sort, different from those who hoped to support themselves by occasional or even regular contributions to magazines, and again from those who aspired to great works of literary art. There was overlap among these three categories to be sure: Ann Stephens and Caroline Kirkland, for example, were prolific contributors to many journals as well as editors; Poe divided his energies between criticism and creation; T. S. Arthur thought of his journal as promoting his didactic reputation. In the main, however, magazinists were people who wrote for the moment, did not write fiction and poetry, and did not expect their work to endure. Nor were they, in the main—though clergymen and professors put out journals—the best-educated, most cultivated, or most leisured members of American society. (Neither, for that matter, were the group of writers now thought of as "major.") In general the state of the art of reviewing was precisely that it was not an art but a service, performed because readers wanted to know about current books; if the review had previously substituted for the book, now it provided guidance about whether to buy.

The reviews in most magazines were by men, though there are significant numbers of women reviewers too. Sarah J. Hale reviewed for *Godey's*, as did her associate editor Alice Neal. Caroline Kirkland reviewed for *Sartain's*, Ann Stephens for *Peterson's*, and Nathaniel Willis's sister-in-law for his *Home Journal*. The proportion of women reviewers may be as high as 20 percent, but they are not represented in the *North American*, the *Christian Examiner, Harper's, Putnam's*, the *Atlantic*, the *Mirror, Knickerbocker*, the *Southern Literary Messenger*, and so on, even though many women published in these journals. Overall one can conclude that the proportion of reviewers who were women was notably lower than the proportion of writers who were women. The gender of a given reviewer is not immediately apparent unless a reference to "our sex" as opposed to "the fair sex" appears to give it away; and the reviewer opinions do not divide along gender lines, even where women's issues are concerned. Except for Margaret Fuller, writing for the *Tribune*, the women reviewers were not radical in their views. Where the novel's potential for forming or deforming the reader's character was at stake, to a man or woman the reviewers preferred novels enforcing Victorian ideals of duty and self-control to those favoring anarchistic, self-expressive tendencies.

My procedure in the chapters that follow is essentially to disassemble the many reviews I have read and reassemble them into one large "overreview" in a structure of eleven chapters, taking up the various topics covered in individual reviews. To give a sense of the flow of an individual review and show how it might be treated in my study, I quote in part a review from the December 1859 *Atlantic* of *Sword and Gown: A Novel*. The review gets under way by calling the work

> rather a brilliant sketch than a carefully wrought and finely finished romance. The actors are drawn in bold outlines, which it does not appear to have been the purpose of the author to fill up in the delicate manner usually deemed necessary for the development of character in fiction. But they are so vigorously drawn, and the narration is so full of power, that few readers can resist the fascination of the story, in spite of the intrusive little digressions which everywhere appear. . . . It is certainly a book in which the interest is positive, and from which the attention is seldom allowed to wander; and is, so far, a success.
>
> But there is also another relation in which it is to be considered. Without being much of a moralist, one may clearly perceive that its tone is unhealthy and its sentiment vicious. . . . Dealing with the subjects it does, it must work good or evil. . . . The moral of such a book is not a good one. The author does his best, by various arts, to make the reader look kindly upon a guilty love, and to regard with admiration those who are animated by it, notwithstanding the hero is no better at the end than he was at the opening, and the heroine is rather worse. And such is his undeniable power, that with many readers he will be too likely to carry his point.

According to the way I have organized my work, there is material in this review for nine of its chapters. In chapter 2, "The Triumph of the Novel," I could note the references to power and influence exerted by the novel as a literary type. In chapter 3 on readers I could point out the use of the word "fascination" to describe a reading experience, and the somewhat patronizing reference to readers in the last quoted sentence of the review. In chapter 4, on plot, I might note the criterion of "interest"; in chapter 5, on character, that of "filling out" as a means of characterization. (This term, borrowed from the vocabulary of art criticism, could also be noted in chapter 8, "The Novel as a Picture of Nature.") In chapter 6, on aspects of narration, I could note the disapproval of digressions; in chapter 7, on narrator presentation, the comment on an "unhealthy" tone. Chapter 9, on morality and moral tendency, could certainly avail itself of the second quoted paragraph. For chapter 11 the blurring of the distinction between the term "novel" and the term "romance" (*Sword and Gown* is subtitled "novel" but is called a "romance" in the first quoted sentence) would be useful. I would probably not use this review for chapter 12, on authors, but one might note that this anonymous work is simply assumed to have been written by a specific male human being, possessed of "undeniable power."

One who has been schooled—as I have—in the belief that "America" was for many reasons hostile to fiction, cannot but be startled at the evidence of a veritable novel industry in this country long before 1860. The small number of American fiction writers who are now called major did, evidently, have trouble supporting themselves as novelists. But the explanation for this difficulty *cannot* be hostility in the public at large to fiction in general. There was a problem with copyright that has not been adequately appreciated in a literary historical mode that deals only with the context of ideas; with no international copyright law, American publishers found it more profitable to reprint European books than to encourage native authors. Virtually every essay on literary nationalism I have read from this period makes the point that lack of copyright hurt American authorship (although this was muted after Dickens turned the tables on Americans during his visit of 1846 and complained bitterly about how much money he was losing through the pirated editions of his works sold in the United States). Still, copyright is not the whole answer, since, as I have noted in my Preface, close to half the novels reviewed were American. Perhaps we have to ask again whether hostility or indifference to *Moby-Dick* really means hostility to novels in general.

If lack of copyright hurt American authors, it may have helped American readers, who had ready access to books written abroad. In the 1840s Americans could read Hawthorne and Poe stories in magazines or books; they could also read Cooper, Simms, Sedgwick, and a host of other American writers; and in addition they could (and did) read Dickens, Thackeray, Bulwer, Gaskell, C. Brontë, E. Brontë, Mrs. Gore, G. P. R. James, Miss Jewsbury, and the Honorable Caroline Norton, as well as George Sand, Balzac, Dumas (father and son), Hugo, Sue, and Bremer, and also German and Italian novelists. They read a great many American works, it is clear, but it is also clear that they had no interest in restricting their reading to native productions, a strategy that some of the more extreme literary nationalist critics advocated. This fact, far from suggesting that Americans did not like novels, implies the very opposite: that they liked them immensely. Thus Hawthorne and Melville did not introduce their works into a literary void, but addressed a market richly filled with *Pickwick Papers, The Mysteries of Paris, Vanity Fair, The Neighbors, Jane Eyre, Wuthering Heights,* and *The Hunchback of Notre Dame,* all in cheap editions within reach of most literate Americans.

The reviewers discussed a variety of aspects of fiction from many approaches, in conversation with assumed readers. Since this book means to be comprehensive, it touches on many issues without attempting to devise an overall system. Certain motifs, however, will recur. First, the novel is universally understood as a formal entity whose principle is plot narrated in prose; all other aspects of the novel are assumed to be subordinate and functional with respect to the unifying story. Second, although (perhaps because) the novel was recognized to be a woman's form—crucially to involve women readers, authors, and characters—yet reviewers continually generalized about novels in ways that made women a special case. Among many ways in which culture entered into their "formalist" discourse, their assumptions about the nature and place of women may be the most striking. Third, between (say) 1820 and 1860, reviews increasingly asked questions about the views of life contained in a novel and judged novels as superior when their views accorded with a vision of a morally governed universe. This judgmental strategy was continually in tension with the idea of the novel as an artistic form as well as with the dynamic principle of plot as the novel's formal essence. It was also the chief source of disagreement between reviewers and readers at large, as critics strove to make novels "better" by praising those that were "serious," while readers apparently continued to buy and read novels that simply told stories and consequently provided more immediate pleasure and entertainment. This disagreement has never been resolved; if anything, it has intensified. "Seriousness" has become the justification for our enterprises of academic literary criticism and literary pedagogy and is the source of their tension with the general public. Once-popular books are plumbed in literature courses for their serious content, not for the sources of the enjoyment that drew people to them; novels designed to give pleasure to the smallest number of people are touted as the present age's masterpieces; readers who read novels turn to authors and works that contemporary critics never read and never refer to except with contempt. The situation is now much more polarized, and the feelings more bitter on both sides, than it was in 1850, but its outlines were emerging clearly before the Civil War, even as the novel was extolled as the literary form of the age.

2

The Triumph of the Novel

No doubt American life in the colonial, revolutionary, and early national periods was inhospitable to fiction. Religious conviction, pragmatic values, and the hardships of settlement life certainly cooperated to make fiction seem a dispensable if not shameful luxury. No doubt, too, American novelists or would-be novelists in the second quarter of the nineteenth century and beyond continued to have a hard time making a living by writing. But for American readers it appears that novels had carried the day long before 1850.

In July 1827 the *North American* described the times as an "age of novel writing." Life before novels was hard to imagine. "We of the present generation can hardly estimate our own good fortune," the reviewer said. "Thrice blessed is the man who first devised these agreeable fictions. The press daily, nay hourly, teems with works of fiction, of no contemptible quality." Less cheerfully, it observed in April 1831 that "novels have broken upon us in a deluge." Throughout the period journals testified that a huge number of novels was available. *Knickerbocker* in January 1836 referred to the "numerous attempts at novel writing with which the American press has of late been burdened," and it commented the next month that "the press is at this juncture so prolific in novels, romances, *et id genus omne*, that to give each the time it deserves for a perusal, would not only consume the entire day, but take largely from the hours usually devoted to sleep." In June 1843 it appealed to its readers, "Think, O think, ye great multitudes of novel-readers that no man can number."

The *New York Review* (July 1840) mentioned "floods" of novels. The *Ladies' Repository* (April 1843) observed that "this age is most prolific in works of fiction. Scarcely a newspaper falls under the eye that does not announce the forthcoming of a new novel"; it wrote again (May 1847) that novels "swarm America as did the locusts in Egypt"; and it used the same image two months later: novels "drop down by millions all over our land." The *American Review* (April 1843) complained about "tens of thousands of miserably written, and worsely printed novels, that have been floating, in pamphlet form, thick as autumn leaves over the country" and referred more matter-of-factly (October 1848) to the "hundreds of novels, published every year." The *Christian Examiner* wrote of a "deluge" of novels "poured upon us from all lands" and again of a "tide" of novels (March 1845, May 1845).

Harper's library of "select" novels issued its 167th volume in April 1852 (the series eventually exceeded 600 titles). The *North American* in April 1856 described "heaps of fictitious works which load the shelves of booksellers" and in October of that year echoed *Knickerbocker* of two decades earlier: "the works of novel writers follow one another in such quick succession, that an immense amount of reading is forced upon those who would keep up with the times in this branch of literature." In September 1859 the *Atlantic* noted that the British Museum had accumulated more than twenty-seven thousand novels written since the publication of *Waverley*. The *Christian Examiner* for January 1860 began a review essay on novels of the previous year with this summary statement: "novel-reading may be misused, but argument for or against it is quite worn-out and superfluous. The great supply which the last year furnished only proved the demand. In Mr. Carlyle's phrase, the 'all devouring fact' itself has eaten up and quite ended the old palaver of fine objections to it, and of fine defences of it." It went on to observe that 1859 was "emphatically a novel-writing year, and we hold it a good sign of the times that so many of its fictions are of such excellent quality."

Though much of this commentary expresses enthusiasm, the language of tide, flood, deluge, and inundation also suggests uneasiness. The novel phenomenon caught reviewers by surprise. Not only was it a new form, it was a popular one; and it was an unprecedented cultural event for the masses to be determining the shape of culture. To follow the public instead of leading it, to surrender critical judgment to the extent of permitting a low literary mode to assume cultural significance, involved critics in new and difficult professional decisions. But the tide, as their language expressed it, really could not be resisted, because successful authorship depended on selling, and novels were what the public was buying.

There are references throughout the reviews to the public appetite for novels. A writer in the *North American* for October 1823 remarked that "a Waverley novel once or twice a year has grown into such a second nature of our intellectual constitutions, that the rising generation must be at a loss to know what their elder brothers and sisters talked about, before such things existed." "We live in such a novel-reading age," *Knickerbocker* said in September 1838, "that every work of romance, possessing more than ordinary excellence, is seized on with avidity, and made popular at once." Less generously, the *Literary World* for June 24, 1848, said that "the great vice of the age in literature is the novel. The whole world is mad for this style of writing." The *Ladies' Repository* complained in April 1843 that novels "are devoured by thousands, nay millions, of men, women, and children" and in January 1845 that "the popular reading of the day consists almost entirely in works of fiction." The *Christian Examiner* (July 1843) called novels the "favorite reading of the day," and the *North American* (December 1849) described them as "the most popular mode of communication with the public."

In July 1840 the *New York Review* asserted that "for every single reader of any work purely didactic, a popular story counts its hundreds." This hardly surprising public preference for novels over lessons is frequently noted and explains in part the qualified endorsement the genre received from reviewers. Those who read novels might not read anything else. According to the *Ladies' Repository* for January 1845, "it is romance reading, more than everything else put together, that has so universally corrupted the taste of the present age. If a man writes a book—a work of profound study and solid merit, no body will read it." The *Southern Literary Messenger* for September 1849 described novel readers as "an enormous class, who have neither leisure, nor inclination, for graver and more solid studies." *Harper's* (June 1853) observed that "hundreds of readers who would sleep over a sermon, or drone over an essay, or yield a cold and barren assent to the deductions of an ethical treatise, will be startled into reflection, or won to emulation, or roused into effort, by the delineations they meet with in a tale which they opened only for the amusement of an hour." The *Christian Examiner* (September 1855) observed, with reference to Dickens's *Hard Times* and Gaskell's *North and South*, that "it is easier to read a novel than to study political economy or theology, and while there are few who are willing to toil along the hard and difficult path of truth, there are thousands ready to lounge along the broad highway."

Some reviewers claimed that the novel had lowered the level of public taste, but more commonly they recognized that public taste itself was something new, since in prior ages taste had been the prerogative of an elite. Attributing the rise of the novel to the emergence of a large class of new readers, they tended to approach it, if not as a cultural improvement, at least as a cultural opportunity. *North American*, writing on Dumas in January 1843, attributed the popularity of novels to "the increase of the reading public, consequent on the diffusion of education and the cheapness of paper and print." Six months later, reviewing novels by Fredrika Bremer, it described novel reading as "the most common recreation in civilized lands." The *Democratic Review* in July 1846 characterized novels as "a mark of an advanced state of society, as far as the masses of people are concerned."

In short, the novel was thought to have originated as the chosen reading of the newly literate masses, and its dominant position represented less a change of taste in an existing audience than a change in the makeup of the audience for the written word. "As we read these records of ministerial life," a reviewer for the *Christian Examiner* commented on novels concerning ministers, "the mind naturally reverts to olden times. . . . We see at a glance into what entirely new conditions society has fallen. Then the minister made himself felt; he was a man of power; he was far more erudite than those around him; the means of acquiring knowledge was far less than now. . . . The printing press had not achieved its present miracles of art, and public libraries were unknown" (November 1853). The minister-reviewer looks back nostalgically to a social era when books were out of public reach and the ability to own and read them conferred power and prestige. Now, in contrast, the minister is dependent on a reading public that gets its information about ministers from novels. "No department of literature has more direct bearing upon the popular mind than that of fiction" (*Sartain's*, September 1850).

If an educated elite was to reassert its role as arbiter of taste, then it had to establish some control over novels, and this effort was described as an attempt to raise their quality. An early statement of this intention appears in the *North American* for July 1825, in an essay predicting that a new type of novel, focused on ordinary life, would "become exceedingly numerous. . . . A large proportion of them will have a considerable circulation, and consequent influence upon the public opinion, taste, and morals. It follows, further, that it is the duty of reviewers to exercise a strict *surveillance* over this department of literature . . . and endeavor to give a beneficial direction to a force, that they cannot resist if they would." Speaking of and to "the wise and the good," the *Christian Examiner* (July 1843) said, "there is no case in which they are more bound to use their judgments for the benefit of the unwise, the impetuous, the unthinking, the susceptible, than in the scrutiny of the favorite reading of the day." And a reviewer in the *Home Journal* (March 24, 1855) said, "it is futile to attempt to prevent the young, and many not young, from the perusal of works of fiction. There is a powerful fascination in such productions which ensures to them multitudinous readers in this reading age. . . . Indeed, I question the utility, while I cannot but mark the utter inefficiency, of the wholesale and indiscriminate proscription of fictitious literature by many well-meaning persons. They meet a natural demand in our intellectual natures which must be gratified. They address the imagination, the most powerful and influential faculty of the mind; and, instead of denouncing everything in this class of literature, we should seek rather to select and provide pure and wholesome aliment in this form for the mental appetite of the young."

Reviewers were joined by novelists in this attempt to make better novels. And by January 1860 the *Christian Examiner* could record some success. "We doubt if readers now-a-days could be content with fiction which serves merely an idle hour's amusement. . . . It is gratifying to find the class of readers on the increase, who, while seeking genial entertainment and recreation from the novelist, will make still larger demands for wholesome sentiment, free and foodful thought, and good impulse to believing the true and doing the right." We should not mistake this praise from a Unitarian journal as referring only to pious, didactic works of fiction by sentimental American women; the remark occurs in a general review of novels including *The Virginians* and *Adam Bede* as well as works by Wilkie Collins and Charles Reade—major figures by "our" standards as well as those of the day. The reviewer was describing a perceived development in the novel's form: novel readers were becoming more sophisticated and, rather than moving on to more weighty forms of literature, were either welcoming or being persuaded to welcome a more weighty type of novel.

Along with an access of "wholesomeness," another change noted by reviewers was a diversification of subgenres; as "the novel" extended its hegemony it absorbed other types of literature and hence began to fracture internally. The tendency of the age, *Graham's* wrote in reviewing Charles Kingsley's *Hypatia* in April 1854, was to present everything in novel form. "We have political novels, representing every variety of political opinion—religious novels, to push the doctrines of every religious sect—philanthropic novels, devoted to the championship of every reform—socialist novels, philosophic novels, metaphysical novels, even railway novels. . . . The opponents of novel writing have turned novelists." The *Graham's* reviewer was not pleased with this development, considering it the proper function of the novelist "to create or imitate individual character, to invent incident, to represent manners, and to convey the cosmopolitan and comprehensive sympathies of the observer of human life." Even these criteria, however, represent an enlargement of expectations for the novel in comparison to pre-Waverley days. That more and more novels written in these years were "serious" seems certain. Otherwise, no writer who aspired to greatness could have cast ambition in the form of a novel. In effect, however, the "serious novel" developed as a subtype of a popular form, and for this to happen the novel had first to establish itself as *the* form of the times.

"Novels are one of the features of our age," *Putnam's* wrote in October 1854. "We know not what we would do without them. . . . Do you wish to instruct, to convince, to please? Write a novel! Have you a system of religion or politics or manners or social life to inculcate? Write a novel! Would you have the 'world' split its sides with laughter, or set all the damsels in the land a-breaking their hearts? Write a novel! Would you lay bare the secret workings of your own heart, or have you a friend to

whom you would render that office? Write a novel! . . . And
lastly, not least, but loftiest . . . would you make money? Then,
in Pluto's and Mammon's name! Write a novel!" The reference to
the novel as a way to wealth is not merely jocular. Discussions of
Sir Walter Scott regularly commented on the amount of money
his novels made, and clearly the chance of becoming rich as well
as famous as a novelist introduced a new element to authorship.
Indeed, the novel was responsible for a new idea of professional
authorship, and the aspiring novelist, even a "serious" one,
launched a career with expectations that owed much to the possibilities of the novel as a popular form.

Accordingly, though uneasiness about the attractiveness of the
novel is expressed in many reviews, and though a great many
novels were reviewed unfavorably, most summary statements
about the novel as a genre are finally favorable. To fly in the face
of a clear public preference would be, in America, to doubt "the
people," and this relatively few reviewers were prepared to do,
especially in journals that themselves were aspiring to mass circulation. Among the twenty-one publications that make up my
pool, only the Methodist *Ladies' Repository* took a theoretical position of hostility to the novel as a form.

This Cincinnati-based magazine announced in its second issue
(February 1841) that "in some instances a desire has been expressed for some '*good moral tales*'; but such wishes cannot be
granted. This periodical must be the vehicle of truth, and not of
tales." In January 1843 it editorialized, "nothing can be more
killing to devotion than the perusal of a book of fiction." In
March 1843 it featured an essay on novel reading that linked the
love of novels to original sin: "Our mental constitution is originally and naturally diseased. It loves undue excitement." The
measure of a novel's pernicious effect was precisely the degree to
which it afforded pleasure; that which was popular was necessarily pleasurable and necessarily evil. The habit of novel reading
would go far not only "to destroy the taste for useful studies, but
also to *destroy* the *power* of severe mental *application*." By giving
false pictures of life, novels made readers, especially young wom-
en readers, unfit "for the arduous duties and stern realities of
life" and also had a tendency "to weaken the barriers of virtue"
by "introducing impure scenes and ideas into pure minds." As
we will see, the general campaign to raise the quality of novels

involved an attempt to make them reflect the stern realities of life and hence in effect to make them less pleasurable, and criticisms like this one frequently occur with respect to particular novels. But only the *Ladies' Repository* condemned the entire genre.

At the same time, the *Ladies' Repository* constantly testified to the number of novels published and the popularity of the genre by its complaints as well as the frequency with which it published antinovel essays and editorials. And it is with more than a little amusement that one observes the appearance, in 1849, of a serial written by the editor, Rev. B. F. Tefft. This historical work, called *The Shoulder-Knot*, was thought by everybody but the editor himself to be a novel. "It is certainly gratifying," he sputtered in December 1849, "to find that there is such a general hostility to fiction, that history itself, if written with a little less than ordinary dullness, excites suspicion. . . . There seem to be some amongst us, and those of some pretensions to knowledge, who do not appear to know when they are reading facts and when fiction. . . . Because the story is somewhat romantic, they can hardly credit it as a reality." And so on. "To allay all fears, now and for ever, respecting the historical character of our story, we will here plainly say, that we have gathered our materials, by a very extensive course of reading, from more than one hundred volumes of authentic history. . . . If we know what fiction is, we never wrote a word of it in our life, and we never shall."

Whatever it was, *The Shoulder-Knot* did the *Ladies' Repository* good, as Tefft made clear in July 1852 when he announced his resignation from the editorship: "complaint was raised against my Shoulder-Knot articles, and it was roundly but childishly asserted, sometimes by persons of official consequence, and by a great many of no consequence, that a continuance of the series would infallibly break down the work. Well, reader, it is now enough to say, that the series was continued, in the face of a great deal of shallow but mischievous talk; and the result was, that, while my annual gain had then averaged about *eleven hundred a year*, the next year's *increase* was over *five thousand names*."

The journal's no longer pure stand against novels was further weakened in the 1850s by the appearance of numerous so-called religious novels that it felt obliged to notice from time to time and found difficult to condemn. And finally, in January 1859, it reviewed a novel called *The Methodist* at great length and with a full critical vocabulary. "It may be thought, however, rather a bold step, and perhaps some will say an ill-advised one, to attempt to use the emotional exercises of religion, and their various manifestations, to give interest to a romance, and to employ Methodist class meeting, love-feasts, and revivals as the machinery of a novel. But this our author has done—with all gravity and good taste—without cant or bombast or sickly sentimentalisms—and done it successfully." The issue is no longer whether religion can accommodate the novel, but whether the novel can accommodate religion.

So much for the *Ladies' Repository*, to which I have devoted this space in order to give voice to the antinovel faction in reviews of this era. It was joined by other sectarian journals, of smaller circulation; and certainly segments of the populace remained opposed to novel reading throughout the period. But in all the other periodicals in my sample, only a handful of attacks on the novel as a type can be found, and all of them before 1850. In the Unitarian *Christian Examiner* for March 1845 there is a jab at "that kind of literature of which so large a proportion is worthless, and a larger still detrimental," but this occurs in a favorable review of Fredrika Bremer's novels. Another essay in the *Christian Examiner* (May 1845) attacks cheap literature, primarily fiction, but insists "it is impossible we should be understood in these remarks as deprecating all works of imagination; pronouncing them all deleterious and immoral; opening a crusade against the whole department of fictitious composition"; rather, the complaint is only against "the abuse of this department." Another essay (January 1847) starts out as a pure attack on novels as such: "it is surprising that so many, even of the influential and conscientious, are apparently insensible to these appalling dangers; surprising, that parents and teachers of the young do not discern the sure process of corruption which goes on, under the ministry of reckless novelists, in the heart of our community." But after this opening, the essay becomes a conscientious review of seventeen current novels, many of which it praises. And though, to be sure, the *Christian Examiner* always preferred novels full of morality and uplift, this is the last attack on novels as such in its pages.

In the nonsectarian publications, hostility is even sparser. The *Southern Literary Messenger* wrote in February 1842 of the "pernicious influence of this fascinating species of productions" but limited its criticism to "highly wrought fictions," the forerunner of the "sensation novel" of the late 1850s and 1860s. In July 1843, in a review otherwise favorable to novels, the *North American* described the taste for novels as unhealthy. The *American Review* complained in May 1845 that novels "have done more than all other causes combined to corrupt our taste, and degenerate our literature." The *Literary World* for December 16, 1847, argued that, though the genre had possibilities, when one assigned literary rank by the "ordinary and average products" of a form, then "novel-writing, a field that lies open to all, and whose fruits may be gathered with less of labor and previous tillage than any other kind, is so overrun with the poorer sort of laborers, that it seems impossible to set much store by it." Note the class implications of this comment. Novels are easier to write than other forms because the genre has fewer rules to learn and master. Thus anybody can write one. Produced by the people as well as for them, the novel's origins destine it for artistic mediocrity.

Few journals were willing to adopt the antidemocratic view expressed in the *Literary World*. The novel form was much more frequently praised than censured, and it was praised for many accomplishments. The favorable note sounds as early as the second year of the *North American Review*'s publishing history; in July 1816 it wrote that modern novels (in which "fiction is brought home to daily occurrences and observations") "give the reader more freedom and play, than he is allowed in any other kind of composition." Reviewing the Waverley novels in April 1831, it rhapsodized that the novel "will embrace all that man ever did, and all that man ever knew; nothing is above it nor beneath it; it includes with perfect ease and gracefulness all varieties of science, information, profession, and character; and as it does not restrain or oppress the writer, it is not likely to change, except by improvement." In connection with Cooper's novels (January 1838) it stated simply, "to write a good novel, we hold to be one of the highest efforts of genuis." "The novel, indeed," it said in a review of *Dombey and Son* (October 1849), "is one of the most effective, if not most perfect forms of composition, through which a comprehensive mind can communicate itself to the world, exhibiting, as it may, through sentiment, incident, and character, a complete philosophy of life, and admitting a dramatic and narrative expression of the abstract principles of ethics, metaphysics, and theology. Its range is theoretically as wide and deep as man and nature. . . . It is the most difficult of all modes of composition." "The successful novel of the present day is strictly a work of art" (October 1856); "fiction has become more and more an art" (October 1859).

Other periodicals took the same line. The *New York Mirror* (April 16, 1836), listing the most eminent contemporary writers in England and America, named eighteen novelists out of a total of thirty writers. On December 28, 1839, it said, "that species of invention which alone could body forth the infinite variety of modern society—the novel—requires much peculiar to its period, and all that the mind has ever possessed of original power." The association of the novel with the age recurs in other journals. "The novel is the characteristic literary effort of the present age. It is more. It is its creature and impression" (*Southern Literary Messenger*, May 1854). "The man, who shall build in living literature a monument of this teeming nineteenth century, will find the novel a far fitter form of structure than the poem" (*Putnam's*, March 1855).

More universal claims were made for novels and novelists by many critics. "Fiction has exercised an important influence over the public from the earliest ages of the world. . . . It will not do to despise that which is so indestructible, and which everywhere exercises such powerful influence" (*Graham's*, May 1848). The *Democratic Review* in February 1852 described fiction as "a department of literature in which it is as honorable as it is difficult to excell" and referred to the "superiority of prose fictions over all other kinds of literature, in inculcating healthy truths and healthy sentiments. Nowhere else can satire be so well directed, fancies so aptly expressed, observations so effectually presented, and style so happily varied, as in fiction." *Harper's* in June 1853 said that "considered merely as artist productions, we are disposed to place the ablest and finest works of fiction in a very high rank among the achievements of human intellect," and an Easy Chair for February 1860 said flatly that "the literature of fiction is the only permanent flower of the imagination. . . . No man's nerves tingle when he hears the name of Aristotle. But to think of Fielding, and Scott, and Dickens, is like grasping a warm hand or leaning against a beating heart. . . . The scope of fiction is as broad as Life and Imagination, and its influence is finer and profounder than that of all other literature." *Harper's*, of course, was published by the house of Harper and Brothers, whose prosperity was founded on cheap issues of foreign novels. It was not disinterested, but neither was any journal that aimed for a large, general audience.

"Life offers nothing better than a good novel" (*Literary World*, July 29, 1848). The *American Review* for December 1849, discussing Jane Austen, commented that "if all literary fiction could be withdrawn and forgotten, and its renovation prohibited, the greatest part of us would be dolts, and what is worse, unfeeling, ungenerous, and under the debasing dominion of the selfishness of simple reason." In October 1854 *Putnam's* ran a major essay called "Novels; Their Meaning and Mission," which stated that these days "novels are judged as art products. . . . Novels are now, many of them, the productions of men of the highest intellectual and moral worth, and are at present more generally read, and probably exercise a greater influence than any or all other forms of literature together." The *Home Journal* (November 10, 1855) praised Dickens and Thackeray as "the two greatest artists of our time." And *Knickerbocker* (September 1859) said that novels constitute "the favorite department, at present, with both readers and writers. There are novels in every style, suited to every taste, treating of every topic, revealing all conditions of life, discussing all branches of learning, rambling through every field of speculation, ordaining the principles of Church and State as easily as the rationale of manners, demolishing and reconstructing society, penetrating all mysteries, unfolding, in short, all the facts and all the wonders of the world which have been since creation, and which shall be while destiny be accomplished. The mission of the novelist is to depict society, and when we reflect that the ideas of all thinkers, the visions of all poetic dreamers, the diverse schemes suggested by love, by ambition, by benevolence, and the multiplied hopes and purposes of all classes of persons are combined and work and ravel together in what may be called the mind of the community, it ceases to surprise us that the domain of the novelist embraces every department of human thought."

This rhetoric sublimates, elevates, or otherwise purifies the basic psychological reality of the human love for fiction, which all critics understood to be the bedrock of the novel's amazing success. "Fiction," according to the *Christian Examiner* for March

1842, "has its origins in man's dissatisfaction with the present state of things, and his yearning after something higher and better, in effort to realize those innate ideas of the beautiful, the grand, and the good, which have no counterpart in the actual world." A more secular approach appeared in the March 1850 issue of *Sartain's*, which described the love of "narratives of adventure or delineations of character" as a "passion." It was "in vain to utter general fulminations against so natural a taste. It were as wise to attempt to extinguish love, or hope, or curiosity." These three earthly passions underlie the novel's power: love for the characters, hope for their good fortune, curiosity as to the outcome of their story. "The appetite for narrative has a solid foundation in the social nature, and must endure. Works of imagination will ever find hearts eager to be made to throb with sympathy for the joys and woes, the physical and moral struggles, of humanity" (*North American*, January 1851). "There is nothing more universal than the taste for fiction, nothing in which all persons more universally agree than love for the imaginative, the marvellous, the ideal—for those incidents and traits of character which transcend the common place realities of life, and find their only home in the regions of the fancy and imagination" (*New York Ledger*, March 19, 1859). "In its essence," according to *Harper's* Easy Chair (February 1860), "story-telling is the earliest desire and the simplest instinct. . . . Fiction is a final fact of human education, and is no more to be explained or defended than the sunset or the rose."

These accounts of the love of fiction converge from different starting points. In the *Home Journal*, *Christian Examiner*, and *New York Ledger* we see a sort of idealism, where fiction is a corrective to real life; in the other journals we observe something more like realism, where fiction is faithful to real life; but both approaches root the love of fiction in social emotions. Whether these be the desire for connection with the social body or with an ideal world, they are always the yearning of self toward something beyond it.

But this is not the whole story. Throughout these statements of praise we may also note an emphasis on freedom and scope for both writer and reader, in implied contrast to other, more restrictive, literary forms. Even though relatively few of the multitude of novels read and enjoyed might reach the pinnacles of artistry envisioned in some of the reviews, almost all of them seemed to gesture toward a kind of personal enhancement. Novels, in some way, attract because they gratify the self. The hostility of the *Ladies' Repository* in this review from April 1843 is founded on such an assumption: "in a well-written fiction there is interwoven so much that is beautiful and fascinating, that young persons often feel themselves bound to the page as by enchantment. The descriptions . . . are so high wrought that they cannot fail to please. And then rare adventures by land and sea, hairbreadth escapes, sudden reverses of fortune, heart-rending separations, and miraculous meetings, in connection with high wrought portraitures of peerless beauty, and extravagant delineations of character, all have a tendency to gratify by excitement. . . . The mind becomes ungovernable."

In gratifying the self, novels foster self-love and a tendency to self-assertion that make the mind ungovernable and thus jeopardize the agencies of social and psychological control. That most readers of novels (and virtually all those who read novels only) were thought to be women and youth made particularly ominous the implications of a novel reading based on self-gratification as opposed to social feelings. Not only in the *Ladies' Repository*, but in other journals as well, reviews of individual novels showed concern about the novel's potential for creating social and personal disruption. The ideal novel would negotiate the claims of the individual writer and individual reader and of the social order: as *Knickerbocker* said, "the diverse schemes suggested by love, by ambition, by benevolence, and the multiplied hopes and purposes of all classes of persons are combined and work and ravel together in what may be called the mind of the community." In such a novel, the competing and legitimate claims of individuals and the commonality might be resolved.

Rather clearly, reviewers considered those novels superior that weighted the claims of the commonality higher than those of the individual. The preference led them to favor what would come to be called the realistic novel, the type that enforces the primacy of the social world by presenting it as natural fact. Those novels that frankly catered to individual fantasy were described, and dismissed, as less serious works. But reviewers were not alone in a preference for the socializing over the individualizing potential of novels. Many authors had an interest in seeing that "better" novels according to society's lights were written, and by no means were these authors exclusively older males, in whom the existing social structure invested power at all levels of life. It was, after all, George Eliot whose anonymous critique in the *Westminster Review* attacked "silly novels" by silly women novelists. Her comments were quoted and discussed in several American journals. *Godey's* in April 1857 quoted this segment of her essay: the silly novel's "greatest deficiencies are due hardly more to the want of intellectual power than to the want of those moral qualities that contribute to literary excellence—patient diligence, a sense of the responsibility involved in publication, and an appreciation of the sacredness of the writer's art." No schoolmaster could have said it better: the religiosity and didacticism of Eliot's idea for fiction corresponds well with the idea of the better novel held by reviewers. Here is the historical moment at which the novel becomes divided within itself, as a subgenre of inevitably limited appeal seeks to emerge from, and claim the prerogative of, the popular form. This is a trend that has continued unabated into our own time, even to the point where the "serious" novel is now openly intended to be unreadable and exists as the occasion of elite academic and critical commentary, yet anticipates a sale of millions of copies.

Indeed, from the vantage point of the contemporary scene the nineteenth-century American reviewers really appear quite broad-minded, looking favorably on a far greater number and wider range of authors than we have permitted to survive in the canon. They never assumed, though they might have feared, that popularity implied poor novelistic quality, and they were prepared to appreciate novels that fell considerably below their own sense of the highest standard. Further, and more significant, if one attempts to extract from all the varieties of praise those terms that persist, one finds a lexicon for individual novels somewhat different from those propounded in the more self-conscious and generalized descriptions of the ideal work.

The concept behind many different words seems to be something connected to *energy*. Here are phrases from the *Home Journal:* "this interesting story will enhance her reputation," "her books are always deeply interesting," "a spirited and well-wrought tale, displaying vigor and discrimination," "deeply interesting," "one of the most spirited and powerful of female novelists," "the incidents are of thrilling interest, and the characters sustained with power," "the story unfolds itself with absorbing interest." *Arthur's Home Journal*, an exponent of didactic fiction, nevertheless praised books that possessed "uncommon power," "vigor of intellectual grasp," or fertility, vigor, power, and vivacity. *Godey's*, designed for women and girls, praised Hoffman's *Grayslaer* (August 1840) as an exciting, interesting, and vigorous production "full of graphic description and stirring incidents," and *Love's Progress* as "a narrative full of interest." The phrases "full of interest" and "stirring incidents" recur in its reviews.

The *Literary World*, reviewing *The Tenant of Wildfell Hall* (August 12, 1848), saw the secret of the writer's "power" as "vigor of thought, freshness and naturalness of expression, and remarkable reality of description. No matter how untrue to life her scene or character may be, the vividness and fervor of her imagination is such that she instantly *realizes* it." The first issue of *Harper's* (June 1850) described Edward Grayson's *Standish the Puritan* as a "narrative of very considerable interest and power" and referred to the "vigor" of its satire. In January 1855 one of its reviews said that *The Lost Heiress* by E. D. E. N. Southworth depicted events with "great power" whose "vigor of conception and brilliancy of description make it one of the most readable novels of the season." The *New York Ledger* described the novels of Anne S. Stephens (June 5, 1858) as "of absorbing interest," containing dramatic fire, intense vitality, and vividness that "enchain the reader's attention."

Taking the opposite tack, *Putnam's* for November 1856 criticized four morally worthy novels for the absence of interest and power: *Household Mysteries* was "not highly exciting, and yet agreeable"; *The Fashionable Life* showed "the strongest religious sensibilities and the kindest intentions in the writer, but [was] quite destitute of originality or power"; *Helen Lincoln* possessed "few remarkable or striking qualities"; *Elmwood* was "a sensible story" that displayed "the most respectable talent without calling for much remark either in the way of praise or blame." Even in the *Christian Examiner*, the journal most consistently devoted to fiction at once decorous and weighty, these judgments appear. George Sand, it admitted, "writes always with beauty, often with singular power" (March 1847). It preferred *The Shady Side* because it had "more power and genius" than two other novels about ministers: "it seizes upon the feelings with a stronger grasp, and makes much greater demands on the reader's sympathies" (November 1853). Melville's *Israel Potter* was faulted (May 1855) because the main character "lacks those elements which arrest and enchain the reader's sympathies; and, at the best, it is only a feeble delineation of a very commonplace person."

Examples of this sort could be greatly multiplied. Whole novels, parts of novels, and novelists were assessed as vigorous or feeble, powerful or tame. Power and vigor were always good, feebleness and tameness always bad, quite independently of any other variables such as the type of novel, the acceptability of its morality, the gender of the author. Domestic fiction was usually not of the first rank because it was difficult to make powerful stories about household routine; but those who succeeded in doing so won high praise. The French novelists were fiercely excoriated because their vicious morality was conveyed in works of extraordinary power, on account of which they were hugely (and deservedly, the reviewers grimly admitted) popular. Women writers were supposed to be less capable of literary artistry because they belonged to the weaker sex. But this theoretical presumption often failed in practice: Ann Stephens, E. D. E. N. Southworth, George Sand, Charlotte Brontë, and Emily Brontë were all exceptions, and their works were praised.

What does the concept of power mean here, and why is it so favorably assessed? It was never defined or discussed, but its desirability in novels and its essential relation to their success were taken for granted. It seems to be a property of writers or texts that calls out a complementary response in readers, a response called "interest." The greater the power of the text, the greater the reader's interest, which at its height becomes enchantment, absorbtion, or fascination. Power is thus experienced as power *over* the reader; but power works by creating interest *in* the reader, so that the reader too becomes strong. Interest refers less to intellect than emotions; as the dictionary puts it, interest is "excitement of feeling, accompanying special attention to some object." The objects of interest in the novel are the story and its agents, who by virtue of their resemblance to human events and human beings have the capacity to create an interest beyond that of any other literary genre. Interest in the novel is a kind of excitement.

So the explanation for the success of the novel lies in the inherent power of the form to generate reader excitement. Novels that succeed realize their formal potential. Such a potential, it should be noted, has little to do with the additional capacity of the novel to—as the *North American* had written—embrace all that man ever did, and all that man ever knew; to include with perfect ease and gracefulness all varieties of science, information, profession, and character. Or with its capacity, according to another review in that journal, to exhibit through sentiment, incident, and character a complete philosophy of life, and to admit a dramatic and narrative expression of the abstract principles of ethics, metaphysics, and theology. These undoubted desiderata were always ancillary. And their ancillary status always left a trace of bad faith in reviews that hoped to utilize the immense popularity of the novel for "higher" aims.

3

Novel Readers and
Novel Reading

By 1850 American reviewers had accepted the novel as *the* literary art form of the nineteenth century. Its preeminence derived from its extraordinary popular appeal, which had been evident in the United States a quarter-century or more earlier. The union of popularity and artistry was something new in the history of literature: since literary art had always been the property and practice of an elite, popular modes had never before entered into critical discourse. Like other major literary forms, the novel was thought to represent the spirit of its age; and the spirit of the nineteenth century consisted of the emergence of the people as a political and cultural force. During the second quarter of the century reviewers and serious novelists introduced the concept of the "better novel." But no matter how vigorously reviewers strove to create public esteem for what they considered superior examples of this form, they could not forget—indeed, as Americans they did not want to forget—that the popular reader who had made the form had to be its final judge.

Deference to public opinion in evaluating particular novels is expressed in many reviews. The *North American*, looking back on the career of Sir Walter Scott in April 1833, recalled that when *Waverley* first appeared, "men beheld it with as much perplexity, as the out-break of a revolution. Critics were in sad straits, having nothing wherewithal to measure it . . . but the public, without asking their opinion, gave decisive judgment in its favor." *Knickerbocker*, attacking what it deemed the inflated reputation of William Gilmore Simms, asserted that "novelists, poets, composers, and all other authors whose productions appeal to the feelings, may snap their fingers at critics and reviewers, for they can neither be written up or written down. The public may be persuaded to adopt a false religion or a false theory in political economy, as they have been often; but all the reviewers in Edinburgh and Westminster could not induce them to read a dull novel or remember prosy poetry" (April 1846). Such deference exists in unresolved tension with the critics' efforts to elevate public taste. Reviewers of the time assumed that without the seal of popular approval a novel could not be put forward as a great work of art. And they also held that, though popularity was by no means in itself the test of artistic merit, one could never assume the opposite: that popularity implied poor art. The automatic correlation, in our own times, of popularity with inferiority involves a cynicism with respect to the popular mind that was not to be found among American reviewers during the 1840s and 1850s.

Although reviewers could not ultimately resolve the tension between aesthetic absolutism and a belief in the role of the people as final judges of a popular form, they did try. Their most common strategy was to suppose that the people were "rising," largely by their own efforts in an enabling society, and that their inherent instincts for quality, increasingly called out by opportunity, would make them appreciate better books as these were called to their attention. So a *Graham's* reviewer in February 1849 observed of Cornelius Mathews's *Moneypenny* that "the work is exceedingly interesting, evinces a strong grasp of character, is well written, and while it deserves and will reward the attention of the more tasteful class of readers, it will tend to give a more important, because more numerous and sensitive class, a higher notion of the requirements of romance." According to the Editor's Table in *Harper's* for November 1859, opponents of cheap literature "affirm that, were it not for this flimsy stuff, readers would take to better books. But this is a mistake. There is no sort of rivalry between the two kinds of publications. . . . It is out of this body of readers—the million—that the widening circle of those who enjoy the masters in English literature is supplied. . . . No doubt it would be desirable for a refined taste, a genuine appreciation of the best merits, to be formed without this intermediate stage of progress. But this is simply impracticable. . . . The safest rule in literature, as in government, is to believe that the people are the soundest judges and the sharpest guardians of their own interest. If left to themselves, they will not go very far astray."

This habit of accepting the people as final judges may account for the lesser severity of American as opposed to English novel reviewing, a phenomenon pointed to on both sides of the Atlantic. Even for American reviewers, however, there were two sorts of limiting case: the extremely popular novel that was trash, and the work of high quality that was clearly not likely to be popular. But a judgment about the trashiness of a fictional work almost always derived from the book's morality, so that questions of artistry could be ignored in such cases. And reviewers usually handled the work of limited appeal by showing how, for one or another reason, it was not really a novel, thus freeing it from expectations of popular success. This is how reviewers presented Longfellow's *Kavanagh* (a critical though not popular success in its day) and Melville's *Moby-Dick*, and this is how Hawthorne presented himself. The strategy was well intentioned, for it tried to ensure that nobody expecting a novel would be disappointed by getting something else. In particular instances, however, such a strategy could lead to a smaller readership. This may have happened with Melville. If authors were pretending to write novels in order to capitalize on the popularity and prestige of the genre, their intentions might be contravened by the "helpful" reviewer who was trying to ensure a fair reading for the work.

Overall, and to a much greater degree than is the case today in journalistic (and even more in academic) criticism, American reviewers of the 1840s and 1850s were sensitive to the reader who completed the novel's reality. They never lost the sense (so lacking in various current academic theories of reader response, including the concept of "interpretive communities," which in practice are composed of students reading required novels and writing about them for a grade and under professorial surveillance) that readers were autonomous beings, selecting novels by choice and for pleasure. Accordingly, too, reviewers were regularly alert (though not, on that account, necessarily correct) to questions of the make-up of the reading audience.

Novel Readers

Who, then, as the reviewers saw it, read novels? In the broadest sense, everybody read them, from the most cultivated and leisured classes on down. Just how far down the social strata the pool of novel readers was thought to go may be sensed in a comment from the conservative *New York Review* for October 1837. The reviewer was assessing Catharine Sedgwick's *Live and Let Live*, a didactic story arguing that servants should be treated like contractual employees rather than inferiors or menials. "We should not quarrel," said the review, "if the book were to be confined to the party whose failures are described. But it will be extensively read on the other side; and in its present form it is precisely the book we should wish to keep out of the hands of a numerous class of servants." Sedgwick was advised to write a companion story setting forth the obligation of servants to their "mistresses" and to bind it with *Live and Let Live* in a single volume. Obviously the reviewer believed that many members of the servant class read novels.

If everybody read novels, then the class distribution of the audience was proportional to the class distribution of the nation, hence consisting largely of "the people." Here we meet a typical American vagueness. In the *Harper's* Easy Chair on cheap literature quoted above, the use of pronouns suggests that *Harper's* did not include its own very large number of readers among the people: if left to *themselves*, *they* will not go very far astray. At times reviewers meant the working class, at other times the middle class, and at times both. Of course, social commentators in America have always been fuzzy where thinking about class is concerned, and novel critics are not cultural theorists. Ultimately, in novel criticism, the audience seems to be divided into two groups, correlated loosely with presumed class membership. First, and more numerous, were ordinary or "mere" novel readers looking for pleasure and reading for story; second, there was a small group of cultivated, discreet, intelligent, educated, tasteful, thoughtful readers who wanted something more than, but not incompatible with (reviewers hoped), the tastes of the ordinary reader. Because this smaller group was thought of as cultivated and educated, its membership was naturally drawn from a higher social class than the ordinary reader. It was the degree of education, rather than class membership, that constituted a distinction between two groups of readers.

But when novel readers were thought of as a subset of the class of general readers the question of education or class became even less important. First, some people read more novels than others; second, some people read novels to the virtual exclusion of any other kind of book. The weight of ordinary readers in the scale increased greatly if they, as novel readers, read almost nothing else and also did most of the reading: if, that is to say, the educated, tasteful lawyer or merchant read one novel each year while the ordinary reader went through fifty. Moreover, if—as reviewers sometimes seemed to fear—that educated man was not much of a reader of *anything*, then the preferences of the "ordinary" novel reader became more significant still. Essentially, it became much more important to bring more or different novels to the people who already read them than to bring new groups of readers to the novel. Reviewers had to spend much more time telling ordinary readers that some worthwhile story was nevertheless interesting than telling readers of taste that this interesting story was nevertheless worthwhile. In this way, the assumed constituency of the novel reader controlled the remarks in reviews.

Yet another aspect of the habits of ordinary novel readers implied by their fondness for reading novels was a preference for the form itself over any particular example of it. They liked to read *many* novels. This approach made it certain that no novel could be written that was so perfect as to make the form obsolete, any more than a superb dinner might mean the end of eating. Readers might, to be sure, read *Waverley* over again from time to time and enjoy it. But how much better was a *new* Waverley novel every year! In other words, the practice of novel reading tended to favor authors who were capable of producing many novels, and the novel itself developed as a form whose individual examples, no matter how beautifully crafted, had to expect to be quickly "used up." (And not because the reader had grasped the meaning of a particular novel, but because he or she wanted repetition with variation rather than a simple repetition of the novel-reading pleasure.) Since some notion of permanence has always attached to the idea of great art, this transitoriness intensified the difficulty of defining the "better novel" within the popular framework. To have a work judged the best novel of the season, or of the month, was perhaps the most an author might realistically hope for.

Other ways of classifying readers than by education or class (though not unrelated to these matters) involved age, gender, and family membership. In this excerpt from a laudatory essay on the Warner sisters from the *North American* for January 1853, such concepts can be seen. "As far as we know the early history of *The Wide, Wide World*,* it was, for some time, bought to be presented to nice little girls. . . . Elder sisters were soon found poring over the volumes, and it was very natural that mothers next should try the spell. . . . After this, papas were not very difficult to convert. . . . We are much mistaken if *The Wide, Wide World*, and *Queechy*, have not been found under the pillows of sober bachelors. . . . They were found on everybody's table, and lent from house to house." The circle widens to involve the sober bachelor at last, but its center is in the home. The novel is at home in the home's heart, with the children and the women. Though the Warners' books, being domestic fiction, were especially home centered, this connection between family and fiction is the one most frequently on the reviewers' minds. "The novel, at present, more than any other variety of literature, becomes a household book, and in some sort a member of the family" (*Knickerbocker*, December 1858). As the one form of nineteenth-century amusement that comes into the home from the outside, it is opposed to amusement that one must leave home to enjoy. "Let us not ungratefully forget," *Godey's* wrote in an Editor's Table on cheap literature (June 1853), "what vast amount of benefit these attractive productions induce, by fostering a love of purer recreation than the young would otherwise cultivate, and by withdrawing the mind from habits of questionable or decidedly pernicious influence, to the sacred precincts of domestic affection."

This connection does not mean, however, that novels functioned as the occasion for family group activities like evening

---

*The spelling, capitalization, and italicization of novel titles have been silently regularized in quoted material from reviews. In many cases books were published anonymously, identified as "by the author of . . . ," and the reviews did not mention the author's name; in some such instances I have supplied that name.

reading aloud. Instances of this use for novels are recorded in nineteenth-century diaries and letters, as is reading aloud to sick people, but reviewers mainly described reading as a solitary activity carried on in the home. The novel is passed from house to house and from reader to reader within the house, but each person reads it privately. The novel thus supports the all-important home by providing pleasures within its precincts, yet at the same time it encourages a dangerous privatism and individualism by providing a solitary, self-centered activity. If it strengthens the home against outside forces, it also weakens the social character of the home itself. In domestic ideology home is a fortress against the world and a corrective to atomistic, nonsocial human tendencies. These goals are in tension, and the home is a fragile construct. Could another fragile construct, the novel, serve the home if it encouraged social fragmentation in its interior? The question that the exciting and self-gratifying content of popular novels raises is duplicated by the isolating nature of the novel-reading activity itself. The matter becomes even more sensitive when we perceive that the two great classes of novel readers, when audience was approached from a family perspective, were the young and the female—those for whom the home is supposed to be all in all and whose domestication is what creates home in the first place. No reviewer, whatever other social, political, or religious approach he or she took, could even briefly entertain an antidomestic thought; hence the role of the novel in the lives of young people and women was an issue of great moment.

In this extract from the *Christian Examiner* for January 1847, these questions emerge clearly. "Profligacy has seldom devised a more cunning or successful scheme for laying waste the pure principles of a people, than when she sent forth her dissolute panderers, in the disguise of scribbling romancers, to enervate and demoralize, with their wretched stuff bound up between yellow covers, the strong-hearted youth of New England. . . . These seductive emissaries create artificial notions of success in life; they spread a bad taste for extravagant manners; they foster bad passions; they break the peace of happy homes; they entice the young of both sexes from the healthful and steady pursuits of the country into the city,—the wide and wicked city, where virtue loses its crown, where temptation plies a double power and all its wiliest stratagems for the stranger, where the freshest hearts are blasted and the bright hopes go out in terrible darkness." Thus where the *Godey's* reviewer sees cheap literature as enforcing the citadel of home, the *Christian Examiner* reviewer sees it as a Trojan horse. But the family is a democracy like society at large: "we are aware," the review continues, "of the difficulties that beset every effort to correct this abuse. We know how ill-advised a direct attempt at its suppression might prove, and that the very earnestness of a prohibition, either parental or civil, might only stimulate curiosity, and cause that reading to be done clandestinely, in the spirit of theft, which is now done openly. In fact, we cannot look for any sudden check to be interposed. The art of printing has been invented."

This rhetoric is more like that of our own day, and less like that of the Puritan era, than might at first glance be supposed. It attributes no more than weakness to the youthful mind. Depravity is an adult quality entering the home in which youth is protected and innocence preserved. The young person's response to fiction is different from the adult's, because youth is less experienced, less knowledgeable, and much more excitable and impressionable. A *Peterson's* review of *Evelyne; or, The Heart Unmasked*, said, "we question the propriety of such novels, when we remember how very young most of their readers are"; another review of a novel called *The Two Families* said that "in an age like this, when so much harm is done by improper fictions, a writer like this should be welcomed to every fireside, and receive the thanks of every parent" (August 1845; August 1852). The "danger to be apprehended" from French novels, according to the *New York Review* (August 1846), "is almost exclusively confined to the more youthful class of readers, whose imaginations are excited, and passions inflamed, by the highly-wrought pictures of sensual indulgence with which they are filled and the exuberant life with which they abound. Those of maturer age will find in their coarseness an antidote to their immorality." *The Sunshine of Gray Stone*, "carrying with it a certain quiet and pleasing interest . . . may be safely recommended to American parents" (*Arthur's*, May 1854)—not, of course, for their own reading, but for their children's. In our time such rhetoric is seldom applied to novels but is commonplace with respect to those new intruders into the home space, television and popular music.

All reviewers who distinguished youthful from mature au-

diences assumed that the mature were the wiser and better readers. Youth had less experience, greater love of pleasure, and
stronger passions. These passions were chiefly, though not exclusively, attributable to emerging sexuality. Thus the distinction between youth and adult suggested a split between body and
mind, with the youthful mind less capable of artistic discrimination because it was still enmeshed in its physical casing. The
adult stage, at which passion had presumably been mastered,
called for a more mental and consequently superior novel.

On occasion, however, youth and maturity were contrasted as
different mentalities. *Sartain's,* reviewing George Sand in November 1847, observed that "notions in reality crude and narrow, seem in the light of her genuis and expressive power, full of
generous, all-embracing humanity, and remedial wisdom. Young
and ardent minds, fascinated by her grace, her noble sentiments,
her tenderness, her sympathy with all those passionate feelings in
which so many young people believe happiness to consist, adopt
her as a leader. . . . Next to the pleasure of talking about one's-
self to a sympathizing listener, is the expression of one's secret
thoughts by another and a superior mind. It is a gratification of
egotism without the shame. . . . We cannot consider her a safe
companion for youthful or excitable minds." Here the leading
aspect of the youthful mentality is its egotism. In other reviews it
is idealism, though, interestingly, idealism and egotism are seen
as related qualities. "At sixteen," a reviewer in the *Southern Literary Messenger* commented, Lamartine's *Confidential Disclosures*
"might have enraptured us. . . . But at the period of the present
writing, we have years enough over our head and have seen
sufficient of this naughty world of ours to cause us to lay aside
some of the frivolity and nonsense of our boyhood" (June 1849).
The young prefer Dickens, but the old, "who have 'seen the
skeleton,' who know how hollow a thing life is, will choose
Thackeray; and though not yet very aged ourselves, we must
confess to being better satisfied with the realities we find in
Pendennis, than with the visionary, though beautiful creations in
most of the novels of Boz" (*Peterson's,* January 1853). Where sexuality is at issue, reviewers complain about novels that are too
adult; where mentality is at issue, they complain about novels
that are not sufficiently so. Questions we might wish to consider
about the development of better novels during the second quarter

of the nineteenth century need to be put in the context of this audience division. Did the novel get better, in reviewers' eyes, because it became less truthful and hence more adapted to its function of preserving youthful innocence, or because it became more truthful and hence more capable of initiating youth into life's realities? And in either case, what had these effects to do with the form of the novel or the purpose for which youth read novels?

The second category of ordinary novel reader besides the young was the female. Her taste was supposed to reflect a fastidious delicacy: the *American Review* assured her, for example, in April 1846 that in the works of the Vicomte d'Arlincourt "all is chaste and correct." It recommended "to the fairer portion of our readers" that they "procure and read his novels, in which they will find abundance of romantic incident, a fund of historic information, and much of the honey of sentiment, untainted by the poison of a refined sensuality." In November 1851 it judged that a book called *Sunbeams and Shadows, and Buds and Blossoms* "would be a great favorite with all lady readers. The authoress wields a graceful pen, and paints characters with no little skill. There is a fine undertone of religious sentiment and earnest feeling pervading the whole, and elevating it above the ordinary novel."

This view of the female reader is only what we would expect, but it implies a very different reader from that excitable, impressionable, sensually vulnerable youth for whose innocence the reviewers were so much concerned. Yet, since half or more of the novel-reading youth were females, these two imagined readers must be identical. Indeed, the two ideas of readership are incompatible when referring, as they do, to the same group of people. In one case the reader is attracted to, in the other repelled by, the intense, passionate, and exciting. Were the reviewers reporting on a real personality change that came over young women as they reached adulthood—one precisely opposite from that which came over young men? There is unquestionably a real gap in American Victorian thinking concerning the transition from adolescence to maturity in women. But this gap may be the result of willful blindness, a reluctance to perceive (in the particular case of novel reading) that young women were prominently among those who loved dangerous novels. Moreover, for passionate novels of dubious morality to be tremendously popular they had to be read avidly by females of all ages. Even if, however, the grown woman relinquished the beloved reading of her girlhood, it *had* been a part of it, and hence the dream of female innocence involved a measure of falsification. If novels were the nineteenth-century version of the apple in the home's Garden of Eden, then women were the great apple eaters. In this sense the prevalent ideology of domesticity was grounded in a deep, though possibly unconscious, hypocrisy. The realities of novel reading contradicted popular theories of the female character, a matter that male reviewers may not have noticed. Though it is difficult to imagine that the women reviewers completely failed to see the inconsistencies, their silence on the topic is easily understandable.

Novel Reading

However they might elaborate on this idea, all reviewers acknowledged that the basis of the novel-reading experience was interest, which might vary in intensity but could never be entirely forgone and which, at its greatest, could be so exciting as to be painful. People liked novels because they alone among literary types produced this experience. They did so by telling stories about sympathetic, humanlike beings beset by difficulties, thus engaging curiosity and arousing suspense. Of course mimesis of some sort was at the heart of the novel, and not until much later in critical history—when theory became able to think of novels apart from readers and hence apart from affect, as well as to question the very idea of the human being—was it possible to conceive of nonrepresentational novels. At the same time, strict "realism" was not necessary for novels to be effective; indeed, as we will see, realism might well reduce interest. Mimesis thus could be thought of with no difficulty as utterly conventional and schematic, a set of gestures defining the novel's agents as human beings and their surroundings as the real world.

The heart of the experience of reading novels, the *North American* asserted as early as April 1828, lies in "the interest, the natural, irrepressible interest, which the passions of men will always take in lively descriptions of passion, the absorbing heed which their affections will render, while the world stands, to writings which address and excite them." Like calls to like, and human passions respond to their own description. "For every man recognizing in himself the elements of character delineated," *Harper's* wrote in an Easy Chair for February 1860, "recognizes also the fidelity of the picture of their inevitable operation in life—sees himself openly revealed—his secret sympathies, impulses, ambitions—his vices, his virtues, his temptations; and follows with terrible fascination the course of his undeveloped future—passes thoughtful and alarmed, and hangs back upon the very edge of sorrow and destruction."

Whether the basis of interest in the representation lay in action, in character represented by behavior, or in "the secret springs of passion," the fixed concept was that of interest. *Knickerbocker* praised Bulwer's *Zanoni* for "the deep interest which it excites" and the "curiosity awakened, stimulated, enhanced to almost painful excitement" (May 1842). Eugene Sue's *Martin the Foundling*, according to the *Democratic Review* for October 1846, "abounds in those picturesque scenes, startling incidents, and novel mysteries which, in the works of Sue, rivet the attention, and lead us on from page to page with alternations of pleasure, doubt, and thrilling expectation." *Jane Eyre* "will create a deeper interest and seize more strongly on the hearts of the reading public, than any work of fiction that has appeared since Miss Bremer's *Neighbors*. . . . The story is of singular interest, and rivets the attention to the last. . . . whoever commences it will not lay it down until the spell of enchantment is broken by the ending of the book" (*Literary World*, January 29, 1848). "An absorbing fiction," a *Peterson's* reviewer wrote of *The Divorced*, by Charlotte Bury. "No one can take up the book without perusing it breathlessly to the end." Emerson Bennett's *The Forged Will* was "a story of absorbing interest, and one that will have an immense sale. The author seizes the reader's attention, in the very first chapter, and triumphantly retains it until the very last" (both March 1847). A later *Peterson's* review speculated on the popularity of E. D. E. N. Southworth, deciding that "she owes this eminent success to the absorbing interest which she infuses into her narratives" (November 1854); another said that her *Retribution* "is one of the most intensely absorbing stories we ever read" (October 1856).

At the point where the interest of the novel became positively painful, the ordinary reader and the reviewer tended to part company. While acknowledging the inevitability of the popularity of tremendously exciting books, reviewers often felt that their educative responsibilities required them to qualify their praise. A *Southern Literary Messenger* review explained in November 1843 that the appeal of Sue's *Mysteries of Paris* lay in "its *fulness* of incident and the *intensity* of its interest" which "have procured and will procure for it thousands of readers" but "render it objectionable to a pure, moral taste." Taking a complementary approach, a *Harper's* reviewer approved of *The Watchman* because it made no appeals to "an imaginative craving for unnatural excitement" (September 1855), while the *Tribune* praised Catharine Sedgwick because she "has never appealed for the interest of her works to the morbid love of excitement" (August 15, 1857). The problem for these reviewers was to draw the line between natural and unnatural excitement, and this problem was essentially unsolvable. Only the *Ladies' Repository* with its view that *all* excitement is unnatural—or more precisely that all excitement, though natural, is a mark of original sin—could escape the issue, and it did so, inevitably, by condemning the novel genre as a reprobate form. Those reviewers who wanted to justify novel reading, and those who even more ambitiously wanted to elevate the form and claim the rank of artist for novelists, could only waffle around the agreed-on fact that the novel was based on and directed toward the secular passions. They could not finally separate aesthetic from moral value, and on many occasions morality called for a different end from that of pleasure, and hence for a different aesthetic form.

It was a feature of this pleasure, as I have already noted, that it created the desire for more novels. In January 1839 the *New York Review* referred to "those who rely on works of fiction for their intellectual food"; in April it said, "the thirst for light reading is fed and not quenched by being gratified." Reviewers often observed, with disapproval, that love of novels was itself likely to become a passion. They emphasized this point by consistently describing it, as in the review above, with metaphors drawn from bodily appetites implying physical stimulation, intoxication, and addiction. Drinking and eating were the activities most compared to novel reading. Of course the *Ladies' Repository* used this rhetoric: "rum and romances are just about equal in their power to intoxicate and stultify their victims." "The vain stories of the fugitive press . . . produce a moral intoxication. . . . The novel reader becomes little better than a lunatic, and passes his hours in dreams of rapture, or of anguish." "Man is a reading animal. . . . He will have something; and if he cannot obtain sound food, he will devour the infected and poisonous" (December 1843, September 1844, July 1847).

But the *Repository* was not alone. The *North American* referred to "multitudes of men, so-called, besides women and children, who fall, with a wolf-like appetite, on husks, which, if the animals were readers, would appear intended for creatures much lower than mankind" (January 1846); sometimes "the appetite for fiction becomes a sickly craving, from much cramming with crude, unnatural food" (January 1851). As for the popularity of foreign novels: "thousands, nay, millions of readers and writers drink from this bounteous source, and feed on this foreign aliment, till the whole complexion of their thoughts is tinged with it" (January 1852). The *Literary World* referred to French novels as "highly-spiced and unhealthy French dishes" (March 17, 1847). A *Southern Literary Messenger* review compared the effects of highly wrought fictions to "the honey gathered from the flowers of the rhododendron; it creates a madness in those who taste it" (February 1842); another said that "the rank inveterate novel readers have been stuffed to surfeiting" (August 1843).

Knickerbocker said *Howard Pinckney* had "stirring adventures, and love scenes enough to satisfy the most craving appetite" (November 1840). The *American Review* in April 1846 likened reading Eugene Sue's novels to "literary dram-drinking" and deplored the "large class of readers . . . who crave excitement and seek to stimulate their palled appetites with something highly spiced." The *Tribune* wrote of the "spiced wine" of popular modern fiction and "the taste of many readers, pampered and spiced up with all manner of heating condiments" (April 28, 1849; August 15, 1857). *Graham's* said that "the feverish power" of Bulwer's *Zanoni* "exacts a feverish interest, which is as unhealthy as it is stimulating; but this intellectual dram-drinking is now so common that the charge of morbid sentiment brought against a book operates as a puff" (August 1850). A later review referred to the "popular craving for stimulants" in the class of novels (April 1855). *Putnam's* in May 1853 referred to the "feast of fiction" and said Thackeray's was "like good sound old wine, though we have tasted them a thousand times, the actual smack upon the lips is always a new and luscious sensation." *Harper's* in April 1853 called *Villette* "a piquante luxury to the sated taste of regular readers of fiction."

Images of eating and drinking were not confined to instances of censure; on the contrary, those arguing for "wholesome" fiction did so with the same metaphors. In June 1844 *Peterson's* called for better novels: "the heads of families would do well to consider that the taste for what is called light reading is natural, nay! inevitable in youth—that it will usually gratify itself, in one way if not in another—and that the wisest course is to feed it with proper aliment instead of leaving it to 'gorge on garbage.'" The *Home Journal* for March 14, 1855, proposed that those concerned with improving public taste provide "pure and wholesome aliment in this form for the mental appetite of the young." Fiction, according to the *Literary World*, may act "as an intellectual cordial to restore the healthy action of other faculties" (June 12, 1847); we "lay Scott aside, refreshed and invigorated" (June 24, 1848); "however torpid and inactive the inventive faculty may be in any individual reader, if there be any life left in him, the administering of *Kaloolah* will be an admirable dose to rouse it into full vitality" (June 24, 1848); fiction is generally praiseworthy because it provides one's "higher faculties" with "nutriment denied them in real life" (November 24, 1849). When you read a good novel "your heart aches, your soul smiles, you feel the delight and satisfaction streaming along your nerves" (*Harper's*, May 1854); the "quiet pictures" of *Wesley* "make an agreeable and soothing impression on the mind" (*Harper's*, July 1854). *Godey's* in June 1853 described the mission of good light fiction: "to invigorate the intellect without fatiguing it," affording "that relaxation the mind requires."

In all these examples the good novel seems to have a medicinal effect, either tonic or soothing, in strong contrast to the exciting novel, which agitates and irritates. But discussion of both effects shares a conception of the novel as a substance taken into the body, there to work an effect beyond the reader's control. The good book is one that "tastes good" or "is good for you" in a physical way. Occasionally, most circumspectly, and mostly before 1850, reviewers approximated novel reading to sexual excitement, perhaps suggesting that novels gave occasion for masturbatory activities. For *Knickerbocker*, reviewing *Richard Hurdis*, "the object of novelists in general . . . appears to be to seize the public mind, and hold it with a sort of enchantment; a fascination which arises from the power which a master will exercise over the volition of inferior spirits, leading them captive, and exciting them with the stimulus they love most. Accordingly, there are no novels so saleable as those which lead the affections step by step into a sphere of irritating tumult, fevering the blood with uncontrollable sympathies, and steeping the interior man in a sea of voluptuous sensuality" (September 1838). The *American Review* commented that Sue "excites those evil impulses, which slumber in the hearts of the purest like the hidden embers within the volcano. . . . No virtuous woman can or should read the sentiments and feelings exhibited . . . without feeling the blush of shame and indignation mantel on her cheeks" (March 1846). Observe that "can or should"; in all this rhetoric of jaded appetites and stimulated curiosity we may well forget that the chief readers of fiction were supposed to be the pure of heart—the young and the female. The *Democratic Review* wrote of the "delightful involuntary thrill which the pathos of Sterne and Dickens so often produced" (October 1848); *Graham's* praised *Wesley* because "there is no attempt to produce striking effects by jerks or spasms of diction or incident" (July 1854). If women and children were what ideology held them to be, they would not be reading for the pleasures here imputed to the novel.

This description of cheap literature from the *Christian Examiner* for May 1845 certainly reads like a pamphlet on masturbation: "there are loads of books emptied daily into the market, which instead of imparting to the reader's intellect, will, or affections any healthy spring, kindling in him any pure emotion, or nerving him for any manly struggle, only enervate and defile him, eating away all the elastic energies of his being. There is just attractiveness enough in their style, or just fascination enough in the succession of incidents they narrate, to make them palatable to a diseased, unnatural appetite." The *Ladies' Repository* declared (January 1845) that popular fiction was "prostituted to the gratification of the grossest sensuality," its object "the murder of time, the dissipation of the intellectual energies, and the corruption of the heart; whose tendency is to habituate the mind to a morbid excitement which totally unfits it for healthy and rational action."

Clearly this language, whether of gustatory or sensual appetite, goes far beyond the elaboration of the submerged metaphor of literary taste. It testifies to the reviewers' belief in the compelling impact of the novel on its readers, an impact the novel seldom has in our own era of far more explicit stimulations. Both the subject matter and also the reading process itself were believed to be sources of an intense pleasure that reviewers distrusted yet had to accept as the basis of the novel's success. In order to champion a better novel, reviewers had to persuade the public to accept a different kind of pleasure as the proper base for the reading experience. The novel offered a unique opportunity for "improvement" of the people; and reviewers, being didacts at heart, eagerly seized the chance. But it was a question how far the novel might be "improved" before it lost its popular appeal. Only if readers improved along with their novels could a new interaction be established on a higher, more intellectual level. And the issue was fundamentally confused by the lack of fit between various presuppositions about the audience, especially with respect to its age and gender composition.

In retrospect it appears likely that the desire of didacts, whether critics or authors, to raise the novel above its basis in pleasure had the eventual result of splitting the genre into the popular and elite forms we know today. (Of course one could argue that "elite" fiction, distinguished by earnest seriousness, is in reality middle-class.) The deliberately elite novel, and those earlier novels that can be reconstituted as elite productions, now hold sway in the academy. The public, if it reads novels at all, continues to read for story and for pleasure verging on painful excitement. In the 1840s and 1850s that result was still in the future, however, and the golden age of the novel was thought to be dawning. Reviewers saw that age as the age of the domination of fiction by the "better novel," whereas, as it now appears, it was rather the age in which a great variety of novels—intellectual and emotive, serious and ephemeral, moral and immoral—were all widely read by the ordinary reader. Like other golden moments, it was a moment of balanced tensions rather than consensus.

On the other hand it is true that reviewers in the mid-nineteenth century, though speaking for a reading elite, were much more hospitable than their counterparts in our own day to a wide range of fiction and believed that the first test of any novel was its ability to create an unforced interest. And never—not in a single instance—did they talk about the act of reading novels as one of producing meanings, interpretations, or readings. The novel was a told story, not an expository genre; in whatever way they thought to improve the novel, the reviewers of this earlier day did not aspire to change its essential generic nature.

The closest they got to what academics take as the norm of reading fiction today—that is, interpreting it or constructing (or deconstructing) its meaning—was in discussions of the second reading, which novels occasionally merited. The second reading was a critical reading and different in kind from the first. It did permit a certain liberation from the bonds of the story. "We have not had time to read the book critically, but hurried through it for the story, by which we were led along and which does not flag at all" (*Mirror*, October 8, 1836). A critical reading was slower in pace than the first, but it was still based on pleasure and desire: "how many of the hundreds of novels, published every year, leave any impression on your mind or give you one after-thought about any character in them?" the *American Review* asked, considering *Vanity Fair* in October 1848. "Say what you will, the book draws you back to it, over and over again." One goes back for a second reading because the book's interest is not exhausted by the first; the second reading provides new *pleasures*. *Hands Not Hearts* "will bear reading twice or thrice," the *Literary World* wrote on March 9, 1850, "first, for the story, which has a dramatic terseness, and afterwards for the study of character by means of a captivating style deprived of all mannerism." *Julia Howard* is "emphatically one to be read at a sitting, for the sake of the plot; and then to reread at leisure for the sake of the style" (*Literary World*, September 14, 1850); Kingsley's *Hypatia* is "en-titled to two readings, one for its animated, stirring incident, another for the moral underneath the story" (*Literary World*, December 10, 1853). This review went on to comment that "for our own parts, we hold the story to be much the more legitimate object of the two for a writer of fiction."

The proper object of the second reading, which was agreed to be a test of the worth of the novel, was the author's artistry, appreciation of which, like the tonic or intoxicant or soothing effect of the first reading, was essentially pleasurable. "It possesses the great test of excellence, that it well sustains critical examination, revealing new beauties, upon familiar acquaintance, that were not obvious to a superficial inspection" (*Harper's* on *Leather Stocking and Silk*, August 1854). Hawthorne's tales "always deserve a double reading, one for the story and one for the art"; *Amabel* "merits reperusal as a study in the art of effective writing" (*Home Journal*, January 14, 1854; December 30, 1854). All these pleasures rose from the foundation of the novel's primary appeal as a story, and it was altogether inconceivable that the second reading could replace the first. It was also impossible to imagine a novel without readers, for if the pleasures of the novel created a sort of dependency in its audience, the novel itself was formed to the shape of reader desire and thus contained the reader as an aspect of its form.

4

Plot, the Formal Principle

The reader was an aspect of the novel's form, to these reviewers, because among literary genres the novel conformed most immediately to the shape of a human emotional experience: the action that structured the plot and the characters who carried it out interested, attracted, stimulated, intrigued, intensified, and finally satisfied such basic human drives as curiosity, affection, dislike, hope, and fear. Because works that called out these basic emotions were fun to read, people went out and bought them. The reader in the text of the nineteenth-century novel is a real person who *buys* novels and likes to read and own them. Reviewers frequently conclude reviews by advising a reader to "purchase" the novel; a pleasant physical appearance—a handsome cover, good paper, nice print—and a reasonable price frequently figure as elements in a positive review, especially in the women's magazines.

The reader was not in the text as construer of meanings, interpreter of value systems, or supplier of bridges over gaps in signification. These concepts of reader behavior lay far in the future, and they imply a profoundly different kind of activity from that assumed in nineteenth-century reviewing. For one thing, our current academic theoretical concepts of reading do not imagine it as pleasurable. It is not merely that the construction of meaning is an "academic" activity, it is even more that the concepts of reading in use today do not imagine anybody voluntarily purchasing the books she or he reads. The kind of novels that are still bought and read for pleasure are not considered worthwhile—indeed, one aim of the college literature teacher (like that

63

of some nineteenth-century reviewers) is to improve taste, to detach students from preferences for inferior works of fiction; accordingly, the activity of reading for simple pleasure receives no weight in literary-academic descriptions of reading or the reader. That this should be the fate of the novel is particularly ironic, since the reason so much contemporary critical activity centers on novels to the exclusion of other genres is precisely that, historically, the genre crowded out the others by virtue of its powerful emotional appeal.

A second important point in which the reader-concept of today's academy differs from the reader-concept of these nineteenth-century reviews is that the activity of reading was seen to take place at a much higher level of organization than the meaning-construal basis of most postmodernist criticism, including structuralist, reader-response, and deconstructive. That is, these modern theories locate the reader activity at the level of getting meanings out of individual lexical units, in understanding language at no more than the level of the sentence. Attempts to go beyond the sentence do not work very well because at least one and possibly several hierarchical layers, with their own organizational rules, have intervened. The reader in nineteenth-century novel reviews is thought to be responding to a very high level of the structure rather than to the lowest level. And of course you *must* be responding at a high level if, as a reader, your experience is controlled by the knowledge or expectation that the work you take up is in fact a novel and not another literary mode. If you ground your theory in the lexical or sentence level, that is, you cannot distinguish a novel from any other literary form, and indeed you have a theoretical apparatus to *prove* that such distinctions are untenable, regardless of what people do or say.

The classroom teacher who has not yet absorbed, or who has decided to resist, today's advanced theoretical approaches usually conceives of her or his activity as helping students learn how to get the themes out of novels; themes are taken to make the novel worthwhile, and finding them makes reading a worthwhile activity. The classroom teacher, then, is a clear descendant of those nineteenth-century reviewers who were engaged in the campaign to improve fiction. But there is one striking, perhaps all-important difference—that while nineteenth-century reviewers discriminated worthwhile from worthless fiction on the grounds of moral content (which we now call theme), they did not think of reading novels as the process of retrieving such content from the work. The promise of retrieving a moral meaning from a novel could never explain the novel's appeal—even the appeal of better fiction.

This view of reading holds whether or not the nineteenth-century reviewer was an academic (though few were). Of course, contemporary novels were never taught in the college classroom in those days. Reviewers today who write for the popular press retain much more interest in such aspects of the novel as story, character, and excitement than professors do, so that the contemporary discourse about novels is partitioned. The rather striking hostility toward the literary academy expressed in popular novel reviews and by many successful practicing novelists as well may be a reaction precisely to the methods by which novels are taught (and hence constituted for students) in the classroom. Other novelists, of course, depend on the explications of professors (and the sales to students) for what currency they have. But the results of professorial explications, ingenious as they are, all too often produce students who, believing that novels exist to embody hidden moral messages, will never read one after graduation.

No matter what kind of novel the nineteenth-century reviewer liked best, she or he invariably assumed two things. First, novels were read because they were novels and not something else. Second, novels were constituted as such by their character as invented stories of a certain length, narrated in prose. No narrative in verse, and no unnarrated story (like a play), qualified as a novel. And a minimum length, though never specified, was required if a work was to be acceptable as a novel. These limiting conditions follow from the understanding that *narrated plot* is the formal essence of the novel. An author choosing verse as the medium signaled to the reader that beauty of diction, splendor of imagery, and elevation of sentiment—in a word, matters of style and thought—were to receive more attention than in a novel. An author choosing the drama form signaled, of course, the absence of narration. The tale and "nouvelle" belonged to the same family as the novel, as house cats and lions are related, but their brevity necessarily involved radically simplified plot structure. Tales were more commonly associated with unplotted sketches; the two types often appeared in a single volume and were thought of in the same terms, because plot requirements were less stringent in shorter forms.

It is impossible, because the point is iterated so often, to overlook the assumption that plot was inseparable from the idea of the novel in these reviews. One sees it in the *North American* for July 1822 as an issue on which there is already consensus, in this commentary on Irving's *Bracebridge Hall*. "We have no hesitation in pronouncing *Bracebridge* quite equal to anything, which the present age of English literature has produced in this department. In saying this, we class it in the branch of essay writing. It may, perhaps, be called a novel in disguise; since a series of personages are made the subject or authors of the sketches of life and manners, which it contains, and it is conducted to a wedding, the regular *denouement* of a novel. The plot, however, is quite subordinate." In a January 1838 review of Cooper, the *North American* said that for a novel "unity of action is essential; the story must have a beginning, middle, and end. A string of events, connected by no other tie, than the mere fact, that they happened to the same individual, or within a given period of years, may constitute a fictitious history or memoir, but it does not make a novel."

The *Mirror*, on December 8, 1838, called Cooper's *Home as Found* "an imposition upon the public, put forth, as it is, in the form of a novel, when it has about as much claim to be ranked under the head as a fourth of July oration, or a book of travels. . . . There is neither plot nor interest in the narrative." A *Knickerbocker* review in August 1839 of Joseph Holt Ingraham's *Lafitte: The Pirate of the Gulf* observed that "it is not a novel, proper. There is no regular tendency of incident to a single point; the events are not made to conduct to a general end. Scenes are introduced that do not, in our judgment, seem necessary to the progress or interest of the story." It said that "as a novel proper" Cooper's *Home as Found* was, "to say nothing of more venial faults, plotless and desultory," and it referred to "the art of the novelist, in the conduct of the story proper" in a review of *Afloat and Ashore* (September 1848, December 1844). In Hawthorne's *House of the Seven Gables*, it said, "the story is regularly convergent to a denouement, after the manner of a novel proper" (May 1851).

In May 1842 *Godey's* complained about *Cecil* and *Cecil, a Peer:*

"the provoking manner in which the reader is tantalized with the expectation of coming to something like a denouement—something having the elements of consistent action—something like unity and design—is past all endurance. The parts are well enough executed. . . . But as a whole, each of the books is a failure. That learned critic, Dionysius of Helicarnassus, says that a history should have a beginning, a middle, and an end. So should a novel; and we would suggest to the author of *Cecil* the propriety of taking a few lessons in the art of constructing plots, before he attempts the concoction of another work of fiction." An Editor's Table in *Godey's* for March 1855 sets out a concise and standard definition: readers are accustomed to apply the term novel "to a series of adventures, having one plot and one interest." The *Literary World* for December 16, 1848, borrowing from the *Westminster Review*, said, "the first and obvious business of the novelist is to tell an amusing or interesting story; this alone is his peculiar province; and if certain gifted minds have embellished and dignified this task with jewels borrowed from the wardrobe of poetry or philosophy, it may perhaps be said that in so doing they have wandered out of their sphere, and ceased to be mere novelists." It characterized Longfellow's *Kavanagh* as "a thread upon which to hang some very pretty pearls, with an occasional sketch or suggestion of character, rather than such elaborate handling as we are accustomed to on the broader canvas of the modern novel" (May 26, 1849) and thought *Lady Alice; or, The New Una* "a genuine novel, with a plot and a catastrophe" (July 7, 1849). Its issue for November 22, 1851, found the problem with *Moby-Dick*, as well as "one or two other of Mr. Melville's books," to lie in "the double character under which they present themselves. In one light they are romantic fictions, in another statements of absolute facts."

To the *Democratic Review* for March 1849, *The Prince*, by Henry Cockton, was "rather a series of amusing anecdotes than a novel." *Graham's* on Longfellow's *Kavanagh* said that "considered as a novel, it must be admitted that the story is but slight, the characters hinted rather than developed, and the whole framework fragile; . . . the purpose . . . was evidently not the production of a consistent novel, but the illustration of an idea through the form of a tale" (July 1849). "As a novel," it said again of Kingsley's *Westward Ho!*, "the events have little connection with each other, having no other bond than the casual one of the presence of the hero in each" (July 1855). The *Tribune*, writing on Kimball's *St. Leger*, felt that "judging this unique composition by the ordinary rules of novel-writing, most readers would pronounce it barren of incidents, and without a sufficiently developed plot to give it the excitement demanded in a work of the imagination. . . . It is not to be read for the interest of the story" (December 25, 1849). Plot here is identified as a sign of the work's status as an imaginative (rather than intellectual) product. In Alice Carey's *Married Not Mated*, according to the *Tribune*, "the plot is destitute of consecutive interest. . . . As a collection of sketches, the work merits more cordial approval than as an attempt at connected novel writing" (May 3, 1856). Plot as connective distinguishes the longer from the shorter fictional form, allows for the creation of interest and excitement, and also demands a degree of skill in execution in which claims for the status of novelists as artists can be grounded. On March 24, 1860, the *Tribune* commented again that *Compensation*, by Ann M. H. Brewster, was "without ambitious pretensions as a novel—the simple and inartificial character of its plot almost taking it out of all that class of literary productions." A *Putnam's* reviewer wrote that *Oakfield*, "having for its end an important moral rather than an agreeable narrative, will not elicit the admiration of regular novel readers" (November 1855).

In the *Christian Examiner* for July 1849, *Kavanagh* received standard treatment: "those who expected a novel which would illustrate New England character and life have not been gratified. *Kavanagh* is a sketch, and not properly a rounded and completed story." Kingsley's *Hypatia* was not "properly speaking, a novel; indeed, to an inveterate reader of novels, the plot must seem provokingly simple" (January 1854). In this commentary the reader envisioned is different from the voracious novel devourer described in chapter 2. This is a connoisseur who reads for the exciting story but is also a sophisticated judge of plot artistry. Connoisseurship is based on pleasure; a badly plotted novel will not produce excitement or interest. Attacking Thackeray in May 1856, the *Christian Examiner* appealed to this sophistication. "We think it questionable whether the popular 'novelist' can be called a novelist at all, in the pure, artistic meaning of that term. We do not see any quality, in the quantity he has written, that proves the ability of composing a thorough novel, properly so called. That class of works . . . must have a carefully arranged opening, development, and winding-up. . . . It must be a whole, with complicated and interlacing parts. . . . A series of events, set in single file upon a highway, with nothing to look at on either side of the road, can hardly be called a novel. . . . Mr. Thackeray is nothing so much as a sketcher."

A formal distinction between story and plot seldom functioned in this criticism, though on occasion one reads something like this from *Arthur's Home Magazine* on Mrs. Moodie's *Mark Hurdlestone:* "regarded artistically, it betrays evidences of a hand unaccustomed to novel writing; while, as a story, it is singularly full of interest. The great defect of the work arises from the perfect nonchalance with which the authoress deals with her characters and incidents. Personages who were alive and in famous health to-day, are found killed off tomorrow . . . with far less than the ordinary amount of preparation. . . . We have always hitherto been accustomed to be forewarned. . . . So with the incidents; they are introduced with the same unexpectedness, take place just in the very nick of time, and are always found to be of the kind exactly suited to the wants of the moment" (October 1853). Plot, as distinguished from story, is an arrangement that simultaneously satisfies such formal conventions as foreshadowing and also conceals its artifice. This novelist, failing to understand the relation of artifice and artlessness in a novel, produces a bad plot behind which one can still see an interesting story.

More frequently (as in several extracts above), reviewers used the terms plot and story interchangeably but then discriminated the plot as a well-managed—a good—story. We see this in a *Putnam's* comment on *Bleak House:* "the thing which Dickens has yet to do, is to write a good story. Hitherto he has attained his brilliant successes by the production of novels, which have lacked one of the essential qualities of that species of literary manufacture" (November 1853). And in its claim that neither Stowe's *Uncle Tom's Cabin* nor her *Dred* were "stories, in the proper sense of the term; that is, they have no plot which begins, and develops, and culminates. . . . Both of Mrs. Stowe's novels are a series of sketches. . . . There is no story, no novel . . . no artistic sequence or unity. As a work of art, therefore, or as a pleasure to mere story readers, *Dred* is not successful" (November 1856). The assumption of plot's double function as a source of artistry and of pleasure should be noted. The *Atlantic*, in December 1858, grumbled that in Robert Lowell's *New Priest in Conception Bay* "a fair proportion of the novel might be called with strict propriety a series of sketches connected by a slight thread of narrative. . . . The faculty of making a well-constructed story, in which every event shall come in naturally, and yet each bring us one step nearer to the journey's end, is now one of the lost arts of the earth."

The concept of plot distinguished novels from other literary modes and, within the mode, identified artistic success. It was neither good nor bad for a work to be, or not to be, a novel. Some of the reviewers thought that the formal necessity to feature plot made the novel inferior to such genres as philosophy or poetry. Others thought the prominence of plot made the novel superior to the more desultory sketch or tale. But they were less concerned to arrange modes in a hierarchy than to establish whether a given work belonged to the genre. Such a desire derived partly from the taxonomic enthusiasm that gripped all fields of thinking in the middle of the nineteenth century. It also derived from the desire to make sure that the work was properly—one should note the recurrence of the term "novel proper" in the extracts—approached by readers. If a work signaled itself as a novel and then produced a bad plot, the reviewer was bound to fault it; if a good work of another sort might mistakenly be read as a novel, then it was the reviewer's job to provide the appropriate context. If the work was understood not to be a novel, then the reader, freed from expectations regarding plot, would be able to appreciate the work on its own terms.

Major authors like Cooper, Dickens, and Thackeray were said on occasion to have written books that were not "proper" novels. Even Sir Walter Scott, acknowledged by most critics to be the founder of the modern novel, did not escape this criticism. "The standing objection to Scott's novels," wrote the *North American* in a retrospective on the Waverley novels in April 1831, "is their want of a story consistent in all its parts. . . . We have certain traditional notions of the unity required in a poem or novel, which are regularly insisted on by critics, and as often disregarded by every successful writer." Given the marginal success of most writers who ignored genre rules and the tremendous popularity of any number of modestly talented writers who wrote to rule, the *North American* seems wrong here. But it is pointing to the obvious fact that the "great" writer can generally ignore rules or remake genres without suffering. The great writer gets an audience even when breaking rules. Perhaps even by breaking them.

In fact the truly great writer was expected to transcend (not transgress) the limits of genre, and even a lesser, but good writer marked his or her works with traces of individuality. The criterion that enters here is, of course, the nineteenth-century idea of genius, which exists in interesting and productive tension with the idea of genre. On the one hand, that the novel had so few genre requirements made it a particularly suitable form for displays of genius. On the other, the very paucity of formal requirements made reviewers likely to insist strongly that its *one* requirement, a plot-grounded form, be fulfilled if a work was to be thought of as a novel. But again, they did not limit their search for genius to the novel form and did not feel (as critics tend to today) that they first had to call a work a novel before they could allow that it was the product of genius. Thus, identifying boundlessness as the property of genius rather than genre, they could impose definitional boundaries on the novel form without thereby disabling themselves as critics in search of artistic excellence.

If narrated plot defined the form of the novel, plot itself was defined by various formal features: a completed action with beginning, middle, and end. Because it was lengthy, it was complicated; complications meant that the plot did not consist of "a series of events, set in single file upon a highway, with nothing to look at on either side of the road" but was made up of events whose linear relations were not always immediately evident. The mark of a good plot, however, was that ultimately all events were seen to cohere; the denouement gave them significance. The denouement functioned doubly (as so many terms in this discourse do) with respect to the action and the reader, completing the action and satisfying the reader's curiosity.

As the *North American* put it early on in a review of John Galt's *Lawrie Todd*, plot was "a concentration of action and incident to [a] particular consummation, at which the interest terminates . . . one series of action, with a uniform tendency, disguised until the denouement explains all" (October 1830). Events interesting in themselves would cease to hold the reader's interest if they did not somehow, mysteriously, gesture toward a denouement; thus denouement was the final cause, in an Aristotelian sense, of the novel, controlling every aspect of the action as well as of its presentation. The "want of unity" in Bulwer's *My Novel*, the *Southern Literary Messenger* said, "materially mars the symmetry of that work. We look in vain for that central conception from which all the minutiae should emanate as their source, to which they should tend as their result, and from which they should obtain their vitality" (May 1854). In like manner, the *Christian Examiner* complained of a novel that "there is no intricacy of plot, and no development of plot, and the denouement is not provided for in the elements of the story. Some personages who seemed to promise very well disappear very soon, and others annoy us all along as disagreeable and intrusive. Though spun out to an intolerable length, the story is not finished after all. It stops short just where the interest begins to revive and there are signs of a fascinating complication" (January 1858). In fact, the process of reading a novel, for the nineteenth-century reviewer, is the process of plot construal (rather than meaning or theme construal). And hence the reading experience is inseparable from the form and genre of the work.

"Denouement" and "interest" (and their synonyms) are the two most active critical concepts in discussion of plot; they are terms oriented toward both the text and the reader, denoting the reader's engagement in plot as well as the plot line itself. Here is a statement of the concept from a discussion of *St. Leger* in *Graham's*, where the reviewer is distinguishing the German from the Anglo-American novel. German novels, so-called, "have no regular sequence of events—no relation of parts to a whole—no dramatic bearing of character upon character, to produce an ultimate result—no apparent effort to close the story at the very start, which an influx of conflicting circumstances alone prevents, and toward which it ever struggles, overcoming obstacles and softening down discordances, until the end is gained by an unforced blending into one harmonious mass of all the opposing elements of the plot" (April 1850). A critique of *Vanity Fair* from the *Democratic Review* clearly connects interest and denouement, reader and form. Midway through the work "the story becomes dilatory, diffuse, and its loses much of its interest. . . . Laugh as

we may at Aristotle and the classic school, some *unity* is absolutely necessary to make a plot interesting" (October 1848).

Another good example of the intertwining of closure and interest is this from *Putnam's* in April 1854, unfavorably reviewing
The Barclays of Boston by Mrs. Harrison Gray Otis. "Everything
turns out not just as it should be, in a novel, but just as it should
not. In these perversities Mrs. Otis has shown a lack of true
artistic management of her puppets, for the reasonable anticipation of the reader must not be disappointed in the denouement of
the story, or his feeling will be one of disappointment and disgust
instead of pleasure. The perplexities of the reader must arise
from the developments of the plot, from the unanticipated events
which the art of the writer uses to bring about the denouement
which all parties anticipated at the outset. In the *Barclays* there is
no plot at all, and the surprises are in the denouements which are
constantly happening, and destroying the interest which should
be felt in the final explosion of the last chapter." A reviewer in
the *Tribune* stated the criterion succinctly: "a deftly constructed
plot enchains the reader in a delightful suspense, until the various
and apparently conflicting lights of the scene verge toward a
common focus in a brilliant denouement" (December 6, 1855).

Examples abound. "It has become quite too common to inter-
polate a string of unconnected events upon a pre-conceived nu-
cleus, with no bearing on the main plot, but which are introduced for the mere purpose of bringing in characters and conversations, which only serve to distract the attention, and lessen the
interest, of the reader" (*Knickerbocker*, April 1837). From
Graham's, approvingly, on *Bleak House:* "the moment we discern
the blind way in which so many separate and separated characters are working to one result, we feel a new and more eager
interest in the story" (December 1853). From the *Southern Literary Messenger*, on John Esten Cooke's *Henry St. John, Gentleman:*
"the plots of Mr. Cooke's novels are singularly ill-contrived. He
is not wanting in invention . . . but the reader is kept in no state
of pleasing and excited doubt, alternating between satisfaction
and despair, as to the fate of the heroine" (October 1859).

Reviewers did not often try to uncover the psychological basis
of this need for closure that dominated the conception of plot. On
June 26, 1858, the *New York Ledger* reprinted a moving explanation of the phenomenon by Charles Kingsley, which it titled

"Novels and Romances." "A novel," Kingsley had written, "is a species of drama, or complete history. . . . It is this which distinguishes the drama from history or biography. . . . The life of any one individual leaves a most unsatisfactory and deep void, which makes it appear like a mere episode or fraction of history, terminating without a consummation or winding up either the affairs or the principles on which the life was engaged. . . . It is very different with a novel, romance, or a drama; in these, there is a completeness—a winding up of all affairs. The whole subject-matter of the plot is explained; the mystery is unriddled . . . even the most trifling circumstances are discovered to have a meaning. . . . In reading a novel, it is the belief of this completeness, this final winding up, that creates the interest in our minds. Were we not assured, from experience, that every difficulty would be removed at the conclusion of the tale, we should not have any interest whatever in reading it. The interest is a pure offspring of faith—faith in the completeness of the history and the importance of all the incidents as they occur in succession." Kingsley went on to say that "nothing is more common amongst skillful novel-readers than to exercise their ingenuity in attempting to divine what may be the consequence of such apparently trifling circumstances in the commencement of a play or tale. . . . But it is generally acknowledged, that the plot which conceals itself to the very last scene of the piece is superior to that which is easily detected before the general consummation takes place. . . . The love of perfection, or completeness, is at the root of the passion for novel-reading." The *Ledger* was at this time the nation's most popular fiction weekly, claiming an amazing circulation of some 400,000. We may be sure that this extract corresponded to an acceptable ideology among its many readers.

It is noteworthy, then, that the grip of the novel is located in its formal rather than its representational character; the formal aspect is seen to correspond to a fundamental human need, so that form is a function of the human psyche. The remark about the superiority of plots in which the mysteries are not guessed before the author chooses to reveal them shows how plot, in this conception, turns as much on the interaction between reader and author as it does on the sequence of narrated events in itself; or rather, it iterates the congruence of plot design and reader response. If plot is structured as mystery and clarification, these terms acquire meaning only with reference to a reader who is first mystified and then enlightened. Plot is fundamentally a matter of secrets withheld from the reader; this configuration may be represented in the action by plots of concealment and revelation, but such plots are imitating the reader's desires rather than external reality, or more precisely are instances of the novel's content imitating its form. Indeed, Kingsley makes clear that in his view external reality does not possess a satisfactory shape and that the novel is appealing because it repairs a damaged real world. Verisimilitude in the novel would produce no pleasure without the novelist's skill in imposing the corrective of plot on recalcitrant reality so that we appreciate not reality itself, but reality made better. If we prefer "true-to-life" novels to improbable ones, it may be owing to the very *improbability* of their achievement.

However this might be, the formal principle of the novel had little to do with verisimilitude and much to do with desire. The *New York Review* said about a Balzac novel that "the interest becomes thrilling, when the reader finds himself among a world of human hearts, linked together by an invisible chain, a mystery half palpable, half volatile, of which the enigma is the author's secret" (April 1839). The *Tribune*, reviewing Edward Grayson's *Overing*, wrote approvingly of "the numerous threads crossing and intertangling with each other in a way that requires a dexterous hand to prevent confusion—but in the sequel, all apparent mysteries are happily cleared up, and the connexion of events which at first seemed to have no bearing on each other is explained to the satisfaction of the reader" (January 1, 1853). Reader, text, and author (not narrator) are all implicated in the notion of plot, for the test of authorial skill and the artistic challenge of the form involve presenting material in a way that maximizes the reader's inherent pleasure in following increasing complications to their effective resolution.

Individual segments of the plot were called "incidents," and plot artistry consisted of two specific achievements: first, inventing incidents; second, arranging and proportioning them with respect to the winding up. Some of the more theoretical reviewers distinguished novelistic talents into the "inventive" and the "combinative" faculties. Although the inventive was the rarer and greater talent, it was the combinative that made effective novels. The most common criticism has to do with the placement of the denouement. It may come too early in the action, eliminating interest in the later pages. Or, if the insertion of irrelevant incidents has surpassed the capacity of the work to sustain interest or the complications introduced betray too clearly the author's desire to keep the plot going, it may be felt to come too late.

The more common of these two errors was the premature denouement. The *Mirror*, reviewing G. P. R. James's *The Robbers*, noted that "there is much that is artist-like and dramatic in the introduction of the characters and the disposition and management of the various scenes. The climax, however, occurs about the middle of the second volume, in the discovery of the parentage of the hero, and all that comes afterward is wearisome and forced" (June 2, 1838). The *North American* observed in a plot summary of George Sand's *Lélia* that "the novel should end here, for the point of interest on which the whole plot turns . . . is now exhausted, and no apparent obstacle remains to the union of the lovers. But the writer injudiciously protracts the story" (July 1841). The *American Review* explained that in *Kavanagh* the early love of Alice Archer, "crossed by that of her friends, and ending in death, constitutes the romance proper of the tale; but her death, instead of being reserved for the denouement, occurring as it does in the middle of the book, and at a time when other interests are paramount, the little sympathy which her ill-fated passion has excited is lost, and she forgotten" (July 1849). Protracted denouements created another kind of tedium. The plot of an anonymous novel called *Blanche Dearwood*, according to *Putnam's*, "is utterly improbable, and full of mystery where there need be no mystery; yet the incidents are developed with dramatic skill. But as one sees the end a long way ahead, the details of the last chapters are painfully protracted" (June 1855).

Another common plot defect was the crowding of incident. *Knickerbocker*, reviewing *Rombert*, said, "the plot is overcrowded, overcharged, and to a certain extent, unintelligible; there are half a dozen heroines, and twice that number of heroes, circumstances which destroy a connexion of interest, and prevent the reader from knowing exactly whom to follow with his good wishes" (February 1835). It criticized William Gilmore Simms's *Mellichampe* on the same grounds: incidents "are literally crowded into the narrative, from the commencement to the close. Many of these are almost entirely disconnected with the main plot, and tend, as we think, to distract the attention of the reader" (December 1836). The *Mirror* said of *Hamilton King*, "the action is too crowded, the characters too numerous, and the plot too confused and compound. Mysteries, involvement, and desperate adventures, which lead to nothing, and have no dramatic adaptation to the story, follow one another in a whirl, which at last dizzies the attention" (October 5, 1839). *Godey's* observed of *Howard Pinckney* that "one half the incidents in a practiced hand would answer the purpose" (November 1840). *Blanche of Brandywine*, by George Lippard, introduced "such a crowd of events and characters . . . that the unity of the story seems to have been somewhat neglected" (*Democratic Review*, October 1846). *Harper's* complained that in Carolyn Chesebro's *Getting Along* "the materials employed in the construction of the plot are sufficient for half a dozen novels. Such a profuse outlay on the part of the writer indicates a consciousness of power, of a rich store of resources— but not the talent for organization which is essential to the success of a great imaginative work" (May 1855). It found the plot of Kingsley's *Two Years Ago* "encumbered by a variety of characters, which serve only to distract the attention without conspiring to the unitary impression of the whole. Indeed, the plan of the work embraces the materials for no less than three distinct stories, and the attempt to combine them in a single narrative was injudicious" (May 1857).

One particular kind of crowding was known as "hurrying," a crowding near the denouement that signaled the writer's impatience or fatigue. The *North American* wrote of Cooper's *The Spy* that "nothing but unpardonable haste can account for that sad huddling into confusion, toward the end, of a plot so well laid at the outset" and, in a review of Sedgwick's *Clarence*, noted more generally that "the denouement of a novel is the part which most severely tries an author's ingenuity; for it is very possible that a story may have been skillfully constructed to a certain point, and then be wound up in the most hurried and clumsy manner" (July 1822, January 1831). *Graham's* complained that Dickens, in *Hard Times*, "evidently was tired himself of his materials and huddled them up to a conclusion long before his original intention" (November 1854); the *Tribune* thought the catastrophe of *Little*

Dorrit was "hurriedly and obscurely worked out" (June 23, 1857).

These comments focused on the need for the writer to identify and highlight a unitary plot if reader interest was to be engaged and maintained and implied the importance of pacing and of the positioning of incidents along the route to the denouement. A novel might also err in its plotting at the other extreme by being too simple or sparse in incident to create curiosity or suspense. A *Knickerbocker* reviewer doubted whether a simple "succession of events converging to a final point" could really be called a plot, since such a structure lacked complication; and another raised the same point in a review of *Kavanagh*, which could "hardly be said to have any plot proper," since it proceeded by "regular convergence to the end" (July 1837, June 1849). The operative word here is "regular"; matters untoward or unforeseen must be introduced if novels are to be interesting. "There must be unity with ever shifting changes," the *Christian Examiner* explained, "a regular progress through the midst of doubts and surprises; various clews running tortuously to meet in the same point of common effect; some ingenuity of contrivance to keep the mind of the reader suspended and engaged, and swept forward, while it is swayed to and fro, by curiosity and emotion, and a constantly heightening sympathy" (May 1856). For a *North American* reviewer Hawthorne's works continually missed the mark: "his plots are seldom well devised or skillfully developed. They are either too simple to excite curiosity and attract interest, or too much involved for him to clear them up to the reader's satisfaction" (January 1854).

The artistic arrangement of incidents in plot did not extend to breaches of chronological order; in fact, departures from what was called (naturally) the "natural" order of events were perceived as signs of lack of skill. An additional criterion—probability—which later critical discussions of the "realistic" novel (a term that, by the way, does not appear in any of these reviews) were to make much of, was distinctly secondary in significance in defining the novel as a genre, though for a group of reviewers it was of considerable importance in determining the eventual value of any given work. Most reviewers of the day agreed that the novelist who made an artistic and interesting plot out of the probable had achieved something qualitatively superior to one who relied on improbabilities to wind up a story or deliver characters from complications of incident. But there was less consensus that a more probable story was also inherently more interesting, since readers did not behave in a way that would make such a proposition self-evident. Thus, though the *Tribune* found the "great defect" of *Ida May* in "the improbability of its leading incidents," asserting that "the intrinsic improbability of the whole conception greatly mars the interest of the work as a consecutive story, and leaves the reader dependent on the energy and pathos of isolated passages" (November 22, 1854), it had also written earlier (of Mrs. Marsh's *Castle Avon*): "complicated, and, in some respects, improbable, as is the plot, it is developed with such admirable grouping of incidents and richness of coloring, that the interest of the reader is held in a perpetual fascination" (February 19, 1853).

Improbabilities in a plot diminished but did not obliterate reader interest, and other aspects of the presentation could more than compensate. E. D. E. N. Southworth's *The Deserted Wife*, according to the *Literary World*, "will owe its popularity to the dramatic power with which a complicated and not unoriginal plot has been managed. . . . As often happens in dramatic pieces, this novel sacrifices probabilities to the intense" (August 31, 1850). It repeated this judgment on later occasions: there is "no lack of interest in Mrs. Southworth's tales, and although somewhat wild and improbable, once commenced they are never thrown aside as tame common-place"; "the plot of Mrs. Southworth's novel is highly interesting and ingenious, though she does not stop at an improbability for the sake of extricating a favorite character from a dilemma" (May 24, 1851; August 7, 1852). *Harper's* also found Southworth's excesses a fault: "in the construction of her plots, she has not regard for probability; nature is violated at every step; impossible people are brought into impossible situations; every thing is colored so highly that the eye is dazzled"; but it described these excesses in language revealing their appeal. "Let her curb her fiery Pegasus with unrelenting hand," the reviewer counseled, "and she will yet attain a rank worthy of her fine faculties, from which she has hitherto been precluded by her outrages on the proprieties of fictitious composition" (October 1852). Reviewing Ann Stephens's *Mary Derwent*, *Harper's* remarked that "the plan of the work is bold—

not to say audacious—involving demands on the faith of the reader which defy all sense of probability; but the incidents are wrought up into a succession of striking scenes, forming a sort of tragic unity which excites both the imagination and the sympathy of the reader" (August 1858). The dates of these extracts suggest that the demand for probability was no stronger at the close of this era than it had been earlier. And the word "proprieties" in the *Harper's* criticism of Southworth suggests that the need for probability was less strongly felt by readers than by critics—suggests even that the criterion was connected to reviewer preference for propriety as a virtue in itself. In sum, the inveterate novel reader preferred excitement and interest to probability; the reviewer hoped to elevate taste.

Again we return to the criterion of interest, a persistent term describing identically a formal aspect of a novel to be identified, isolated, and described and an experience or response in a reader. The *North American* employed the term in its almost technical formal sense as early as July 1825 when it observed of *The Refugee* that "the interest is also divided by episodes and underplots, till it is nearly reduced to nothing." In October 1837 it commented that "artificial complication of plot . . . is necessary to sustain the interest of a long story." *Emma*, said *Knickerbocker*, "may be a fine and delicate conception, but it has been embodied at the sacrifice of what we prefer—that of interest. Of this essential quality in a novel, *Emma* is so seriously deficient that all the talents of its author have proved incompetent to make a story which the most determined patience can peruse"; in Simms's *Yemassee* "the interest . . . is awakened, without circumlocution, in the opening chapters, and though perhaps too often changed from one train of moving events to another, is yet powerfully excited, and sustained, throughout the work"; Ellen Pickering's novels were "all richly endowed with the one most indispensable quality, interest" (August 1833, April 1835, April 1839).

Theodore Fay's *Countess Ida* "is well told, the plot is well-laid and well developed, and the interest is sustained throughout" (*New York Review*, July 1840). "The interest of a romance should continue, let it be remembered, throughout the whole story" (*Graham's*, January 1841). The *Southern Literary Messenger* complained that in Cooper's *Wyandotte* "what little interest there is in it is terribly delayed," found Bulwer's *Lucretia* "deficient in the first quality of every novel—interest," and, though commending the morality of his *Harold*, observed that "as a story, it is a very wearisome affair" displaying "an entire want of continuing interest" (November 1843, January 1847, August 1848). *Peterson's* thought that the "interest of the story is not sustained" in Bulwer's *Last of the Barons* (April 1843). The *Literary World* found "the interest [of *Dombey and Son*] not so well sustained as the author's previous efforts"; in *Laneton Parsonage* "interest, in the ordinary sense of the word, is not to be found"; and the "interest" in *St. Leger* "is considerably injured by the introduction of characters foreign to the general design" (September 25, 1847; March 10, 1849; January 5, 1850).

Godey's said that in *Sybil Lennard* "the interest commences on the first page, and is continued throughout the book" (January 1848). *Sartain's* noted that in Brontë's *Shirley* "the interest is divided between too many, and being divided it is of course weakened" (February 1850). The author of *James Mountjoy* has "unwisely deprived his book of the advantage of unity of interest. He has too many leading personages, whose separate adventures engross too much of the reader's attention" (*American Review*, April 1850). *Harper's* declared that in McConnel's *Talbot and Vernon* "details are managed with a good deal of skill, developing the course of the affairs in such a gradual manner, that the interest of the reader never sleeps, until the final winding-up of the narrative" (June 1850). In Mayo's *The Berber*, according to the *Tribune*, "the different interests of the story are admirably blended"; the paper also said of *Overing* that "the interest of the plot is well sustained," and of Chesebro's *Getting Along* that the novel "gains consistently in interest as it advances" (November 13, 1850; May 22, 1852; March 30, 1855).

In sum, the formal principle of the novel was plot, and the basic principle of reader response—interest—also derived from plot. The "novel," in a basic sense, existed only when the distinction between it and the reader disappeared, when the novel initiated and the reader completed a single experience. Thus formal criticism and reader-response criticism (of course neither of the terms existed) were the same act, since reader response was a function of form and form was a modeling of reader responses.

5

Character

All plots in fiction require agents to carry out and register actions. In the contemporary novel, according to reviewers in the second quarter of the nineteenth century, those agents could only be human beings. Over time, discussions of verisimilitude with respect to the depiction of human beings in the novel became an increasingly significant aspect of reviewing. From this basis, critics assessed the creation of memorable characters as an achievement unique to, and characteristic of, the best novels and novelists.

Histories of English (though not American) fiction take it for granted that an emphasis on character emerged as the hallmark of the better nineteenth-century novel. According to some, individual character really did have freer play in the nineteenth century than ever before; according to others, it was convenient for one or another power group to imagine that this was the case or at least to persuade others that it was so. But though reviewers after 1850 talked more about character in novels than they had earlier, an emphasis on character or the presence of characters asserted to be human was never the element that defined the genre. Character was discriminated for purposes of plot: in order properly to construe the action, auditors or readers had always to be able to tell the important agents of a story apart. Purchasers must also be able to tell specific examples of the novel apart. Character, in the sense of an assemblage of personality traits and associated behaviors, increasingly became the method chosen for achieving these psychologically, formally, and commercially necessary ends. But character in this sense was more a particular cultural solution to formal and psychological problems than a representation of reality.

The requirement that characters be human beings at first meant no more than that: the novel was not to contain any agents who were recognizably *not* human, for the temper of readers had turned against fictions of the supernatural, as we see in this review of Cooper's *The Pilot* from the *North American* for April 1824. (The reviewer is talking about auxiliary characters who help out the heroes and heroines of a "modern" novel, precisely the sort of character that Natty Bumppo would be and in which, more generally, Cooper excelled.) "Characters of this description are substituted for what used to pass under the name of the machinery of epic poetry; for the gods of the ancient writers, and the witches, fairies, and other supernatural beings, introduced into the older of the modern writers of fiction, to bring the other personages into situations, which would otherwise be too improbable, or help them out, when they could not retrieve themselves. But a giant, a wizard, or spirit . . . makes but a sorry figure in a modern story, in which the author affects any regard to probability. Yet the reader must be interested, and his feelings must be disturbed by imminent perils, desperate situations, and hairbreadth escapes; and it is rude and inartificial in the author, to resort only to good fortune in these emergencies. . . . Some extraordinary and powerful agent is needed for the trying occasions."

If plots involving supernatural beings were no longer interesting, writers had to turn to other subjects for their stories. Apparently people had become interested in themselves in a new way. "Human nature concentrates all that is permanently interesting in this world," the *North American* wrote in an October 1830 review of John Galt's *Lawrie Todd*. "It is quite a subordinate achievement of genius to accumulate obstacles, and carry the actors further and further from the haven, until by a lucky change of the wind, they make the port under full sail." According to a reviewer in the *Mirror*, "every fiction is popular, in proportion to the degree in which it interests the greatest number. . . . To interest is to excite the sympathy of the reader with one of the persons of the fiction—to be anxious about his fortunes, to exult in his success and lament his sufferings" (June 1,

1838). "The novel of the present age differs from that of the preceding more particularly in its plot," a reviewer in the *Southern Literary Messenger* explained; in earlier works "the experienced novel-monger could see afar off the coming catastrophe, and could predict with unerring certainty the fate of the principal personages of the action. In times when the history of any man might have been written out before his birth on knowing his circumstances, talents, acquirements, and associations, by the unerring operations of social laws, these plots were true to nature. . . . But now, when under the more inconstant laws of a more rapid civilization . . . the author's plot should be more complex and his catastrophe more startling. . . . Novels, in comparatively recent days, have had their gypsies, their witches, and their haunted castles. They were then necessary to excite and retain interest. They are not so now. Follow the natural, and at the same time astounding revolutions of every day life, and interest will never flag" (May 1852). There is an evident contradiction in this theorizing, since we are told that the old-style predictable novel, true to an earlier time, also had witches, gypsies, and haunted castles that were true to no time. The real emphasis, which renders this contradiction irrelevant, is on exciting and retaining interest: when the course of life could be predicted even before birth, stories of human beings were not particularly interesting. The reviewer's explanation is no better or worse than dozens offered to account for the shift in public taste; nobody really knew why, but all were sure that a change had taken place.

But loss of interest in nonhuman characters did not mean that readers demanded elaborate verisimilitude in human characterization. It was a matter more of exclusion than inclusion, of structure rather than content, and, as the review from the *Southern Literary Messenger* makes clear, of plot rather than character as such. If no supernatural agents were to be allowed in novels, matters had to work themselves out entirely through human agencies. Even the most perfunctory gesture in the direction of anthropomorphizing was often enough to satisfy the reader that a given character was a human being. At the point where character emerged as a focus competitive to plot, readers tended to opt for plot. Even as late as 1858 character was second to plot with readers, as a comment from the *Atlantic* in December of that year indicates. Finding that the interest in Lowell's *The New Priest in*

Conception Bay "derived more from marked and careful delineations of individual character than from the march of events or
brilliant procession of incidents," the reviewer remarked that
"novels constructed on this plan are less likely to be popular than
those in which the interest is derived from a skillfully-contrived
plot and a rapid and stirring succession of moving events."

In fact an important aim in American (and British) novel reviewing toward the middle of the nineteenth century was to
impose the criterion of perceptive characterization as a means of
discriminating better from worse novels. "The novelist who succeeds in creating and describing an imaginary character, that ever
after remains in the memories of men ranked among the real
existences of the past, both illustrates his own merit and secures
his fame," the *New York Review* wrote in January 1842. "An
ingenious plot, with a variety of incident, may make an interesting tale that will occupy the attention pleasantly, and leave
agreeable impressions upon the mind. But that these impressions
may be lasting, our sympathies must be excited by the characters
that are introduced; and if, when we lay down the work, there is
not one of the persons described in it with whom we part as we
would do with a familiar acquaintance, the chances are a hundred
to one that our first perusal will be our last." (Of course this
criterion was of more interest to a critic than to an average reader,
who wanted more new novels rather than a second reading of an
old one.) The province of the novelist, a reviewer in *Knickerbocker*
asserted, is "to create characters, and if he fails to do this, he fails
utterly, though he may produce two or three romances yearly,
like Mr. James, or a dozen in as many years, like Mr. Simms"
(April 1846). A *Graham's* reviewer praised Thackeray for representing "those evanescent and unconscious transpirations of
character, in which a novelist's capacity is most truly exhibited"
(November 1848). According to the *North American*, "it is in this
absolute creation of character, that our modern novelists so far
exceed all that their predecessors were able to accomplish. In
variety of individuality, in successful delineation of the action of
one character upon another, or of internal will upon external
circumstance, or the struggle of earnest natures against adverse
influences,—in these, the themes of the modern novel, nature
herself is almost rivalled. . . . It is now . . . the development of
character which commands attention" (October 1856).

But though reviewers talked as if they had succeeded in winning readers to this criterion, they argued endlessly with each other and with their readers over which novelists created believable characters and which characters were in fact believable. The point is that whichever authors they liked, those were the ones they claimed had created good characters; whichever they disliked they faulted on the same score. Of course, reviewers liked authors whose portrayal of characters conformed to their own views of what character was. There are thus two theoretical issues here: first, how important, in general, characterization is to the novel; second, what is, and what is not, an example of artistry in character depiction. Reviewers tended to agree among themselves on the first and to differ on the second of these issues; and on the first they tended by their own account to differ with readers.

Reviewers generally agreed on a hierarchy of good character types in the novel. The highest type was both "original" and "true" in the sense of being recognizably human. An April 1837 *Knickerbocker* review praised Robert Montgomery Bird's *Nick of the Woods:* "no creation of any modern American novelist can lay claim to the originality, the strictly *sui generis* qualities" of the two principal characters. The *North American* said the "finest character" in *Vanity Fair* was "Miss Rebecca Sharp, an original personage, worthy to be called the author's own, and as true to life as hypocrisy, ability, and cunning can make her" (October 1848). The *American Review* concurred: "Becky Sharp is an original creation, not the representative of a class, though there are traits about her that remind you of several classes" (October 1848). A *Peterson's* reviewer commented on the "originality of the real characters" in *Villette* (May 1853); one in *Putnam's* observed that for handling of character Dickens "stands second only to Shakespeare. . . . There is nothing so rare in literature as the creation of a new character" (December 1853). The character of Christie Johnson in Charles Reade's novel of that name was, according to the *Southern Literary Messenger*, "a *creation*—not an adaptation, or a weak or strong copy, or an imaginary personage out of real life. She lives and breathes, and is delineated with a vigor which carries the reader along with surprise and delight" (July 1855). "To mention all the characters deserving of notice for their originality and truth," *Graham's* said of *The Newcomes*, "would be to give a master role of names" (December 1855). An *Atlantic* review complained that "of all the popular novelists, not more than half a dozen have ever created characters that survive"; Leatherstocking was one of them, "a creation which no reader ever can or would forget,—a creation for which the merely accomplished writer would gladly exchange all the fine sentences and word-pictures ever put on paper" (September 1859).

Somewhat lower in achievement were characters who, though manifestly typical, were yet unique in some way. This, according to the *Democratic Review* for September 1853, was Scott's achievement. "His fertile fancy ranged through every class and variety and description of men . . . and what is most wonderful still about these endless developments of the human race, and varieties and forms of life, is the fact that each individual is stamped with its own marked peculiarity—each has a character of his own, original and self-sustained,—and no two are similar." Paul de Kock's characters, according to an April 1843 review in the *North American*, are "imaginary beings, but they are still human. . . . Not a particular portrait drawn from life, but a combination of the most familiar and striking traits that characterize a whole class, and forming, therefore, a better representation of that class, than any faithful picture of an individual." Characters of this type fitted the demand for greater seriousness in novels, as the reviewer went on to demonstrate: "we regard novels as vehicles of instruction,—as furnishing the means of enlarging our experience,—as increasing our knowledge of men and things. This effect is not the chief object of the writer, we admit; but he aims at it as subsidiary to his main purpose, and it is essential to his success." Here the reviewer, linking characterization with better fiction, also makes the point that character and instruction are not formal necessities in fiction.

Indeed, at the level at which character is a formal necessity in the novel it is simply a specification within the frame of cultural norms sufficient to enable a reader to tell one character from another. We are accustomed to maintain that the idea of individuality or individualism is a nineteenth-century or at least an Enlightenment concept underlying and making possible the treatment of character in the great fictions of the nineteenth century. (From a liberal-historical viewpoint, this ideological development is good, from a Marxist approach, bad.) Yet clearly it is a transhistorical formal and psychological requirement for any narration or representation that its agents be differentiated; the chief cultural matter is the content of the distinctions rather than that they are drawn. When we cannot tell characters apart in fictions from other cultures or eras, it is usually because we are ignorant of the right categories.

Individualism has, to be sure, a certain substantive force in this nineteenth-century discourse: self-awareness and a sense of one's uniqueness are character traits that emerge with increasing importance in the repertory of traits from which character is constructed. I find, however, only three formal criteria absolutely required for specification: first, differences are matters of inner traits that are expressed in outer actions (and stress on inner traits becomes stronger as the era advances); second, the traits that make up a given character are all consistent with each other; and third, they have an inseparable moral aspect to them, on account of which characters may be not only told apart, but placed as sympathetic or unattractive. Of course reviewers thought the traits they identified, as well as this moral quality, corresponded to human nature; and of course they thought the discriminations that the form called on novelists to make corresponded to real human differences. But the formal effect was known to be the point in all this: "he seems to be afflicted with a want of knowledge of human nature," the *North American* complained in reviewing Cooper's *The Water Witch* in April 1831, "which prevents him from giving a proper degree of distinctness and individuality, and, above all, variety to the persons of the drama." The "proper degree" being called for here is a formal demand connected to the needs of the fiction: distinctness and variety.

It is perhaps necessary, then, to distinguish between characters in novels who are individuals and those who are simply individualized. The art of the great novelist consisted in achieving the first, by means of the invention of unusual though still acceptably human traits, and the combination of a large number of these into a totality. The formal requirements of the novel meant that every successful novelist had to achieve the second. And hence "individualizing" is the most common way character is talked about in novel reviews. In this way of talking, characters are thought of in relation to each other rather than as separate

entities; of course in a novel with only one character (if such a
creation could have been imagined to exist) no individualizing
would have been necessary. "The great defect of Mr. James as a
novelist is his lack of skill in the creation of accurate delineation
of individual character," the *North American* wrote of G. P. R.
James in April 1844. "We want a forcible conception and consistent development of individual minds, with traits and peculiarities which constitute their distinction from other minds.
They should be drawn with sufficient distinctness to enable the
reader to give them a place in his memory, and to detect all
departures, either in language or action, from the original type."

I cite briefly some of the numerous applications of this criterion. "His characters want that distinctness and individuality,
which we so often meet with in those greatly dramatic authors"
(*Southern Literary Messenger*, June 1847); "the characters are drawn
with a masterly hand, and individualized with singular power"
(*Literary World*, January 29, 1848); "all the characters that aid in
the development of our author's plot are drawn with a strong
dramatic distinctness, and have something more than their mere
names to distinguish them from each other" (*Sartain's*, March
1850); "a rare talent in individualizing character; his groups consist of distinct persons, without any confused blundering or repetition" (*Harper's*, October 1850); "the chief defect of it is want of
variety in the personages introduced. There are no less than three
or four heroines, and quite as many heroes, different from each
other, of course, yet not very decidedly different" (*Putnam's*,
October 1855); "it will be objected to her men . . . that they are
not sufficiently discriminated, being made too much on the same
pattern" (*Putnam's*, March 1856). "Every character introduced is
a distinct and appreciable personage" (*Home Journal*, January 6,
1855); "crowded as the scene before us is with complicated scenes
and various actors, they all preserve their identity with wonderful exactness" (*Knickerbocker*, October 1855); and in December:
"these personages . . . are grouped with exceeding skill, and
have many a touch of individuality about them." "The characterization evinces that the writer has an instinct for individualities,
and a power of embodying them so distinctly that they readily
take shape and life in the reader's imagination" (*Graham's*, July
1854); "the characters are not only individually and strongly
marked, but are contrasted—placed in apposition to each other in

the various scenes—with very striking effect" (*Graham's*, September 1858).

The chief question asked about verisimilitude in characterization was whether the character was mixed, compounded of good and bad qualities. It was necessary that the traits in one character amount to a consistent whole, and bizarre assemblages of traits were signs of authorial ineptness; but novelists more often erred, according to reviews, by making characters overly consistent, in the interest of achieving pure sympathy or animosity on the reader's part (that is, of clarifying the mutual relations of protagonist and antagonist). The art of characterization consisted in making the character as mixed as possible before the whole disintegrated or the obvious positions of protagonist and antagonist were confused.

"Martin Faber," according to a *Knickerbocker* reviewer considering the novel of that name, "is a most fiendish, gratuitous villain. . . . Such characters are unnatural. Men are neither fiends, nor angels, but a little of both" (October 1833). "Novels are pictures of life," the *North American* opined, "and the characters presented in them must have that diversity and even contrariety of feeling, motive, and conduct, that inconsequence of thought and action, which we daily witness among our friends, or we do not acknowledge the fidelity of the imitation" (January 1838). "It is vastly easier," commented the *New York Review*, "to represent your personages with two hues, like the black and white men on a chequer board. . . . The author has conceived no shading, blending, or softening to any of his creations" (July 1841). Of *Who Shall Be Heir?* by Ellen Pickering, *Godey's* objected that "the characters of Rosaline and Vivian are almost too perfect, as is that of Cottrell too bad"; and it found that the hero of Bulwer's *Night and Morning* was "a noble fellow . . . almost too good for every day life" (March 1841, April 1841). The "truthfulness" of Sedgwick's *Alida*, according to the *Democratic Review*, was "confirmed by that natural admixture of fault in the persons for whom our affections are elicited" (May 11, 1850).

Reviews in the *Literary World* frequently criticized novelists for their failure to present mixed characters: "the demon of the piece . . . has the demoniac perfection which is never found in nature" (February 13, 1847); "there is also a want of shading in some of the characters; they are out and out villains of the melodramatic stamp, such as we seldom find in human nature" (May 11, 1850). Dickens's "characters do not present the mixtures of good and bad in the same proportions as we find in nature. Some of his characters are thoroughly and ideally perfect; others are thoroughly and ideally detestable"; while Thackeray's "study seems to be to give the good and bad together, in very nearly the same proportions that the cunning apothecary, Nature herself, uses" (June 7, 1851). Thackeray gives us characters "as they really are, as the whole world is, with a mixture of good and evil, hopes and fears, selfishness and generosity" (*Home Journal*, April 26, 1851). A *Harper's* reviewer thought *The Tutor's World* defective because it painted "an ideal of heartless egotism on the one side, and of generous self-sacrifice on the other"; in *Villette*, however, "the characters are purely human. They make no claim to angelic virtues; nor do they disgust the sensitive reader by any demonic manifestations" (January 1852).

In these comments we observe the reviewers' interest in the moral aspect of character; all traits carried a known moral charge. The reason for the great reviewer interest in characterization as a higher achievement than plot in the novel is closely connected with the desire of this group to improve the novel by making it a more "truthful," that is, moral, form. Nevertheless, in a well-intentioned but inept novel an author might choose the easy way to distinguish characters: to give each only one trait and make a contrast between good and evil that quickly enables readers to tell characters apart. Marion Harland's *Alone*, according to *Putnam's* for June 1855, evinces "a sharp insight into the workings of human nature, making the nicest distinctions and shades of character with a keen, firm touch, and without those strong and exaggerated contrasts, which are too often evidences of confused conceptions, and imperfect execution." The unmixed character implied such marginal forms as caricature, melodrama, and allegory.

Reviews of the time clearly distinguish the allegory as a different form from the novel, primarily on the basis of unmixed characterization, with the novel judged a superior form. We know, of course, that Poe excoriated allegory; as he wrote in *Graham's* when reviewing Bulwer's *Night and Morning* in April 1841, "pure allegory is at all times an abomination." But Poe's was not a lone voice, though his rhetoric was much harsher—on this and every other issue where he took a stand—than that of other reviewers of the era. "His allegorical design," the *Mirror* commented ironically on a novel by G. P. R. James, "may excuse him for making his villain a perfect demon" (July 16, 1842). "The moment the incidents and the characters are made allegorical," the *Literary World* said of *Lady Alice; or, The New Una*, "they lose all the interest with which their previous reality has invested them" (July 21, 1849). *Hugo*, by Elizabeth Oakes Smith, was, to a reviewer for *Harper's*, an "allegory of a very refined and subtle character, appealing but indirectly to the mass of human sympathies" (December 1850). A *Graham's* reviewer of Mrs. Marsh's *Ravenscliffe* noted that "the characters are only seen in their passionate moods. . . . Though this gives emphasis to the ethical intent of the authoress, she sacrifices to it some of the most important principles of the true method of characterization. Her persons are apt to slide into personified passions" (April 1852).

Unlike melodrama, which was only a crude type of novel, allegory embodied a different formal principle. The novel's formal principle was plot, its reader connection the interest of the story; the allegory's formal principle was exposition, and its reader connection the interest of ideas. Where characters in fiction were devised as the agents of action, in allegory they were vehicles for concepts. In one sense the allegory was simpler than the novel, in another more subtle. Above all, however, it was not and could not be a popular form. Hence, much as our reviewers wanted better novels, they did not want them to become allegory.

This distinction explains some assessments of works by Hawthorne and Melville, since these authors were seen at least in part as allegorists. A *Tribune* reviewer said that the story of Melville's *Mardi* "has no movement, no proportions, no ultimate end, and unless it is a huge allegory . . . no significance or point" (May 10, 1849). A reviewer in the *Literary World* explained that the multiple formal character of Melville's works created critical problems. "When to [romantic fictions and statements of absolute fact] is added that the romance is made a vehicle of opinion and satire through a more or less opaque allegorical veil, as particularly in the latter half of *Mardi*, and to some extent in this present volume [*Moby-Dick*], the critical difficulty is considerably thickened. It becomes quite impossible to submit such books to a distinct classification" (May 22, 1851). A *Harper's* reviewer wrote of *Moby-Dick* that "beneath the whole story, the subtle, imaginative reader may perhaps find a pregnant allegory, intended to illustrate the mystery of human life" (December 1851).

The case of Hawthorne was more complex than that of Melville, for whereas Melville's allegories were about the mystery of human life, Hawthorne's were about human character itself and hence shared many points with the novel while perhaps belonging to a different genre. *Knickerbocker* referred in May 1850 to Hawthorne as "skilled to these allegorical, typical semblances." The *Literary World* interpreted his distinction between novel and romance as claiming "license . . . in favor of a process semi-allegorical, by which an acute analysis may be wrought out and the truth of feeling be minutely elaborated" (April 26, 1851). The *North American* said it was difficult to refer Hawthorne "to any recognized class of writers" because, "so far as our cognizance extends, he is the only individual of his class. . . . Plain story-telling, whether true or fictitious, is entirely beyond, or rather beneath, his capacity" (January 1854).

The mixed character called for by reviewers was not, in general, a changing character; the mixture was static. From time to time a critic noted, and always approvingly, that a character developed over the course of the novel. "The gradual change of the heroine, from the self-willed school girl to the intellectual and self-sacrificing woman, is portrayed with a skill that shows an intimate acquaintance with the secret springs of human nature" (*Godey's*, May 1848); "the progressive development of character is admirably depicted" (*Home Journal*, November 22, 1851). But for the most part the only change in character expected was a change in the reader's knowledge of that character, an increasing discovery of what was already there. Character, like plot, would be revealed in the course of a fiction; and against that criterion even Dickens was vulnerable to criticism (as in these remarks from *Putnam's*, November 1853): "Our first sight of Dickens' characters makes us perfectly acquainted with them, and we can know nothing more about them: they are shown to us over and over again, but always the same. . . . It is this permanence and fixedness of character which makes it necessary for Dickens to introduce new personages continually to keep up the interest of the reader." Though the character itself did not have to change in the course of the novel, the novelist was expected to conceal some aspects so that the impression of the character might change. Not character itself, but the psychological process of coming to know a character, was the focus of mimesis and its evaluation here.

The ideas about character and characterization I have been discussing thus far remained constant during the second quarter of the nineteenth century in American novel reviewing; but, we need to remember, novel reviewing was a practical activity existing in interaction with the novels that came to hand and the evident preferences of readers. In the period between 1840 and 1860 reviewers saw something new and important happening to character in novels. Increasingly defined by means of inner traits, character behavior became dependent rather than primary in characterization, and attention turned to the inner life as the field of action. Before 1850 reviews have little to say about the inner life of characters—traits are congeries of actions. After 1850 the inner life increasingly takes precedence. The instigator of this change seems to have been Charlotte Brontë. Reviewers even proposed a new subgenre of the novel, the "subjective" or "psychological" novel, originating with her work. Once identified, the genre could be applied retroactively to explain the works of others, like Thackeray and Hawthorne.

"The author of *Jane Eyre* and *Shirley* is prodigious in character," the *Literary World* wrote on December 18, 1849. "Assuming that people have been overdosed with the fiction that is all romance, and plot, and catastrophe, on the one hand, and that which is all satire and exaggerated humor on the other, Mr. Currer Bell resorts to new elements of interest and intensity, and finds them in the study, analysis, and development, of the passions, motives, and impulses, which make up the individuality and vitality of strongly marked characters." A reviewer in the *Southern Literary Messenger* commented in June 1855 that "the most successful novels of the present day have been those in which the trials and sorrows, the love and despondency, the reverses and triumphs of this life, as they are experienced by women, are thrown in an autobiographical form before a sympathizing world. Charlotte Brontë initiated the new mode in fiction, in those wonderful narratives wherein she exposed to view the inward workings of a restless and fiery nature. . . . Since Miss Brontë, many other writers have essayed the same

psychological style of fictitious composition." A connection between this type of fiction and a female viewpoint was also noted
in an Easy Chair on novels in *Harper's*: "the modern novel is
reproached for its subjective character—for its constant tendency
to explore the secrets of action—and a kind of masculine excellence and robust healthiness is claimed for the novels our fathers
read and liked." The change might be attributed to the entrance
of ever more women, whose lives were less eventful and range of
perceptions more restricted than men's, into the field of novel
writing and reading (August 1859). Certainly the characteriza-
tions of Scott, Bulwer, and even Dickens looked much cruder to
reviewers in the 1850s than they had seemed only a decade
before.

The earliest American comment on the interior life as such
that I have found occurs in an unfavorable review of G. P. R.
James's *Morley Ernstein* in the *Mirror* for July 16, 1842. "There
may be those who can throw aside the veil which hides the
human heart, trace the windings of its tortuous, self-returning
labyrinths, coolly watch the fierce conflict between the passions
that inhabit them, and then, returning to 'this upper light,'
spread before us a faithful map of their wanderings, and a graphic picture of their struggles; but if such there be, Mr. James is not
one of them. It is true that he constantly speaks of the 'motives'
which actuate his characters, and gives a superficial analysis of
their thoughts, but the more subtle and refined vibrations of the
soul are hidden from him." Comments like this one, sparse in the
1840s and virtually absent earlier, became commonplace after
1850.

Knickerbocker, in a famous phrase, called *The Scarlet Letter* "a
psychological romance . . . a study of character, in which the
human heart is anatomized" (May 1850). The *Literary World* saw
in *The Scarlet Letter* "a subtle knowledge of character in its secret
springs and outer manifestations" (March 30, 1850). *Sartain's* described Charlotte Brontë as "not merely a keen observer of the
externals of humanity, but a psychological chemist" (February
1850). A *Home Journal* reviewer praised a novel that "analyzes
with a microscopic eye, all the subtleties of the human heart"
(November 1, 1851). *Godey's* iterated: an author "has evidently
studied the human heart"; "these tales are from the pen of one
who has evidently made the impulses of the human heart her

study"; a novel "manifests a familiar acquaintance with the motives and impulses of the human heart" (February 1853, December 1855, May 1858). The *Ledger* praised Southworth for her "keen insight into the workings of the human heart" (June 5, 1858).

Gaskell's *Cranford* inspired a "pleased attention . . . which is altogether due to the exquisite nicety with which the human heart is exhibited" (*Graham's*, October 1853). *Christian Examiner* reviews referred to "large insight into the motives of human conduct" and "rare insight into human motives" in Charles Reade's novels (November 1855, November 1856); recalled how "*Jane Eyre* took the public by surprise with the wealth of its revelations of interior life" (March 1859); and praised *The Virginians* for "faithfulness of the revelation of interior life" (January 1860). "Novel-readers now-a-days," the *North American* said in connection with the Brontës, "are not satisfied with pictures of external and social life, however brilliantly colored they may be, or however various in style. . . . We ask for deeper insight into character, for the features of the mind and heart rather than of the face and figure. . . . The author plays the part of anatomist, and dissects the heart, brain, and nerve, to lay them before the reader for examination and analysis" (October 1857). If novels had always involved concealments and revelations, secrets and mysteries, they continued to do so in this new mode but located these secrets in the human heart instead of in strongboxes or lost letters. The novelist, who had recently emerged as a recorder of the social scene and human behavior, now became a chronicler of a part of the world that could not be observed, so that her or his powers were functions of insight rather than observation.

Of course these many expectations regarding the treatment of character had to be relaxed for minor characters, since equally elaborate handling of all agents in a story would confuse the interest. In discussions of minor characters one finds stereotypes described as instances of psychological acumen: "The character of the foolish, romantic mother is admirably drawn; the Aunt is a bold, original portraiture; in Henriette the fine lady is described to perfection; and cousin John is a noble ideal of manhood, skilfully, yet truthfully portrayed" (*Peterson's* on Emilie Carlen's *John*, March 1854); *Harper's* called A. S. Roe "one of most most natural and effective delineators of American character," in support of which it offered "the substantial country gentleman, the village clergyman, and the rustic beauty as well as the industrious farm-laborer, the honest mechanic, and the genteel loafer from the city, who poisons the purity of the mountain atmosphere by his corrupt presence" (May 1855). Even more telling is its comment on *Saratoga:* "the characters brought upon the scene bear the decided marks of individuality, showing that they are not merely the productions of fancy, but have been suggested by actual prototypes"; these include a garrulous groom, an old Continental soldier, and a half-breed. "It is clear," the review wound up, "that the writer has made himself perfectly at home with Cooper" (September 1856). The real-world prototypes have suddenly become stock literary characters. Expectations of new insights into character have changed to expectations of standard literary treatment.

These remarks about minor characters bring to our attention certain important disjunctions, or potential disjunctions, in the reviewers' commentary. We of course expect that all the revelations or secrets of the human heart exposed by the supposedly new interest in individual character will be constructed within categories made possible by the culture even if they operate at the margins of cultural discourse. But the comments about minor characters raise the question whether the vaunted revelations of novelists were even supposed to disclose anything new or whether they were rather to confirm what was in the air about human nature. This question is raised in a different fashion by the stress on the moral aspect of character traits, a stress that makes clear that the revelations of the human heart had to conform to a moral framework if they were to be accepted as truthful. The demand for mixed characters involved moral mixtures and incorporated the era's belief that there was good in all, though none were all good.

And the question is even more urgently posed by female characterization—indeed so much so as to put the entire matter of achieved characterization in fiction in doubt. Virtually every novel, of course, contained women characters as major or central figures. Love and marriage were not the only *topoi* of a plot, but they were the most common; even if stories concentrated on a male protagonist, they required significant heroines. And in many novels a woman was the main character. Thus it is not a minor matter when it turns out that the general rules laid down by critics for constructing and evaluating character are overridden, modified, or ignored in the case of female characterization. The highest examples of female characterization, according to reviewers, approximate the woman to a type. The "best" women characters are not individuals, are not mixed, and certainly have no secrets to be laid bare. They are "Woman." In the discourse on characterization of women the substitution of norms for observation or discovery is so pervasive that one feels oneself close to a major cultural deception. When we recall that women, especially young women, were taken to be the main consumers of the genre, it is difficult not to believe that the potential of the novel as an agent of female acculturation seemed more important to reviewers than its potential as an instrument of new knowledge of human character.

It is of course impossible at this distance to begin to know whether reviewers were consciously or unconsciously hypocritical; perhaps they did believe that "women were like that." I have already shown (in chapter 3) how their visions of novel readers' "appetites" were not congruent with an idea of women as pure, innocent, self-sacrificing. And there is plenty of commentary in which the female character praised is deliberately offered to young female readers as a model or ideal, not as a perceptive description of a likely woman. The particular belief in the essential nature of women appears quite a bit like willful blindness. However that may be, there is no aspect of novel discourse in which the cultural is more intransigently "naturalized" than in commentary on female characters. *Mary Seaham*, according to *Peterson's*, is "marked with all that delicate perception of the varied phases of woman's character, in which Mrs. Grey so eminently excels in depicting and laying bare. The struggles of the heroine, in loving not *wisely*, yet *too well*; and the gradual yet natural transfer of her affections to a nobler object; are all colored with that rare tact and fidelity of narration, which only the most consummate knowledge of a woman's heart could have achieved" (November 1852). If the key word operating here is "natural," equally key words are missing, with such euphemisms as "not wisely yet too well" substituted. Mrs. Grey's achievement is not only in her knowledge of a woman's heart, but in the "tact" with which she does not speak that knowledge, thereby achieving the "fidelity" to an image of woman that involves both keeping her secrets and denying that she has any by substituting proprieties for description.

It seems to me of equal importance that descriptions of certain stereotyped traits were promulgated as the essence of an artistic handling of female character *and* that roughly half the characters in any given novel were thus not only excepted from the criterion of individualized portrayal but were faulted if the criterion was followed. I do not mean to propose as new the observation that our cultural heritage did not and does not give women fully human status (however that status is defined). But the talk about novels in this crucial era—when the mode of fiction later to be canonized as the "great" novel *on account of characterization* made its appearance—does provide a striking example of the phenomenon. We see this most crudely in the existence of the asymmetrical category "female characterization." "Female" is the only class of characters singled out on the grounds of content rather than structure. "In the delineation of character—especially of female character—he exhibits remarkable power and a wide acquaintance with human nature in its most secret depths," the *Christian Examiner* announced of Charles Reade in November 1855. "The delineation of the female characters in this novel is especially admirable," the *Atlantic* wrote in November 1857 of his *White Lies*, and again in July 1859: "his portraits of character are capital, especially those of feminine character, which are peculiarly vivid and *spirituel*."

In fact, when female characters *were* strongly individualized, reviewers were apt to object. *Graham's* complained about the attitude toward female character evinced in Charlotte Brontë's novels: "the authoress, in fact, is a strong-minded woman, a hardy, self-relying egoist from the very strength of her individuality; and she has stores of vitriolic contempt and scorn for her weak sisters." Conversely, however, *Putnam's* for June 1857 asserted that "the triumph of *Jane Eyre* is the splendor of its vindication of woman as woman, deprived of all the accessories which generally inveigle interest." These reviews come to contrary judgments that imply the same assumptions: that individuality in a woman is aberrant and hateful; that woman is most accurately portrayed in her "weakness" as a type; and that this type, even though admittedly weak, is both adorable and admirable. "The heroine . . . is a fragile, beautiful, lovable specimen of womanhood," the *Literary World* remarked of Mrs. Marsh's *Ravenscliffe* on February 28, 1852. A very nice plot line, according to many reviewers, was one in which a potentially individual woman matured into a type. The heroine of *Villette* "reminds us, in many things, of Jane Eyre. She is the same strong-minded woman, yet when she comes within the sphere of a strong-minded man, she becomes, in a similar manner, his 'loving satellite,'" *Peterson's* told readers in May 1853. The individuality of the woman gives way to the category, and all is well. The very category of "female character" hypostatized such a character; and even in our relatively liberated world that category retains reifying power though almost every traditionally accepted trait within the category is queried. At the time it was first promulgated in fiction reviewing, the situation in America was that most novel readers were believed to be women; close to 40 percent of the authors whose novels were reviewed were women; and the matter of women's rights was constantly in the air and on people's minds. The conception of the "true" woman's character was to some degree deliberately obfuscatory, since it was acknowledged to be an ideal even while it was promulgated as natural. This character was defined in relation not to individualism but to an inclusive social totality in which a domestic ideology supposed a certain kind of social stability. In brief—and reductively, I admit—if an emergent ideology was encouraging men to think of themselves as individuals, to do and dare, women were being made responsible for the coherence of the social structure that such individualism threatened.

A *Christian Examiner* reviewer, writing on Alston's *Monaldi* in January 1842, openly collapsed the real and ideal woman, the exemplary and the natural, in praising the heroine. Described as "too pure and too trusting even to suspect that she was suspected," she "is no common-place novel-heroine whom any school-girl may imitate, made up of roses and ringlets, useless sensibilities, and unrestrained enthusiasm, the creature of circumstance or emotion. . . . Let us pray our young countrywomen to study this portrait of calm, dignified, exquisite grace, gleaming upon us in a heavenly light—yet not so etherialized as to be unfit for the earth to which it belongs. And let them copy it as they can." The commonplace heroine who can be copied by any schoolgirl must be a realistic portrayal; no need to copy her, the schoolgirl is already that heroine. Just how she may study and emulate an "unsuspecting" character when the very activities prescribed put the character out of reach, we are not to know. In point of fact, the heroine of Alston's book functions mainly as the occasion for the reviewer to give girlish readers a scolding—that is, to play schoolmaster. Thus an ideal of female excellence is presented as a real character, character in the novel is lauded for its exemplary—rather than realistic—intention, and the reviewer is defined as enforcer of moral values and appropriate behavior for young girls.

Here is the *Democratic Review* for June 1843 on a character in a Bremer novel: "the active, pleasant, frolicksome, serious, affectionate, charming little wife, who always does and says the very thing she should, and has the faculty of making all comfortable and joyous around her, who has a smile or a tear for all, as one or the other is proper, and always energy to aid all who are in trouble, and that too without obtruding her sympathy, or suspecting herself of being a prodigy, is one of the finest female characters in the whole range of fictitious literature." What has happened to the demand for mixed character, or the interest in real character rather than prodigies? And in what sense of the term can this depiction be one of the "finest"? It is, of course, a depiction of the ideal wife—not a person but a role—that is presented as a fine psychological study of an individual. "St. Leon's wife," rhapsodized the *American Review* about Godwin's works, "is a pattern for all women, wives, and mothers; an example of as pure, generous, and devoted love, as ever warmed the human heart. . . . It makes one proud of existence [*sic*] to think that a being of such lofty purposes, wisdom, kindness, radiant loveliness, consoling her husband, cleaving to him in his broken fortunes, watching over the welfare of her children, and moving about like a guardian angel, ever had existence here on earth" (September 1848). We never find a reviewer recommending a male character as a "pattern"; in fact pattern heroes are faulted for their lack of verisimilitude, since they are unmixed. Nor, of course, is any male character ever discussed as a husband.

Examples can be multiplied. "We know nowhere, in the range of fiction, a more sweet and engaging heroine. . . . Such a female, cheering the domestic fireside with her smiles, and diffusing around her a very atmosphere of peace and happiness, is our *beau ideal* of a wife or daughter" (*Peterson's*, May 1847). Reviewing Elizabeth Stuart Phelps's clerical novel *The Sunny Side*, the *Christian Examiner* observed that "the good man's crown is the 'virtuous woman' who has cast in her lot with his. Her character is beautifully drawn. The cheerer of her husband in despondency, the kind and wise guide of her children in the right way, with modesty prompting the wish to shrink from publicity, but high principle curbing the indulgence of that wish, she appears the true pastor's wife, ready when occasion calls to be the friend and counsellor of those around her, but finding her peculiar sphere of duty in her own home" (September 1852). "If it were commanded that no author should create a heroine whom he was not willing instantly to marry," *Harper's* editorialized, forgetting that close to half the authors it reviewed were women, "how the 'ideal' would go by the board, and the good, generous, noble women of reality and daily life come by their own again" (May 1854). The reviewers were not substituting the real for the ideal, but one ideal for another—no longer the beautiful, useless, passive, delicate clinging creature of the eighteenth century, woman is now a hardworking, busy, tireless, resilient, ever-cheerful helpmeet: kind, wise, consolatory, sympathetic; a workhorse wife and mother—mainly wife—whose self-subordinating toil and attention support individuality in others.

If there was but one female character, and if plot derived from character, then woman could have but one story. In these reviews the story implied is of the testing of femininity: how far might it be subjected to trials and obstacles *and yet remain womanly?* "The character of Edith is a beautiful conception of human patience, as well as of the virtue and dignity of true womanhood, under the severest trials" (*Godey's*, May 1856). "Rose Clark," said a *Harper's* reviewer in January 1856, "develops a sweet feminine nature, and wins both sympathy and admiration by her noble womanly bearing in the most perplexing circumstances"; in *Sylvan Holt's Daughter* "every new trial only proves a new revelation of her sweet womanly dignity . . . until at length she is placed in a position which shows that her strength of character is equal to her gentleness of disposition" (February 1859). Despite the important substitution of activity for passivity, this story is structurally similar to the eighteenth-century woman's story of retaining or losing virginity. Instead of holding to a corporeal sign of one's value as a woman and of one's value *only* as a woman, the heroine now must retain her feminine character. This is a more spiritual, but perhaps a no less coercive story than the one it replaces, and it is still about preserving, keeping, saving something in the self that is valued by others, only because it is valued by others.

And while the eighteenth-century story offered women who kept their virginity the security of marriage, this one implies that marriage is no security at all. In fact, the discourse offers women no reward for striving to attain this cultural ideal, or indeed even for attaining it, except praise. Reviewers used female characters in fiction to provide samples of the praise a woman could get were she good like the heroine. "The character of the heroine is the most beautiful conception of the womanly virtues that could be presented"; "the character of the heroine is a masterpiece. There is a sweetness, a grace, a naturalness, a living, perennial freshness. . . . She thinks, feels, talks and acts like a true woman, and as such endears herself to every reader" (*Godey's*, May 1858, August 1858). *Peterson's* was especially prone to these effusions: "There have been heroines, perhaps, as lovely in character ideally. There have been others as true to life. But we can recall no one, we repeat, who unites such reality with such surpassing excellence. She convinces the most skeptical reader that it is possible, even in this world, to be 'but little lower than the angels'" (April 1853); "the heroine . . . is the charm of the novel. Sweet, pretty, Belinda, inexperienced and imaginative, yet full of sound common sense, where, in any late fiction, have we a delineation so fresh and true?" (March 1854); "in the whole realm of modern fiction there is not a more lovely creation than Hildegarde. . . . Her conduct, under the most trying circumstances, is ever noble; but ever natural also to her character" (March 1855); "the character of Anne, the elder sister, is most beautiful. She is one of those unselfish beings, those daily martyrs, of whom the ranks of the sex are full. We recommend the work to our readers, satisfied that they will be delighted with it, in proportion to their taste, culture, and true womanhood." Readers of such rhetoric may see how psychoanalysis came to define the female character as "naturally" masochistic and narcissistic, for only the pleasures of such drives are allotted to women.

I do not want to say that novels *themselves* took this approach to female characterization; I am talking only about the terms in which novels were described. In fact, this is not the story I believe the most popular of the "woman's fictions" of the time were telling. The critical discussion, however, is virtually univocal in its approach to female characterization; even Margaret Fuller's dissent in the *Tribune* betrayed many of the dominant presuppositions. While most reviewers were highly critical of George Sand's writings, Fuller defended them on the ground of their portrayal of an essential female character that she assumed to have real existence. *Consuelo*, she wrote, "is entirely successful, in showing how inward purity and honor may preserve a woman from bewilderment and danger, and secure her a genuine independence. Whoever aims at this is still considered by unthinking or prejudiced minds as wishing to despoil the female character of its natural and peculiar loveliness" (April 25, 1846). While Fuller hoped to enlarge the appropriate sphere of women beyond "the usual home duties" to include an "intellectual calling," she did not want to deny woman her particular nature. If the would-be intellectual heroines of such novelists as Bremer, Dumas, or others "ended as they did, it was for want of the purity of ambition and simplicity of character" that George Sand's heroines are allowed to possess. In the sequel to *Consuelo*, *The Countess of Rudolstadt*, the heroine's "native strength, her loyalty, her depth, grandeur and delicacy of feeling, her courage and generosity, seem to belong alike to the actual and the ideal world. In her we recognize the true features of woman as she should be, as she may be even now" (February 4, 1847).

Authors who were criticized for failure in the department of female characterization were faulted according to this new ideal of woman as formed to serve rather than be served. The women in Cooper's novels "are utterly characterless and insipid," a *North American* reviewer asserted. "There is no variety, no grace, no life in them. . . . The tenderness of her spirit, the depth, and strength, and purity of her affections, her real power, her influence over the course and issue of events,—these are things that our author either does not understand, or cannot adequately set forth. Female characters are introduced, as beings *for* whom something is to be done, but who themselves do nothing, and say nothing—to the purpose. They are constantly in the way, constantly in difficulties,—the cause of exertion in others, but never effecting any thing for themselves" (January 1838). We might applaud the reviewer for criticizing a passive, insipid characterization, until we note that he devalues passivity because he likes women who are active on behalf of others. And note how plural female characters quickly modulate to a single female figure: "her" tenderness, "her" strength, "her" powers. No female liberation was implied in this active ideal: as a later *North American* reviewer wrote of Cooper, "the most rabid asserter of the rights of woman is scarcely more ignorant of woman's true power and dignity" (January 1852).

The character most troubling to reviewers was (not surprisingly) Becky Sharp in Thackeray's *Vanity Fair*. Not only did Becky ignore the pattern of the true woman; she was a convincing and artistic characterization, and (even more alarming) readers liked her, not least because she was like a man: that is, self-directed, individualistic, assertive. "Our favorite," the *Democratic Review* wrote in October 1848, "is Rebecca Sharp, clever, keen, pliant little 'Becky.' What though she is heartless, selfish, designing, intriguing; we love her because she is talented, energetic—and successful." The *Christian Examiner* for January 1856, in contrast, fulminated that "no modern writer has done more to strip from the very name of woman all associations of moral beauty. . . . One would imagine that it had never been Mr. Thackeray's privilege really to know, intimately to appreciate, and absolutely to recognize, a truly noble, gifted, lovely woman." Another reviewer for the journal argued in September 1860 that "if Thackeray is sharpsighted to detect the foibles common to the sex, no man has truer sympathy with woman's peculiar trials, nor has any one reverenced more those virtues peculiarly her own." Attack and defense are over neither the artistry of the creation nor the achievement of memorable individual portraiture, but rather the degree to which the character represents something "common to the sex"—trials and virtues peculiarly woman's own. Of course no parallel mode exists for talking about male characters.

Were women really so different from men in this basic particular? Did they really lack individualities of their own, so much so that the wonderful achievement of the novel in individual portraiture had to be suspended in their case? Was it possible that men too lacked individualities, and that the false ideal was of the individual rather than the type? Such questions were not asked. Not a single reviewer in the period seemed to notice that two entirely different systems of evaluation were operating when character in the novel and female character were discussed. Accordingly, none thought to notice that each evaluative approach put the other in question.

And only two critics even seemed to see that the question was, at the least, a vexed one. Both wrote in the *North American*, one in July 1826, the other in July 1853. The earlier reviewer was talking about Cooper, and he said that there is "no task of the novel writer more difficult, we suppose, than that of delineating a good female character . . . whether it be, that the softer sex is less marked by striking and individual character, or because we are less accustomed to see them in scenes which call it forth, or because their genuine peculiarities are of too ethereal a cast . . . or because our tastes are somewhat capricious upon this interesting topic." The later reviewer, writing about Thackeray, commented that "no portraiture of the female mind that shall be complete, and altogether satisfactory, is to be expected from one of the other sex. It is hardly possible that any being should see deeper into the mind of a being of another race, than the point where those qualities lie from which arise the interrelation of the two races. . . . If men are unable to penetrate the important secrets of the sex, women are no less unwilling to reveal them. It is only one who has herself overleaped the bounds of tyrannical custom, who ever ventures to depict that struggle which, at some period of life, a proud and ardent woman can hardly fail to pass through. And when such a picture is presented . . . the sex itself is always foremost to cry out against it, as unfeminine and monstrous. It is in fact a betrayal—a revelation of internal weakness to the common foe."

These comments put the matter of characterization in the novel in question in various ways. If the inner nature of one gender is closed to the other, how can the novelist pose as a discoverer of profound interior truth? And if truths that are known cannot be uttered—for whatever reason—how can the novel be celebrated for its revelation of psychological secrets? In effect, then, the genre that critics were praising for its revelations they knew in the most important instance to be rather a concealer than a revealer of secrets: men could not, women would not, and both sexes should not, tell. The real function of at least female characterization was to deceive—for some, in order to inspire women to strive toward an ideal; for others, to screen women from the betrayal that the new demands of psychological characterization could not but lead to if they were seriously heeded. In either case the issue of female characterization so far as the genre of the novel is concerned makes it seem possible that the novel—even and perhaps especially the "best" examples of the genre, by which I mean those that were most praised by reviewers for their characterological content—never really could achieve what it was praised for, fidelity or insight into human nature.

The issue can be expanded beyond women—on whom I have concentrated because there is so much, and such disingenuous, discourse—to the companion issue of sexuality, which in all these purportedly revelatory novels had apparently no place at all. While Foucault may be correct that our talk about sexuality to some degree has "invented" it in modern times, it has surely had *some* role in human behavior and motivation through the ages; but one would not guess so from any discussion of character in these journals. As we shall see in chapter 9, novels treating sexual matters were generally condemned; the right way to treat sex was to ignore it. Novelists who ignored it were considered superior as psychologists to those who dealt with it; the latter were sensationalists. But since novel readers, according to reviewers, continued to read for story, they may not have been fooled by those who sought to instruct them by presenting ethical norms as psychological realism.

6

Aspects of Narration

Novel reviewers in America before the Civil War did not discuss the novel as a verbal construct. While they showed an awareness that novels were composed of words, they entered the field of the novel at a far higher level of its organization than the verbal base. The assumption that the phenomena named as plot, character, and the like were properly understood by studying the lexical and syntactic units of the text—in other words, by reducing it to elementary particles—did not yet exist. Although it is impossible to know what their response would have been to such a notion, my guess is that they would think (as certain holistic biologists do today) that intervening levels of organization made the reduction of the novel to its basic particles of doubtful value for explaining its highest functions. And the highest functions—that is, the effects of the whole on the reader—were their concern. Mid-nineteenth-century novel reviewing also lacked many of the intermediate language-centered levels of hierarchy that constitute such an important part of present-day practical novel criticism in scholarly as well as mass-circulation journals. There was, for example, no talk of symbols, metaphors, or imagery. Narrator and point of view had only a dimly perceived verbal existence. Even style, which all reviewers discussed, was treated at some remove from specifically identified language features.

Reviewers did recognize, however, that a number of different kinds of language acts contributed to the narrative totality, and they had a vocabulary for discerning and commenting on these. The chief evaluative criterion was subordination of such elements to the organizing principle of plot. All narrative elements were contributions; if they became intrusive, if they dominated the work, then the work became less like a novel. A predominantly descriptive novel, for example, was too much like an essay; a mainly conversational novel too much like a drama; a chiefly reflective novel too much like a sermon or treatise—and so on. While, however, each aspect of narration was functional with respect to a whole organized as a plot, and the best novelist was one who mastered and employed all of them, particular novelists might show particular abilities. Hence consideration of these subsidiary or dependent narrative features permitted reviewers to make specific judgments and to create useful critical descriptions of individual works and authors.

This commentary on *Eastford* from *Graham's* for April 1855 conveys a reviewer's conception of the narrative totality. The author "has endeavored to make his book a representation of the common aspects of New England life and character. . . . The interest of the volume depends in no small degree on the exhibition of the struggle, now going on in every New England village, between old and new fashioned opinions. . . . The hero and heroine have the same rigid truth to actual life which characterizes the other personages. . . . The style of the volume is pure, sweet, graceful, and vigorous, indicating a practiced hand in composition. It is equal to all the demands of description, narration, conversation, and discussion. . . . The power of description is quite noticeable." This is a novel because it has a plot, a struggle involving a hero and heroine. The interest of the plot is enhanced because it refers to a real-life state of affairs, and a secondary, subordinate interest is created by the depiction, in local color fashion, of "aspects of New England life and character." Narration itself divides into description, narration proper, conversation, and discussion; style is a different, overlapping category separable from yet active in all these narrative tasks.

Description, as anyone who reads or writes narrative theory knows, is at best a problematic concept. It is difficult to distinguish from narration, since in the novel everything must be described. Reviewers in nineteenth-century American journals spoke of description when the object of narration was static, and of narration proper when it was active. Of course there is a not-too-fine line where this division blurs; and the most common narrational faults in novels—diffuseness and overminuteness—

occurred whether the subject was an event or an existent. Diffuseness simply meant writing too much and therefore slowing the action or bringing it to a halt even when action was the subject of discourse. George Sand, according to the *North American*, "refines too much, and overdoes the work with a minuteness of detail, that spoils the effect" (July 1841). The *Literary World* complained that "the fault of *Margaret Percival*, as a work of fiction claiming to be received in the literature of the language, is its minuteness, even to tediousness"; it noted in another case that "the minuteness with which the characters are sketched, and the fidelity in conversation which they possess, are apt to weary ordinary readers eager for development of plot" (March 6, 1847; February 9, 1850). It identified the chief fault of Warner's *The Wide, Wide World* as "diffuseness. She tells a story or describes a scene with a woman's indiscriminate minuteness"; and it found the same problem in her *Queechy*: it is "too diffuse to please the hypercritical stickler for strictly artistic construction" (December 28, 1850; May 8, 1852). "Diffuseness is the main fault of Miss Chesebro', as of many other lady writers," it announced (December 18, 1852). "By putting 'too fine a point' on many of the incidents, the author provokes a feeling of impatience," a *Tribune* reviewer complained of Cummins's *The Lamplighter* (March 28, 1854).

Reviewers liked to associate diffuseness with women writers, in accordance with the stereotype of women as generally less well organized and less able than men to keep an ultimate end in view. But they did not claim that only women writers had this fault. Even such a master of narration as Cooper might be diffuse. "One capital defect," the *North American* wrote in an early (July 1822) review of *The Spy*, "is that excessive minuteness which leaves nothing for the imagination to supply. The enumeration of little unimportant actions—mere necessary consequences—and full length descriptions of the exact tone, look, and gesture, with which something, or nothing, is uttered, the precise graduation of this or that emotion . . . are prodigious *weakeners* of style." A *Graham's* review of Cooper's *Afloat and Ashore* noted that "at times his attention to minutiae is so close, that, although it does not fatigue, it is still calculated to irritate a reader who is clamorous for incident, and desirous of being borne onward quickly to the completion of the story" (October 1844). The concept of *pacing* was not named, but it is some sense of a proper pace for narration that controls the assessment of diffuseness.

Because narration itself, the chronicling of event, was so basic to the success of a novel, most reviewers took it for granted and wrote little about it, though they occasionally singled out a particularly powerful narrational ability. Cooper, despite occasional minuteness, was widely considered to have an unusual gift for narration though, interestingly, not for plotting: while overall his stories were not coherent, event by event they were fascinating. The *North American* in January 1838 noted that Cooper "has that skill in narration, the first requisite of a novelist, which, fastening the reader's attention on the issue of events immediately before him, will not allow him to observe any improbability in the plot, or incongruity in the character and actions of the agents. . . . It must be owned, however, that the author abuses his power." A retrospective review in July 1850 in the same journal made the same assessment: "his strength consisted chiefly in his descriptive power and his skill as a narrator. Many of the scenes and incidents created an interest that was almost painful. . . . The remainder of the story through which these fine sketches were distributed was generally a curious piece of patchwork." A *Southern Literary Messenger* reviewer wrote similarly of G. P. R. James: "he has the art of interesting you in his narrative. He has the genuine talent of the *racounteur*. This is a talent of the first necessity to the writer of fiction. . . . The peculiar gift, of which we speak, is not inventiveness, for which it might be taken, but rather something which manages, blends, conducts, and adroitly makes the most of, invention. It is indeed a talent to itself, and by itself . . . an absolute necessity to a greatly successful novelist" (September 1847).

A writer distinguished for his pacing was the popular Alexandre Dumas, whom the *Southern Literary Messenger* found "remarkable for the curt and rapid management of details, which leaves no feature of his picture wanting or blurred; and yet with all his particularity he is never tedious. He really consumes less space in his minute and full narratives than most authors consume in that style of general description which pretends to dash off scenes with a few bold strokes" (September 1847). Unlike Dumas, many writers attempting to avoid minuteness or diffuseness produced narratives lacking in consecutiveness. Disraeli's novels "want that adroit linking and sequency which should be present everywhere to secure and conduct the attention" (*Southern Literary Messenger*, December 1847). *The Matchmaker* is so "abrupt . . . that justice to the authoress obliges us to conjecture that the work has been despoiled of its original proportions" (*Literary World*, March 9, 1850). "In reading his scenes we always seem to have a play before us," a *Graham's* review commented on Reade's *White Lies*. "There is a rapid shifting of scene, without sufficient connection—for a novel" (December 1857).

Description

Although it is impossible to tell just where narration leaves off and description begins, the distinction did enable reviewers roughly to separate aspects of narrative designed directly to advance and develop the plot from aspects concerned rather to explain or decorate it. Minimal descriptiveness was artistically preferable to diffuseness, but no plot could be interesting if it lacked elaboration of events and characters; and a plot would not be coherent without narrated transitions and connectives. "The author should remember," the *Southern Literary Messenger* admonished Charles Reade, "that what is called *autorial comment* must in romances supply the place of scenery, dresses, and acting in the drama" (July 1855). The basic way of evaluating description was to consider whether it ultimately strengthened or dissipated the interest of the plot. When an author had a gift for description reviewers liked to point it out. Where description was overdone, they pointed that out too.

The reader's interest in Simms's *Guy Rivers*, according to *Knickerbocker*, is "kept down, it may be, by a little stateliness and minutiae of style and description in the first few pages" (August 1835). "One great fault of the author," it wrote on Simms again (November 1839), "is too much description. He does not leave enough to the imagination of the reader." And again: Simms winds "envelopes of dry bombastic description" around his scenes and characters (April 1846). One *Peterson's* review observed of Eugene Sue, "there is no author living who can surpass this man in force and brilliancy of description" (July 1845); another attacked Reade's *It Is Never Too Late to Learn* for "tedious prolixity" (December 1856). *Graham's* found "too much of quietly elaborated still life" in *Marmaduke Wyvil* (July 1843). "Historical and pictorial details" in Child's *Philothea* "are managed with much grace and adroitness, so that we are not wearied," a *Tribune* reviewer approved (June 3, 1845). *Harper's* noted that the subject of *Agnes Sorel*, by G. P. R. James, "affords an admirable opportunity for the exercise of the descriptive powers for which the author is remarkable" (April 1853). The *Christian Examiner* found Kingsley excelling "in description more than in dialogue or in narrative" (May 1857). *Putnam's* commented that Simms's works "have an undeniable tendency to prosiness, and the interest of description in them, which necessarily soon tires, is superior to that of characterization" (March 1857). Reviewers assumed that readers were interested in description only to a limited degree; "interest" remains supreme, and the safest authorial practice is to link all description firmly to the story.

Landscape description occupied a special place. Partly because of some persistence, especially in the earlier years of the period, of the eighteenth-century notion of the sublime, partly because Scott devoted space to scenic description, and partly because literary nationalism in America was associated with landscape, set pieces of landscape description appeared frequently, especially in American novels. Reviewers expected them, noted them, and assessed them as they did description more generally, for adding to or detracting from the progress of the narrative.

The *North American* (April 1825) approved the scenic descriptions in Sedgwick's *Redwood* while clarifying the rules by which it was judging: "there is much beautiful and striking description, but it is never so drawn out as to be tiresome, nor introduced so as to interrupt the interest of the story." It generalized about American novels in January 1853 that "the new circumstances of our position, and the feeling that our country is too little known to other countries, have prompted a descriptive tone—both as to scenery and manners—an appearance of the attempt to give information—which has almost put them out of the pale of fiction and within that of travels." The *New York Review*, in a largely favorable review of Kennedy's *Horse-Shoe Robinson*, observed that "the descriptions of scenery are eminently graphic, but they are too much in detail, and perhaps there are too many of them" (January 1842). *Knickerbocker* likewise objected, in June 1849, that in *My Uncle the Curate* "the scenic features of the landscape, and of the transitions of day and night, are a little over-described" (June 1849). And the *Home Journal* found a fault in "the too great exuberance of fancy in the descriptions of external nature" in Ann Stephens's *The Old Homestead* (October 27, 1855).

In February 1852 *Godey's* carried an essay by one of its contributing editors, Alice B. Neal, containing advice to would-be authors. She wrote that "the descriptions of natural scenery [should be] few and delicately handled—we say few, because readers generally are not interested in a geographical description of mountains and valleys that never existed, and that do not increase the excitement of the plot, or hasten the development of character. It is a form of amplification that too often serves only as a cloak for poverty of material." This general view was echoed by the *Atlantic*, whose reviewer complained about Anna Mowatt Ritchie's *Twin Roses* that "the defect, which especially mars the latter portion of the volume, is the absence of any artistic reason for the numerous descriptions of scenery which are introduced. The tourist and the novelist do not happily combine" (May 1858). An *Atlantic* reviewer also faulted *The New Priest in Conception Bay* because "descriptions of scenery are too frequently introduced, and pushed to a wearisome enumeration of particulars and minute delineation of details. . . . Scenery-painting in words is a characteristic of most recent American novels. . . . Every rock, every clump of trees, every strip of sea-shore, every sloping hillside, sits for its portrait. . . . When human hearts and human passions are animating or darkening the scene, we do not want to be detained by a botanist's description of plants, or a geologist's sketch of rocks" (December 1858).

But judicious scenic description merited praise. A *Knickerbocker* review praised Maria McIntosh's *Two Lives* because "her descriptions of scenery and the phenomena of the elements are clear and not over-labored" (October 1846); *Peterson's* liked the "descriptive passages, scattered everywhere through the pages, which bring before us the scent of clover, the hum of bees" in Warner's *Say and Seal* (June 1860). *Godey's* praised one novel for "many a beautiful picture of natural scenery," another for "pictures of western scenery," and another still for "beautiful scenery" (November 1850, August 1854, December 1856). The *Tribune* wrote of A. S. Roe that "few writers excel him in the delineation of American rural scenery" (October 12, 1858). Thus reviewers thought that descriptions of natural scenery, if not too lengthy or too detailed, might make pleasurable reading, but usually thought them an excrescence more likely to annoy than interest. They took a more relaxed line toward local color. While there was no formal need for rich detailing of setting except in the special case of the historical novel, a novelist might, they agreed, establish a strong secondary interest by presenting the manners and customs of a given place. American novelists, self-conscious about the uniqueness and transience of many aspects of their national life, might particularly aim for such a subsidiary interest. To some degree the presence of such an interest constituted a fictional subgenre.

Godey's, which had a strong literary nationalist bias, was especially concerned to point out and praise local color novels. The reader of *Talbot and Vernon* "will find much to interest him in the descriptions of western life and manners," *Lonz Powers* was admirable for its "various descriptions of primitive society in the West," *Tempest and Sunshine* "makes us acquainted with many interesting features of western life," the novelist Emerson Bennett's "pictures of western scenery, and delineations of western character, and of early life in the backwoods, have rarely been surpassed," *Farmingdale* was a "quiet New England story, in which the domestic manners and the peculiarities of the people are ably and interestingly portrayed," and *Ironthorpe, the Pioneer Preacher* "will no doubt prove most acceptable to that numerous class of readers who desire to be made acquainted with the peculiarities and adventures of western pioneer life in the early settlement of that region of our country" (July 1850, October 1850, December 1850, July 1854, August 1854, July 1855).

Other journals also pointed to local color in novels, again especially American novels. *Graham's* praised *Redwood*: "the best account we know of life among the Shakers"; *Farmingdale*: few books "represent with so much freshness and closeness the ordinary life of New England"; *Eastford*: "a representation of common aspects of New England life and character"; *Richard Hurdis*: "scenes and characters peculiar to the roughest border life"; *The Torchlight*: "American home life as it really is in the country"; *The Border Rover*: dealing with "that spirited and dramatic yet eminently natural life of the West, which, as every one knows, is extremely interesting to the reading class at large" (August 1850,

October 1854, April 1855, November 1855, January 1857, June 1857). *Putnam's* reviewers did not rate *A Long Look Ahead* high "as a work of art," but they found value "in its detailed, truthful delineations of New England life," and they described *Wolfsden* as "a tale of New England domestic life, faithful to local scenery and manners in many respects, and not without merit as a fable" (May 1855, March 1856).

The reportorial interest in local color novels was often viewed as a distraction from rather than an enhancer of the primary interest of plot. Local color therefore called for labeling so that the reader would know that the intense ongoing interest of the "novel proper" was likely to be diluted by accounts of regional life. For those mainly interested in the reportorial material the fable might seem intrusive. Something of the same problem obtained in travel literature; indeed, it is not unfruitful to think of local color writing as an intermediate form between travel literature and fiction. For those interested in actualities the fable might be more than distraction; it could falsify. Therefore the form of choice for local color or regional writing during these years was the sketch, a mode with loose structural requirements. Certainly the bulk of the volumes of sketches reviewed in these years were American collections with a strong local color emphasis: in these instances the question of the "fable" did not have to arise.

Whenever the local color writer attempted to claim either the popularity or prestige of the novel form by composing local color novels, the reviewers responded by a mode of analysis that in effect undercut these claims, suggesting that readers should approach the works for the intermittent rather than the continuing, shapely interest of the novel. In so doing, they made it clear that the local color novel was an artistically and emotionally weaker variant of the novel proper. "A pleasant and graceful little humorous tale of New England life." "Not without merit as a fable." These problems with respect to the handling of local color in long fiction are precisely those that we meet again later in the century when local color and regional writing became, according to standard literary history, a dominant mode in American fiction. In fact it appears that the form was a product of the earlier period, and just as dominant then, already recognized by reviewers as a characteristic American imaginative response to its own experience. Why has it been held to emerge in America only after the Civil War? First, because it has been perceived as a nostalgic reaction to the disruptions of the post–Civil War years and hence requiring those disruptions as a precondition; second, because deferring it to the end of the century has permitted present-day critics to offer the "romances" of Hawthorne and Melville, and hence the "romance" itself, as *the* practice of the American artist in midcentury. Of course, as reviewers of their own day make clear, Hawthorne and Melville were *not* representative American artists of their time.

In what we may think of as a formal struggle between plot and reportage within the local color novel, plot was bound to win if the novel was to remain a novel. If we look closely at the descriptions of local color novels in the reviews above, we observe that the critics were separating out two forms of the mode, the New England novel and the western. Each of these forms carried its own inherent expectations with respect to action and character. New England stories were invariably "quiet"; their settings were rural, their scope domestic. It is clear from the reviews that western stories were extremely popular, and it is difficult not to suppose that the basis of that popularity was the action rather than their fidelity to details of western life. One reviewer, in fact, says as much. This is the *Literary World* for October 5, 1850, reviewing James Weir's *Lonz Powers:*

> It is seldom that we meet with a book upon which it is so difficult for us to express our opinion, as this. The characters and incidents—wild and improbable as they may seem to the northern reader—are true to the life, while the language of the actors is generally unnatural, and entirely out of keeping with the location of the scenes. . . . The different phases of southwestern life, as exhibited in the last twenty years, present a rich, and, as yet, untenanted field for the novelist. That this has not been properly improved is, perhaps, owing, in a great measure, to the innumerable trashy, horrible, and utterly false "raw head and bloody bones" stories of that region, with which we have been inundated *usque ad nauseam.* There exists no necessity for the romancer's drawing upon his imagination to produce bloody-minded but chivalrous robber heroes, or accomplished and amazingly beautiful heroines. . . . Quite enough of the heroic and romantic may be found, ready-made to the author's hand, without his indulging in such ridiculously stupid and outrageously improbable fictions, as many

have done, who, knowing nothing of the ground, sit quietly in their chimney corners and deluge a credulous world with a careless stream of senseless trash.

This review permits us to question the usefulness of the local color novel as a vehicle for information and to propose that, whatever the writers had in mind, readers resorted to them, as to other novels, for story. The fable underlying western fiction had little or nothing to do with the actualities of western life; it was rather an imaginative construct proposing an alternative life, featuring the "West" as a remote place. Its value was precisely that assertions about life there could *not* be tested by the average reader, and thus the newfangled novel's obsession with probability could be circumvented.

If one of the two types of local color novel was unreliable, and really plot- rather than information-based, what of the other? The New England novel claimed fidelity to actualities by the quietness (that is, the dullness) of its material, boredom being an apparent earnest of accuracy where New England was concerned. To some extent we may suppose that the New England novel indeed *was* more accurate; I want to qualify this not unreasonable conclusion, however, in two ways. First, it may be that the very "quietness" of the type represented a fabulous expectation: if the western novel corresponded to the old adventure story, the New England novel was a modern pastoral. Second, we know that, among these New England novels, those that attained the greatest popularity (especially after 1850) focused on young heroines and contained a repeated plot that I have written about in another book; they were "woman's fictions" telling stories about the trials and triumphs of young women and hence structured as mythos.

If we return to a review of books by the Warner sisters (*North American*, January 1853) that I have quoted for other purposes in chapter 3, we may sense that, although these works were commendable for regional accuracy, this was not the reason why little girls, elder sisters, mamas, papas, and sober bachelors were all under the spell of *The Wide, Wide World* and *Queechy*. "As a matter of pure judgment," the review observes, "we must place their pictures of American country life and character above all their other merits, since we know not where, in any language, we shall find their graphic truth excelled." But, it goes on to ask, "what are the grounds of the admiration, or rather love, excited by these books?" (clearly implying that pictures of American country life cannot be the answer). "The interest . . . lies in a most life-like picture of the character and fate of a little girl . . . such as any of our daughters may be; unfortunate in some respects, happy in others; dependent, as all little girls, whatever their station or fortune, must be, on the virtue and affection of those about them; but showing, what all little girls cannot show, a degree of character, a firmness of principle, a sweetness of disposition, by no means impossible under the circumstances, yet far enough raised above common experience and expectation, to excite the imagination and stimulate the sympathy. . . . We care for all else only as this little piece of tender, budding womanhood is affected or influenced." Since this perceptive reviewer was addressing the adults who read the *North American*, she or he is not wrong to characterize Ellen as resembling "our daughters." The point, however, gains in significance when we remember for how many readers of *The Wide, Wide World* Ellen was like themselves.

Dialogue

The reviewers' common term for dialogue was "conversation." Unlike narration or description, it was not thought of as a necessary formal aspect of the novel, yet no reviewer expected to find a novel without it. Conversation served two literary functions. As an alternative to the narration, which was expected to be delivered in a single, conventional voice from a conventional stance, conversation introduced a certain amount of lexical and syntactic relief. In addition, conversation provided an opportunity for introducing wit and repartee enjoyable in themselves. Conversation thus was thought of in relation to or in distinction from narration and description. Addressing aspiring authors, *Godey's* counseled that "the conversations should be spirited or thoughtful . . . but always remember that they are conversations, and in real life one rarely moralizes a whole page without even a comment or ejaculation from the listener. Nor does a colloquial style often admit of sentences Johnsonian in length and finish. It is, more properly, characterized by abrupt transitions, terse opinions, or brilliant sallies" (February 1852). We can see here that a certain norm for spoken as opposed to written language, rather than notation of individualized speech, represents the desired achievement of conversations in novels. In fact, the use of dialogue for character development was not invariably perceived as good artistic practice, as this comment from the *New York Review* for January 1842 indicates: "The necessity of making the individuals introduced tell much of the story, and exhibit their motives and peculiarities in speech, has involved the author at times in discussions that are unnecessarily long, and delay rather than advance the plot."

The great danger that reviewers saw in conversation was tedium; dialogue might be stuffily formal or simply go on too long. "The conversations are not so protracted to become tedious," a *Mirror* reviewer wrote approvingly of Cooper's *Homeward Bound* on August 18, 1838, setting out the criterion for all to see. Looking back on Cooper in April 1850, the *American Review* commented that "the general level of the dialogue among the principal characters in Cooper is what, in our school days, was denominated the 'high-flown' school. . . . The first principle in elaborating a dramatic construction, of whatever description, whether re-related in narrative or represented in a dialogue, or both, is *action*."

Complaints of overextended or stiff dialogue run through the reviews, suggesting that novelists faced a real challenge in trying to handle this aspect of their craft. "She made her ladies and gentlemen talk a vast deal too much, and too much like books" (*Knickerbocker*, October 1855); "the dialogue is often heavy; the speakers make long orations . . . not only longer than any real talker ever made, but in a style such as no good talker ever used" (*Tribune*, March 12, 1845); "the conversations are spun out to a tedious length" (*Tribune*, December 27, 1850); "the book is eked out by long and often tedious dialogue" (*Literary World*, July 6, 1850); "we would in a friendly spirit warn the fair author to guard against prolixity in her dialogue" (*Literary World*, June 12, 1852); "the personages of the tale fail to interest because they one and all 'talk like a book.' Ease and nature are wanting" (*Literary World*, December 18, 1852); "the conversations are singularly stiff and artificial, sometimes regular forensics" (*Christian Examiner*, May 1851); "her only danger, as far as the story is concerned, is allowing her conversations to occupy too much space" (*Godey's*, July 1854); "we must remonstrate with the author, too, for impeding the story with those interminable discussions" (*Southern Literary Messenger*, October 1855); "the style is a little too much diluted with dialogue" (*Christian Examiner*, January 1858); "the conversations are too numerous, too protracted, and run too much into trivialities and details" (*Atlantic*, December 1858); "the plot, such as it is, moves onward through a wilderness of talk, inferior in force, freshness, and dignity to the ordinary conversation extemporized in drawing-rooms" (*Knickerbocker*, October 1859).

The reference to the drawing room makes explicit the implicit assumption that the conversational norm invoked in these judgments is linked with the idea of manners. While stiff formality in conversation is deplored, conversation itself is a sort of ritual conducted according to rules. Perhaps this norm is associated with a now-vanished notion of conversation as a social activity, an association that would explain why conversations were not seen as automatically connected to plot and character but rather were linked to general ideas of wit and vivacity. "The dialogue of this story strikes us as the best part of the book; it has all the vivacity and the *air dégagé*, of the polished circles in which [the author] may be supposed to move" (*Godey's*, November 1840); "contains many sprightly and laughter-moving conversations," "several of the conversations are exceedingly amusing," "the various conversations with which the volume is replete are of the most readable and pleasant nature" (*Democratic Review*, September 1846, October 1846, December 1846). The conversations are "sparkling with wine and confectionery" (*Mirror*, April 15, 1850); "the genial vivacity and sparkling wit of her conversational pages have rarely, if ever, been equaled" (*Democratic Review*, March 1855).

Although we might conclude from these examples that only well-bred characters were supposed to speak in novels, from time to time in this criticism we read that the dialogue attributed to a given character is or is not appropriate to the character itself. The *North American*, for example, objected in January 1846 to Judd's *Margaret* because it made the heroine "speak in a dialect which resembles nothing ever heard in the social world, and which is wholly out of nature in a village girl, whatever the accidental circumstances of her education may have been. It destroys the beauty and truth of the conception." It may be a sign of changing times that the criterion of individuality in dialogue appeared more frequently in novel reviews of the 1850s than earlier. "The actors for the most part, are made to reveal themselves in the brief, pithy, pregnant dialogue" (*Tribune*, July 12, 1854); "characters, young and old, male and female, polished and unpolished, talking with a rare naturalness, and developing their peculiarities in this way, instead of having them described narratively by the author" (*Peterson's*, September 1854); "the dialogues are generally brief, pointed, and appropriate to the interlocutors" (*North American*, October 1855). Complaints about excessive use of characters speaking in the vernacular, common before 1840, also dropped off in the 1850s.

Reflections

Reflections or sentiments, shading off into a moral, were also usual and acceptable ways to vary the narrative surface. The moral (discussed at more length below) was technically a detachable summary statement, usually found at the end of a novel, on which it provided a sort of gloss. Morals were much more common in short tales and stories than in novels, since the complexity of a novel's plot tended to resist easy summation. Reflections or sentiments, by contrast, arose more locally from an incident or occasion in a novel, representing a brief detour from the progress of the action that might have an independent attraction for a certain kind of reader, especially one who kept copybooks. *St. Leger*, according to the *Literary World* for January 5, 1850, contains "many little expressions which are so agreeable to those who keep common-place books, concentrated thoughts, which are not too long to be copied." Reviews, especially in the earlier part of the period under study, tended to feature long abstracts from novels they were writing about, often appropriately titled (e.g., "on beauty") for copying convenience. "The following thoughts are beautiful and truthful," the *Literary World* wrote before beginning its extracts from *The Head of the Family* (March 27, 1852). For some reviewers the presence of reflections indicated the writer's attempt to produce a serious novel that aimed for more than story, and they approved the convention—providing, of course, the reflection was sufficiently lofty.

The *Mirror* disliked Mary Howitt's *Little Coin, Much Care* but noted that the "incidental reflections are excellent in their tendency" (August 6, 1842). *Godey's* reviewers applauded *The Moneyed Man* by Horace Smith for "judicious reflections that are scattered throughout it, and the praise-worthy moral it enforces" (August 1841); found the "reflections" in Bulwer's *Zanoni* "original, profound, and just" (June, 1842); praised the author of *The Lamplighter* for "the just, generous, and charitable sentiments that profusely flow from her pen" (July 1854); and wrote of *The Old Farm House* in September 1855 that "many of the reflections are very fine, and alike honorable to the head and heart of the author." *Graham's* reviewers found the "sentiments" in Grace Aguilar's *Vale of Cedars* "beautiful and pure" and saw "the original and striking observations on life and manners" as constituting "no small portion of the charm" of Thackeray's works (November 1850, January 1853). A *Harper's* review commented on *The Old Plantation* by James Hungerford: "the narrative is occasionally diversified by a vein of reflection, showing the aptitude of the writer for the more serious exertions of the intellect" (March 1859). In *Ida Norman* "the sentiments are just, beautiful, noble, and exalted" (*Home Journal*, March 24, 1855).

But even reviewers who liked reflections admitted that too many destroyed the novel's interest, however admirable in themselves the sentiments might be. And overall, a preponderance of novel reviews disapproved of the convention of the reflection. As early as April 1829, the *North American* compared Bulwer unfavorably to novelists who "do not frequently interrupt the narrative, and suspend the action, with comments and dissertation." It also criticized G. P. R. James for placing "a moral reflection, or a feeble speculation, at due pauses in the march of his story, with a sort of mathematical precision. . . . This is 'from the purpose' of novel-writing" (April 1844). "Excessively annoying," the *Southern Literary Messenger* wrote about James, "is his habit of obtruding passages of reflective writing in the way of his story" (September 1847). *Standish the Puritan*, *Harper's* said, "would have had still greater effect if not so freely blended with moral disquisitions" (June 1850). The *Tribune* for May 15, 1850, shared this view: "he indulges too freely in abstract reflection"; it also criticized *The Wide, Wide World* for "moral and religious reflections" that "are lugged in without regard to propriety or grace," saw *Hearts Unveiled* as "clogged by long didactic disquisitions," and described *My Brother's Keeper* as falling "into a train of pious moralizing in which gentle dulness is too prominent an element" (December 27, 1850; April 30, 1852; May 16, 1855). *Harper's*, again, observed that in *Clifton* by Arthur Townley "the plot has no special interest, and is in fact subservient to the taste for dissertation" and that Martha Wickham's *Sea Spray* is "encumbered by a superfluity of moral reflections" (July 1852, April 1857). While reviewers wanted novels to be more serious than they usually were, over time they also became increasingly critical of reflections and sentiments employed as a means to this end.

The Moral

The moral posed more serious problems than did the reflection to proponents of the better novel, since the latter was at worst an interruption while the former gestured toward a nonfictional organizing principle. Morals, too, were differently situated with respect to readers—reflections were to be admired and perhaps copied into commonplace books, while morals were to be acted upon. "The moral lesson inculcated" in a certain novel is "important and instructive," according to the *New York Review* for July 1840. "Her moral is always good"; "the moral is excellent"; "the lessons it contains are all excellent"; "the moral it conveys is an excellent one"; "the moral is pure and healthy"; "it has pure and blessed teachings for all lives" (*Godey's*, November 1849, July 1854, February 1855, March 1855, January 1856). "Can be recommended for its just sentiments, Christian teachings, and pure moral," "the principles inculcated are of the highest practical importance," "inculcating a good moral" (*Home Journal*, January 14, 1854; March 24, 1855; May 31, 1856). *Putnam's* called a novel's moral "pathetic and impressive" (November 1856); *Graham's* praised Southworth's novels because "the whole invariably tends to a pleasing moral" (April 1858).

We cannot comprehend these critical comments without understanding that they distinguish between a novel with a moral, the moral tendency of the novel, and the didactic novel. The didatic novel is an identifiable subgenre (see chapter 10). The moral "tendency" of a novel is an inevitable, invariable aspect of any novel whatever, resulting from the way sympathy is disposed among morally good and bad characters as well as the way morally sensitive material is handled (see chapter 9). A "moral" is rather more limited than either of these, though more related to the didactic novel than to the concept of moral tendency.

Those who inserted morals into novels were apt, from an artistic point of view, to err in two ways: to fail to assimilate the moral smoothly into the narrative flow, and to assume a strikingly inappropriate narrative tone for a novel when articulating it. As early as July 1827 the *North American* had asserted that a moral "sturdily inculcated or illustrated in every page . . . or which in any degree diverts the current of events from their natural course, occasions a violence to probability, revolting both to the taste and conviction of the reader." "There is one noticeable defect, in the management of the moral," *Putnam's* wrote about *Heartsease*. "This, which was apparently intended to permeate the whole texture, is stuck in in unassimilated, uncomfortable lumps. We come upon them as upon an unexpected jolt" (February 1855). "The moral is an excellent one," the *Democratic Review* wrote of Roe's *A Long Look Ahead*, "and not impaired by being made too manifest, too predominating, and obvious throughout; it is suggested and enforced by the story in a true artistic spirit, but does not stick out through the fiction, like a rusty nail through a butterfly" (April 1855).

Lumps of moral were bad, but a pedagogical tone was worse still. In July 1847 the *North American* pointed out that "we read novels, first of all, to be amused; and we feel rebellious at an over-dose of the didactic smuggled into them against our will. It also seems to us, that an author is taking advantage of his position, when he moralizes too severely." *Talbot and Vernon*, according to the *Tribune*, was free "from that dry and didactic tone which usually ruins an attempt to inculcate a specific moral in a work of fiction" (May 15, 1850). "The moral which is the design of the story is brought forward too prominently" in *Oakfield*, it noted on October 30, 1855, "and at times almost chills the interest of the narrative by its cold, didactic formality." "No man bidden to a feast of fiction expects to sit down to a sermon,"

Putnam's announced in May 1853. "There is a general tendency in the composition of the work to a didactic and somewhat pedagogical method," the *Ladies' Repository* wrote of *The Methodist* in May 1859. Severity, coldness, dryness—these aspects of the didactic tone are inappropriate to the narration of a novel. Novel readers do not want to be returned to the schoolroom or the church and will not accept the novelist as teacher or minister.

The more artistic way to present a moral, then, was to avoid a didactic, pedagogical tone and if possible conceal it in the fabric of the story. According to the *Democratic Review*, the moral of *Grace Lee* by Julia Kavanagh was "more powerful, because it glides into the intellect intuitively, and [is] not thrust on us with any Pharisaic ostentation" (May 1855). The *Literary World* reviewers liked a novel whose high moral aim was "implied rather than forced on the reader's mind," and they approved of Caroline Lee Hentz because the lessons she "inculcates are not delivered in a dictatorial, self-sufficient manner, but ingeniously woven in with the story, imparting to it force and reality, without diminishing its romance or interest" (October 9, 1847; April 3, 1852). Two matters are at issue here: first, the primacy of the story; second, the way the writer talks to (or writes to) the reader. The novelist who assumes the manner of a pedagogue has made the political mistake of situating himself or herself above the reader. In the novel-reading situation power is invested in the reader who has bought the book and having done so may or may not read it, may or may not finish it, and may or may not buy another book by the same writer. An author who assumes superiority either is ignorant of, or is attempting to override, this essential aspect of writer-reader relations.

The writer, then, who wants to push the novel form toward pedagogy can succeed with novel readers only through more subtle and more manipulative methods than openly ascending the platform. The method recommended by reviewers was to get readers to find the moral themselves. Such a procedure would give readers the illusion of control; and what is more, it would mime the shape of a plot where discovering secrets is at the heart of the reading process. Without inculcating "any special moral axiom," the *Atlantic* wrote about *Vernon Grove*, "it embodies . . . many worthy lessons for the mind and heart. This is done, as it should be, by the apparently natural development of the story itself. For, as we have said, the book is really a novel, and will be read as a novel should be, for the story" (January 1859). In the phrase "apparently natural" the review acknowledges the presence of a deception it deems allowable, even necessary when a novelist wants to convey a lesson.

"When we speak of a distinct moral aim as indispensable to the novelist, we do not mean that he should be constantly thrusting his moral into the reader's face,—one of the weakest pieces of folly an author can commit. . . . But there must be that spiritual vitality, that life of the affections, that devotion to human weal, which, revealing themselves insensibly, quicken the reader's resolutions, and leave him with a clear consciousness that his soul has been enlarged" (*Christian Examiner*, January 1847). The novel "inculcates without intruding," the *North American* said approvingly of Mary Jane Holmes's *The English Orphans* in October 1855; and of other novels: "fraught with the highest truths of morality and religion; and these are not obtruded upon the reader, but so incorporated with the whole texture of the tale, that he must either take them in, or leave the book unread"; "lessons of faith and piety are embodied in the life-experiences of the characters, not set forth in formal dialogues or in the author's running commentary"; "this unambitious plot is naturally developed in such a way as to be eminently suggestive of prudent counsel, high motive, and strenuous endeavor, while the author never assumes the didactic form, but moralizes only by the skillful collocation of actions and their consequences, incidents and their issues" (January 1858, October 1858).

Lest we too quickly associate the desire for hidden morals in fiction with a dated gentility, consider what happens to this criticism when the word "theme" is substituted for the word "moral." Then, what these reviewers are recommending is precisely what academics consider praiseworthy in novels today; finding themes is the end and method of teaching in literature classes across the nation. Most college teachers today assume that a student who talks about plot and characters rather than offering an interpretation that involves theme is "naive." For more advanced literary theory we should substitute the word "meaning" for the word "moral" to situate ourselves in the wake of history. In this talk about the hidden moral in fiction we see the origins of modern theme study and modern meaning study, the search for the significance that, being "well wrought into the texture of the work, but never officiously presented" (*North American*, April 1825), justifies the reading act for those who, wishing for various reasons to attach themselves to the novel, cannot accept the pleasure of story as one of these reasons.

7

Aspects of the Narrator

Probably no strategy in academic criticism of the novel has proved more powerful in our own time than the separation of the narrator from the narration. Nevertheless, although the sophistication of this separation remained a task for a literary self-consciousness that had not yet developed by the mid-nineteenth century, reviewers did approach the novel as an expression of authorial voice as well as the recital of a story. It was obvious to them that every novel was written in words, had a style, and implied a teller. As with all other novelistic elements, they assessed this expression in terms of its enhancement, or lack thereof, of the reading experience. What was wanted above all was a style that was lively, a tone that was (as the word implies) tonic, and a narrator who was agreeable so that reading would be fun. Thus, at just the point where some contemporary critics anticipate and applaud differences between novelists as well as between individual novels by a single author, reviewers of this earlier time looked for uniformity.

But then again, since reviewers entered the novel at a high level of its organization and did not reduce it to those transpersonal linguistic elements that the novel would share with all other forms of written language, their commentary on the narrator tended to be impressionistic, subjective, and sensitive to individual differences. Although they may not have intended this, their discussion had the interesting effect of leaving the "magic" of the novel unimpaired; since they did not dissect, they did not murder. Entirely missing from their conceptual universe was the notion that the world language referred to was, in even the slightest degree, a linguistic creation; but in a curious sense this structuralist and poststructuralist notion would be irrelevant to their criticism, since the level at which language might create the world was far below the level at which they were operating. They did not interpret novels, nor did they look to novels as a source for speculation (their own or the novelists') on interpretation itself.

Even the briefest review usually commented on style. The commentary was concerned to describe the effect of style rather than its production, and the vocabulary was narrow. All styles were assessed in terms of an idea of *good* style, an idea with two basic constituents: first, that the language conformed to accepted usage, both syntactical and lexical; second, that the style was animated. Although they never articulated the point, reviewers' comments took style to be the vital principle of the novel in the sense of making its story live for the reader. Distinctiveness of style might be noted or described, but it did not form the basis for judgment unless the style was especially idiosyncratic. When it was, reviewers were more inclined to be critical than commendatory. Thus, for example, though musical cadence and harmony in style were desirable as enhancement of reading pleasure as well as emphasis of the forward movement of the prose, a reviewer would regularly object to a style that was "painfully ornate, ambitious . . . full of musical circumlocution introduced evidently for the sake of the music" (*Southern Literary Messenger*, June 1847, reviewing Bulwer). In contrast, the *Literary World* (November 17, 1849) approved of Melville's style in *Redburn* because it had "no verbosity, no artificiality, no languor: the style is always exactly filled by the thought and material."

The comments above should not be interpreted as implying that style should or could be a transparent envelope for what it contained, for if so one could not tell when the matter filled the style and when style was being exhibited for its own sake. Rather, these two remarks imply a sense of style as instrumental, and as beautiful when (and only when) it is functional. The relatively florid norms of Victorian prose style should not obscure the point that functionality was the criterion. The residue of nonfunctional style could only act as impediment or distraction. Since language was ineluctably representational, it could only point to the author when it did not point to the story, and, more specifically, to an author pointing to himself. Thus non-functional style immediately implied a self-indulgent or exhibitionist author, a disagreeable character who was assumed to interfere with the enjoyment of the novel. In this basic fashion, a nonfunctional style could only be self-defeating. The popularity of egotistical authors like Bulwer did not change this judgment.

The general terms employed to praise a style fall into a few clusters. The most common word of praise was "vigorous," and along with it came such related terms as animated, powerful, terse, bold, nervous, vivid, vivacious, spirited, warm, elastic, impassioned, salient, racy, energetic, original, direct, expressive, sprightly. The second most common operative concept was most often expressed by the word "graceful," along with its relatives: melodious, fluent, flowing, harmonious, sweet, cadenced. Together these two constituents—power and grace—formed the life of a style. Ideally a style combined vigor and grace, but if reviewers had to choose between these two qualities they preferred vigor.

To some degree vigor in style was associated with the masculine, grace with the feminine: "her style . . . though frequently showing an almost masculine energy, is destitute of the sweet and graceful fluency which would finely attemper her bold and striking conceptions" (*Harper's* on Caroline Chesebro', January 1852). Vigor and grace, however, were assessed apart from the author's gender: reviewers expected women and men to write differently but used the same criteria in evaluating their styles. Commenting on style in another of Chesebro's works, *Harper's* said it "is always sinewy and masculine, often highly picturesque. . . . We much prefer the robust and well-compacted phraseology of this work, animated as it is by the workings of an original and active mind, to the soft and polished sweetnesses of many of our fashionable sentence-makers" (May 1855).

Cutting across this set of terms is another, represented at one extreme by such descriptive words of praise as elegant, rich, brilliant, fresh, original, varied, picturesque, and at the other by words like chaste, pure, simple, concise, plain, unaffected. Just as power and grace were constituent elements of style that ought to be combined but also might come into conflict, so in the best styles elegance blended with chastity while lesser writers tended to achieve one or the other but not both of these desirable qualities. Elegance has to do with complexity and subtlety and implies a wealth of lexical, syntactic, and rhetorical resources; chastity is equated with simplicity and austerity. Where in choosing between vigor and grace reviewers preferred vigor, between elegance and chastity they chose chastity. The reasons for this preference are not entirely clear, but of course (though we no longer use the words chaste and pure) we continue to prefer simplicity and direct statement, as any survey of writers' manuals will show. Today, however, we associate directness and simplicity with the masculine and elegance with the feminine, associations impossible to an era in which simplicity connoted purity and chastity.

The chief stylistic challenge in novel writing was also the novel's chief mystery: a dead style meant a dead novel. For in fact neither elegance nor chastity nor both could guarantee stylistic vigor or power, while the deliberate effort to achieve power was likely to create an unpleasant sense of strain. Style was most frequently criticized for being "ambitious," a condition manifested through inflation, mannerism, exaggeration, or labored attempts at "fine writing"—through being studied, ponderous, affected, obscure, ornate, luxurious, diffuse. Striving for more, the writer achieved less. There was something here beyond the power of criticism to analyze, something accepted as magic. Hawthorne's many discussions, embedded in his fictions, of the way the writer "animated" his works, refer to this magical vigor. Melville's late works were particularly subject to negative stylistic assessment on these grounds, and in my view it was much more likely his style than his subject or his morality that hurt him with the public in the instances of both *Mardi* and *Pierre*.

Inflation or ornateness pointed on the one hand to lack of skill or (even more significantly, perhaps) lack of talent; it pointed on the other to a fatal vanity and pretension in the author, an exhibitionism that implied the author had forgotten his place as conveyor of a story, servant both to his tale and to his readers. This is why the word ambitious was so often used to criticize a "fine" style—it betrayed the author's desire to be seen in the work, to be noticed as author. So the *North American Review* for October 1848 wrote that *Grantly Manor* is "stirred too often by an ambition for the superfine, to catch that flowing felicity of style which should be the aim of the novelist,—a style in which sentences should only represent thought or fact, and never dazzle away attention from the matter they convey." And, conversely, it praised Hawthorne's style in a July 1850 review: "his style may be compared to a sheet of transparent water, reflecting from its surface blue skies, nodding woods, the smallest spray or flower that peeps over its grassy margin, while in its clear yet mysterious depths we espy rarer and stranger things. . . . Every thing charms the eye and ear, and nothing looks like art and painstaking. There is a naturalness and a continuous flow of expression in Mr. Hawthorne's books, that makes them delightful to read." The *North American* reviewer clearly knows that this natural impression is the result of great art, going on to describe Hawthorne as "master" of a "wizard power over language." By effacing himself in the service of his art, the writer in fact achieves the mastery that he does not attain when he deliberately displays himself. This is indeed a mystery the reviewer is content to leave mystified, as the vocabulary of magic shows.

The intervention of the colloquial novel between those times and our own—of, let us say, *Huckleberry Finn*—makes it difficult to appreciate that "fine writing" was the greatest stylistic defect to mid-nineteenth-century reviewers, because their "plain style" was so much more ornate than ours. In addition, it is true, reviewers objected to colloquial narration. For them, slang, colloquialism, and "bad grammar," as well as neologisms and foreign terms, all indicated the same lack of skill that a fine style implied. The writer was either ignorant of the resources of language or of the conventions of the form he or she was using, or was knowingly rejecting them. This last was not perceived as admirable, for all reviewers assumed that the language was more than adequate for any use a novelist might want to put it to. The *North American* for April 1851 complained about Judd's *Richard Edney* in this way: Judd is "a genius, but unhappily, he is no artist. His work is full of errors any schoolboy of regular training would be able to correct." It protested against the book's "motley style," its "practice of introducing vulgar idioms and words coined at will," its "use of provincialisms, and the most homely colloquial diction." These, it granted, are "not without precedent in the best writers of fiction. But they are used as characteristics of the inferior personages, or under an assumed name and character, to which they are natural and appropriate. No respectable writer adopts them into his own proper vocabulary, and parades them in defiance of polite usage, whatever may be his theme or purpose."

One can hardly avoid noticing that the norms of polite and respectable society are taken as the norms of fictional style; but it would be wrong to infer from this that the reviewers were taking this style to be "natural," that is, were pretending that these particular cultural norms were in the nature of things or that the style they admired could be achieved without effort and practice. On the contrary, the review makes it quite clear that achieving the convention of the narrator's voice is a test of the author's ability. To drop into a low style is no different, structurally speaking, from rising into labored pomposity: both call attention to the writer *as writer*. The writer who adopts standard English becomes, by convention, invisible. The writer who uses colloquialisms or vulgar idioms or neologisms calls attention to himself as uneducated, unskilled, presumptuous; the work then becomes an instance of the author and loses its own proper life. (It is ironic that as writers more and more claimed the right to intrude themselves into their work by ignoring or disrupting conventions, hence reminding readers that the work was "only a novel," the novel did become a less magical, less lively form; and then, in one more turn of the screw, as critics uncovered hitherto invisible novelists in conventional works by exposing conventions, the magic life of the work passed from the author to the critic.)

Within the field defined by these four clusters—vigor, grace, elegance, purity—authors might naturally and properly achieve individual variations of style, which could form the basis for a reviewer's description and constitute part of a reader's appreciation. But it was the ineluctable tendency of this approach to praise and encourage normative style, as is still largely the case today where expository writing is concerned, even though fiction is now an allowed site for stylistic idiosyncrasy. In the mid-nineteenth-century review, it was rare indeed that a highly individual style was praised for its individuality. Of the several hundred authors noticed in the reviews of my sample, only three are regularly singled out in this way: E. D. E. N. Southworth, Charles Reade, and Charles Dickens.

Southworth's is a particularly interesting case, because at first her works were condemned for their stylistic excesses. As her popularity became manifest, reviewers perceived her appeal as grounded at least partly in that same style, indeed in the very qualities they had objected to; hence they changed their vocabulary when describing it. *Harper's* first review of Southworth (October 1852) considered *The Discarded Daughter:* "the author of this novel possesses a singularly vivid imagination, and a rare command of picturesque expression. She evinces originality, depth and fervor of feeling, vigor of thought, and dramatic skill; but so blended with glaring faults, that the severest critic would be her best friend. . . . With the constant effort to surprise, the language becomes inflated, and at the same time is often careless to a degree, which occasions the most ludicrous sense of incongruity. . . . Let her tame the genial impetuosity of her pen by a due reverence for classical taste and common sense—and she will yet attain a rank worthy of her fine faculties, from which she has hitherto been precluded by her outrages on the proprieties of fictitious composition." But a later *Harper's* reviewer modified this approach, finding *The Lost Heiress* "the most finished production which has come from the pen of this fertile writer" whose faults proceeded "from an exuberant imagination and an excessive facility of language—but its vigor of conception and brilliancy of description make it one of the most readable novels of the season" (January 1855). And in November of that year a review of Southworth's *The Deserted Wife* referred to "the exuberant splendor of style for which that writer is remarkable." The *Southern Literary Messenger* observed more laconically that "the admirers of Mrs. Southworth, and she has created many by her passionately sensuous style, will no doubt find *The Missing Bride* highly entertaining" (July 1855). Southworth's stylistic extravagances matched her outsized characters and brought her improbable plots to life; the whole, being larger than life, provided readers with the sense of power and energy they sought in novels.

The mannered style of Charles Reade occasioned a different sort of critical debate. The *Tribune* found his language "free from the conventionalities of fictitious writing, and often has a salient freshness which goes far to account for their attractions, without referring to any skill in construction of plot, or the delineation of character" (June 26, 1855). A review in the *Southern Literary Mes-*

senger observed similarly that "his short crisp sentences have a brilliancy and point which would not fail to make him popular, even if his subjects and the manner in which they are treated were not equally original" (November 1855). But another review in the same journal (October 1856) proclaimed that "we cannot sanction the absurd tricks of typography and ridiculous brevity of chapters to which Mr. Reade has resorted to produce effect." The *Atlantic*, reviewing *White Lies*, observed that "the early chapters of this novel lack the brisk movement, the sparkling compactness, the stinging surprises of Mr. Reade's usual style, but he kindles and condenses as he proceeds"; it concluded that Reade was "a writer difficult to criticize, because his defects are pleasing defects" (November 1857). The same journal reviewing his *Love Me Little, Love Me Long* found it "pleasant to see how unreservedly Mr. Reade has abandoned his functions as apostle of grammatical free-love. Of tricks of typography there are also fewer, although these yet remain in an excess which good taste can hardly sanction. We often find whole platoons of admiration-points stretching out in line, to give extraordinary emphasis to sentences already sufficiently forcible" (July 1859). A review for the *North American*, too, noted that his "peculiarities of style are strongly marked," that he had "tricks of speech" that "sometimes verge on bad taste," and that his "curt and crispy style, in which he is often very successful, needs but a slight exaggeration to become positively ludicrous as well as weak" (July 1859).

Reviewers faulted both these authors for straining after effect; where strain was noticeable, effect was not achieved. But their commentary implies a gap between them and readers in general; either readers did not object to strain, or their less analytic reading habits led them to overlook it. Since some reviews suggest that elaborate style might be a reason for these novelists' popularity, the possibility exists that readers noted, and enjoyed, an ornamental style: straining after effect in writing, as in declamatory acting, acrobatics, or tall-tale telling, could signal difficulty to readers and thus enable them to recognize an achievement. And it could signal energy too.

Dickens, of course, overtopped all writers in the period to an amazing extent. Every critical review—and there were many of them, for his success inevitably engendered the desire to find something wrong with his work—concluded by acknowledging that even his failures were better than the best most novelists could achieve, and that in each of his works there was matter for a dozen ordinary novels. If there was any democratic hope that a great writer could be greatly popular, Dickens encouraged it; if there was any inclination among writers and critics to believe that the public could not appreciate literary greatness, Dickens undermined it. Dickens's secret—and it was a secret in that nobody knew how he did it—was in his fertility, his energy, his apparently inexhaustible creativity: in a word, the life in his fictions. Certainly one aspect of this life was to be found in his matchless, though far from faultless, style.

"His command over the English language in its most native and idiomatic parts is really marvellous. . . . His style is original, almost beyond that of any writer of English in this age . . . formed from the commonest materials, selected with an instinctive tact and used with singular directness and force. It abounds in racy and expressive idioms, and has a strange flexibility in conveying at once to the reader's mind every variety of thought and passion. It may be said to be unstudied, though it must have required long habits of composition to bring it to its present state of completeness" (*North American*, January 1843). "Why is it," *Godey's* asked, "that Charles Dickens is so universally and unabatedly delightful?" A "principal cause" was "the unfailing spring of original turns of wit, turns of phrase, and turns of thought that give the rare delight of *novelty*, and the pleasure of something unexpected" (June 1851). "Such are the attractive and winning graces of his style," *Putnam's* said, reviewing *Bleak House*, "that he can, when character and incident fail him, always secure the reader's attention by mere profuseness of riotous rhetoric, which has no other use than that of diverting his reader" (November 1853). In contrast, the *American Review*, writing on the same novel, objected to his "use of nominatives without verbs, verbs without nominatives, and pronouns without substantives," querying, "will those writers who are faithfully cultivating purity of style and exactness of finish, become depressed by the superior success of a more careless literature? . . . Will the faults of this wonderful author share the same apotheosis as his virtues?" Of course, the journal admitted, it is "beyond Mr. Dickens' power to make a failure. If he should write a book in ten days . . . it would still be a book worth buying and reading" (September 1852).

The example of these three writers shows that to be individual in style meant, as by definition, that one could not be exemplary; the original stylist necessarily broke rules, was incorrect, improper, verged on the ludicrous, offended a correct taste. The equation of grammatical and moral propriety is not accidental; an apostle of "grammatical free love" opens the door to freedoms in other areas as well. The use of the words pure and chaste to describe a proper style is thus significant. To break rules is to indulge; to indulge successfully is to put rules themselves in question. Whether the novel might be used as an instrument of making people better or not, even to the extent of making them more sensitive to good literature, depended to some degree on whether it might help people appreciate rules. "Slang," the *New York Ledger* editorialized, "is disgusting to every noble and considerate mind. In speech, God has given us our highest gift and grace; and when language is made the pure vehicle of pure and good thoughts, must glorify himself and his kind. It is lamentable and shocking, the extent to which slang phrases have corrupted the current speech of our time. Senseless and idle words have crept in and crowded out their infinitely betters, until there is scarcely a vestige of society that does not daily degrade our sterling mother tongue. . . . Thrice enemies of true civilization are they who cultivate slang" (June 12, 1858).

There was one popular subgenre of the novel that allowed slang and depended, in contrast to the "novel proper," on a certain stylistic laxness. "The mere announcement of any thing from the sparkling brain of the Bachelor of the *Albany*," *Graham's* wrote of one of these, *My Uncle the Curate*, "is sufficient to raise anticipations of brisk and business-like satire, of felicitous expression, and of good-natured representation of the follies of conventional life. The present work evinces more of the novelist, and less of the wit-snapper, than any thing the author has previously written. The story and the characters, though plentifully bespangled with epigrams, are still not immersed and lost in them" (July 1849). The chief example of this subgenre, survivor of the picaresque, was *Charles O'Malley* (1840), by the Irish author Charles Lever. The type consisted of a string of episodes connected through the hero; the episodes might be exciting but were more usually humorous, and the work as a whole functioned mainly as the occasion for witticisms and jokes. Many examples of the type were reviewed in American journals of the 1840s and early 1850s, always in the same way: "we have not, for a long time, found a novel so full of real good and pure fun. . . . There is not a dull page in the book. Incident upon incident, joke upon joke" (*Godey's* on *The Marrying Man*, September 1841). "Quaint and delightful . . . rich and racy, serious and comical, still-life and adventurous, rollicking and frollicking" (*Godey's*, October 1847). "If any of our readers are afflicted with the *blues*, or likely to become so, we recommend to them as a most effectual remedy or preventative, to go and purchase" *The Image of His Father* (*Southern Literary Messenger*, November 1848). Neither *Valentine Vox* nor *Frank Farleigh*, according to *Peterson's*, could be read "without incessant fits of laughter" (September 1850).

Given that the success of these works depended on some degree of linguistic license, it is noteworthy that they were strongly male-centered in story line and involved a good deal of masculine misbehavior. Style and content seemed to coincide: "the interest depends more upon the immediate and unconnected adventures of the hero, than upon the intricacies or ingenuity of the plot. We are no admirers of this facile and rambling style of novel-writing," the *Mirror* commented on an American example, *Harry Franco* (by Charles F. Briggs) on July 6, 1839. "There are, however, many good hits. . . . The slang phrases, which he puts into the mouths of some of his characters, are but too faithful transcripts of the *Americanisms*, in which many of our young men rejoice. We cannot commend *Harry Franco* very warmly to the favorable regards of our fair readers." Oddly, the women-centered journals—*Godey's*, *Peterson's*, and *Graham's*—were more favorably disposed toward these funny books than the other magazines even though it was taken for granted that only men would write them. Insofar, then, as linguistic boldness involves, for American authors, the utilization of slang, or "Americanisms," we do have the beginnings of a sexual demarcation of style in novels, but one that seemed to be working in favor of women writers rather than against them, in that slang or colloquial writing could be neither elegant nor pure. The allowable license of these comic books did not seem to promise literary stature or achievement, and certainly it did not point at that time toward the serious novel or the dedicated artist.

If a purely comic book was a minor subgenre of the novel, humor was nevertheless an anticipated element of all novels.

Reviewers looked for passages of humor, for passages of pathos, and above all for the combination in a novel of both humor and pathos. The term pathos was used by reviewers to denote an emotional response (or its provoking cause in the text) characterized by pity, sadness, or sorrow—"to dissolve the heart in tears" (*North American*, July 1822). The provocation would usually consist of instances of sadness or suffering in the novel's events, creating a sympathetic mood in the reader, but successfully created pathos depended as much on authorial handling as on situation. All good novels were expected to contain pathos. Better novels also contained humor, with the result that a reader moving forward on the track of an exciting story would also oscillate emotionally across that track through experiences of contrasting pathos and humor invested in smaller plot segments.

We see this notion articulated in an early review in the *North American* (of Sedgwick's *Redwood*, April 1825): "parts are written with deep pathos; others display no inconsiderable share of comic power." "If any jaded romance-reader would have an honest natural laugh and cry . . . let him . . . pass to-day with Uncle Philip or the Barclays," it wrote about some other Sedgwick stories in October 1837. It faulted Cooper in July 1850 for an "almost total want of humor and pathos" and praised Mary Jane Holmes's *The English Orphans* in October 1855 because the "pathetic element . . . is highly wrought, yet stops short of mawkishness" while "the comic vein is worked with equal success, and with equal moderation." These examples show a persisting criterion through more than a quarter-century of reviewing in this journal.

And we see it in other journals too. "Sadness and humor,—tears and broad grins,—are sprinkled . . . throughout the whole volume" (*Knickerbocker*, January 1835). "It made us laugh, it made us cry" (*New York Review* on Sedgwick's *Live and Let Live*, October 1837). "Touches of the most exquisite pathos," *Godey's* reported (July 1840), and noted again that a novel had "pathos and beauty" that "cannot fail to charm the reader" (January 1859). The *Democratic Review* found "innumerable touches of pathos" in McIntosh's *Two Lives* (December 1846) and described Cornelius Mathews's *Moneypenny* as "abounding in scenes of great pathos, contrasted with passages of broad humor and laughable caricature" (September 1850). "The humor and pathos are effectively blended" in *Dombey and Son* (*Literary World*, July 17, 1847); a reviewer in the same journal complained that "the pathos and humor" of *Uncle Tom's Cabin* had been "very much overstated" (December 4, 1852).

Graham's, though praising *The Scarlet Letter* (May 1850), added that "in his next work we hope to have a romance equal . . . in pathos and power, but more relieved by touches of that beautiful and peculiar humor . . . in which he excels almost all living writers." *Harper's*, from its first issue on, praised "touches of humor and pathos" (June 1850). "For pathos, we know not her equal" (*Home Journal*, March 22, 1851); "a story of uncommon power and pathos" (*Arthur's Home Magazine*, July 1853); "gentle pathos," "quiet humor and pathos," "frequent touches of pathos" (*Tribune*, July 12, 1854; May 15, 1855; June 23, 1857). "Alternate pathos and humor" (*Putnam's* on Stowe, January 1855); "the narrative is full of humor and pathos" (*Atlantic* on Eliot's *Scenes of Clerical Life*, May 1858); "there is a good deal of humor in the work; in fact the author succeeds in this line better than in pathos" (*Peterson's* on *The Quaker Soldier*, March 1858); "the work is excellent, in all respects, but it is in pathos that the writer excels" (*Peterson's* on *Vernon Grove*, December 1858); and so on.

The stability of this criterion and the frequency of its recurrence in reviews throughout the period testify to the profoundly emotive view of the novel-reading experience. Without spending much time on the issue of how it might be that people enjoyed being made to feel bad, reviewers combined a simple Aristotelian notion of catharsis with a Shaftesburian sense that deep emotion called up on another's behalf was morally uplifting. Humor, with its power to startle, clarified and added the pleasure of surprise. The combination provided an emotional variety in the reading experience that both enhanced and relieved the progress of the story toward its denouement. The point to be stressed is that the chief principle of elaboration within the novel is emotional rather than thematic, and it is the job of the author to handle scenes so as to produce these various emotional responses. As with considerations of style, it is the drift of this criticism to impose a certain uniformity on authors rather than to encourage them in individuality.

The all-important requirement for formal closure, an apt denouement, in the novel, is paralleled by an expectation that there will be emotional closure as well. The plot arouses and relieves a set of emotions including suspense, curiosity, interest, and sympathy; all of these will be satisfied by the outcome of a good novel in a way that finishes the experience but does not end the desire to read more novels. Pathos and humor also call for emotional completeness, the name for which was, simply, tone. This word was deployed more narrowly than it is now, since New Criticism and authors of composition manuals have elaborated it to imply all aspects of authorial attitude. It referred to the author's implicit attitude toward the events and characters in the book viewed as though they were real occurrences and existences, and there were only two tones: healthy and morbid. If the author liked his characters, the tone was healthy; if not, not.

"The highest charm of the book is its pure and healthy tone of feeling" (*North American* on Bremer's *The Neighbors*, April 1843). "It gives cheerful and animating views of human life and the Providence that governs it. . . . The author's mind is an eminently healthy one. . . . She has looked at the world through no false and distorting medium of pride or gloom." "The tone of the book is healthy" (*Peterson's*, July 1852 on Warner's *Queechy*); the *Christian Examiner* complained that Alice Carey's *Hagar* was "nowhere relieved from an unhealthy, painful burden of morbid tone" (September 1852); "the author's tone of thought and sentiment is sound and healthful" (*Arthur's*, June 1855); "its tone is unhealthy" (*Atlantic*, December 1859). In October 1852 *Graham's* wrote about Melville's *Pierre* that "none of Melville's novels equals the present in force and subtlety of thinking and unity of purpose. . . . A capacity is evinced of holding with a firm grasp, and describing with a masterly distinctness, some of the most evanescent phenomena of morbid emotions. But the spirit pervading the whole book is intolerably unhealthy." Morbidity means disease, an unnatural condition. Health is natural, undistorting.

An excellent discussion of a related general principle of importance here occurs in a *Graham's* review of Hawthorne's *The Blithedale Romance* (September 1852). "The ordinary demand of the mind in a work of art, serious as well as humorous, is for geniality—a demand which admits of the widest variety of kinds which can be included within a healthy and pleasurable directing sentiment." In Hawthorne, the journal went on, "geniality cannot be said to predominate. Geniality of general effect comes, in a great degree, from tenderness to persons; it implies a conception of individual character so intense and vivid, that the beings of the author's brain become the objects of his love." The healthy tone, then, implies first that the narrator-author's attention is directed away from himself and toward the beings he has created, and second that his attention to these beings is loving. Conversely, the unhealthy tone may come about either because the author's attention, directed toward himself, fails to encompass (and hence to realize) his characters, or because though directed at those characters it is not loving.

The *Graham's* reviewer suggests that characters realized with sufficient intensity must of necessity become the objects of their creator's love; self-obsession and misanthopy alike might hinder an author from the investment in his characters that brings love inevitably in its train. The formulation shows us how the most self-effacing author can also be deeply and evidently present in a work, in that the characters are now seen to be constructed, in an important way, of the author's attitude toward them. Here, in effect, reviewers acknowledge that characters in fiction, created by language, are essentially unlike characters in real life, in that the mark of authorial love is (or is not) clearly inscribed in them. A secular, real-life fear—of being unparented, or at least unloved—is admitted and rectified in the genial work, admitted and sadistically enhanced in the morbid one.

It is an easy slide from this position to the assertion that human nature is validated or vindicated in the work with a healthy tone. The *Mirror* observed that a "great charm and merit" in G. P. R. James's novels was "the healthy moral tone which pervades them. They have none of that morbid misanthropy, that frantic feebleness, which is too often affected by the authorlings of the day" (February 9, 1839). And *Knickerbocker* praised the "highly moral and healthful tone" of *Kate Aylesford*, which "comes like a refreshing breeze from the bosom of old ocean, to clear away the hot, sickly and foggy sentimentalities of the day. The characters are real flesh-and-blood *individualities*. Every one is drawn so true to life, that no doubt of the writer's fidelity to nature startles the reader's credulity; no suspicion that poor, weak humanity is slandered, arises to disturb the interest of the story" (May 1855). The reviewers' language shows, too, that tone, though rising from the

whole book ("the spirit pervading the book," the "directing sentiment"), is directly referable to the author. "The general tone of
the author" of *Vanity Fair*, according to *Graham's*, "is distinguished by singular manliness, cheerfulness, and generosity";
Charles Reade's "novels are not only good, but have something
peculiar in their goodness, derived from his own character. . . .
One rises from reading his books, not merely with the sense of
delight at his brilliancy, but healthier in mind and feeling. . . .
Beneath all his rapid, brilliant, and varying narrative, his felicitous, though somewhat sketchy characterization; his effective situations, and even his brisk, sparkling epigrams, there is a remarkable freshness, geniality, and simplicity of nature" (November 1848, August 1855).

The healthy, the genial, tone is a matter of author love and
makes the experience of novel reading life confirming and en-
hancing. "The mere power and variety of his imagination cannot
account for his influence," the *Atlantic* wrote on Walter Scott
(May 1858), noting the publication of a household edition of his
works, "for the same power and variety might have been directed
by a discontented and misanthropic spirit, or have obeyed the
impulses of selfish and sensual passions, and thus conveyed a
bitter or impure view of human nature and human life. It is,
then, the man in the imagination, the cheerful, healthy, vigorous, sympathetic, good-natured and broad-natured Walter
Scott himself, who, modestly hidden, as he seems to be, behind
the characters and scenes he represents, really streams through
them the peculiar quality of life which makes their abiding
charm." In a similar spirit, the *Democratic Review* had written in
September 1853 that "one thing peculiarly distinguishes [Scott's]
writings. It is the spirit of broad philanthropy which breathes
through them—the spirit which can only emanate from a kindly
and generous heart."

The issues here are both substantive and formal. The lovability
of human nature itself is at stake. It would not matter so much that
a writer not convey a "bitter or impure view of human nature and
human life" if the reviewers did not think such a view might have
some truth to it, and fear that truth. Formally, since the dynamics
of all plots depended on sympathy and interest, a novel without
sympathetic or interesting characters could not but be a formal
and experiential failure. And, too, an author who presents unlova-

ble characters, or who presents lovable characters without loving them, probably does not love his readers either, and it is difficult to see how engagement with such an author could be the occasion of a pleasurable experience, or why readers should choose to read novels that subject them to an author's contempt or dislike. In essence, the wrong authorial tone pointed to a sort of egotism on the writer's part, where he asserted that he was more interesting than the story he had to tell. The morbid author loves himself.

Here is the repeated point at which a formal judgment of narrator efficacy and an ethical judgment of authorial character intertwine. "The habit of intense brooding over individual consciousness, of making the individual mind the centre and circumference of everything, which is common to many eminent poets of the present age, has turned most of them into egotists, and limited the reach of their minds," the *North American* explained in a review of G. P. R. James (April 1844). "The greatest novelist should be a poet, philosopher, and man of the world, fused into one," it continued in a review of *Dombey and Son* (October 1849). "It is evident that this exacting ideal of a novelist has never been realized. In most of the novels written by men of powerful talents, we have but eloquent expressions of one-sided views of life. In some, the author represents himself, ideals of himself, and negations of himself, instead of mankind." "Each author has drawn what he saw, or knew, or did, or imagined; and so has preserved something worthy, for those who live upon his plane and see the world with his eyes. The difficulty is, that the vision of most men is limited; they observe human nature only in a few of its many aspects; they cannot so far lift themselves above the trivial affairs around them as to take in the whole of humanity in a glance" (*Atlantic*, September 1859).

Given the inevitable limitations of the human grasp, the narrator, though apprised of all the secrets of his story and presumably skilled in knowledge of human nature, was not expected to assume the stance of a deity in the story. But neither was he or she expected to take up the novel's space with self-display and self-characterization. What was looked for was an exemplary stance, a representation of the large-spirited, generous, magnanimous human being who is thought of as an ethically admirable character. The author in the novel, then, is a type rather than an individual, and strategies that individualized the narrator were perceived as both morally and technically defective. We realize, all the more since this time period represents a crucial stage in the development of the idea of the individual, and since indeed individualizing was the chief criterion by which characterization in the novel was judged, that the narrator spoken of here must be a wholly fictive representation devised for the sole purpose of effective storytelling. Each narrator is judged against a fixed ideal of narrator presence. There is no thought that different stories might call for different kinds or representations of narrators. But paradoxically, the narrator is assumed to be the model of a real human being, faithful as far as it goes to the state of mind of the real author writing the novel. Certain states of mind not only are judged to be more efficacious for the purposes of good storytelling but also are assessed in and of themselves, for their moral worth. The distinction between better and worse novels becomes, or begins to become, a distinction between the quality of the moral vision as exemplified in the representation of the author through the narrator. The drift away from story, which we perceive emerging whenever reviewers try to sort out novels by quality, can be seen clearly here.

Judging the moral vision of the narrator, reviewers assumed they were talking about the real author. Were there any instances in which the equivalence of narrator with author was not taken for granted? Criticism of the time recognized only one deviation from a novel narrated by its author, a form they called the "autobiography," and by which they meant what we now call first-person narration. References to this form abound in the 1850s, though they are very rare earlier, a fact that suggests a change within the novel itself. In all probability the development can be traced to *Jane Eyre*. The *Christian Examiner* blamed that novel for the immense popularity of the autobiographical mode: "the introspective autobiography has been overdone. No person of original genius or force of mind can indulge further in this style of thing, unless a new path is opened, or new depths revealed, unexpected heretofore" (March 1859). *The Tenant of Wildfell Hall* was an autobiography (*Literary World*, August 12, 1848); so were *Florence Sackville, Villette, Jane Eyre*, and *The Heiress of Greenhurst* (*Harper's*, February 1852, April 1853, July 1857), *Berenice* (*Home Journal*, May 31, 1856), *While It Was Morning* (*Ladies' Repository*, January 1859), and many more.

The autobiographical form was associated largely, though not exclusively, with women writers and even more with novels featuring a female as the leading character. But *Peterson's* and *Graham's* both used the term for Thackeray's *Henry Esmond*, the latter journal commenting in February 1853 that the novel was "in autobiographical form, and all the incidents and characters are viewed through the medium of an imagined mind—one character giving the tone to the whole representation." A *Knickerbocker* review for January 1854 praised Wilkie Collins's *The Bloodstone* for combining "the charm of an autobiography with the high-wrought interest of a tale."

The formal difference between the autobiography and the dominant mode was, simply speaking, that the former was narrated by a character while the latter was narrated by a representation of the author. What were the attractions and limitations of the autobiography in comparison to the normal mode? Given our interpretive interest in fiction, we tend to approach a question like this in an epistemological mood, thinking about how we are granted access to and knowledge of events in the novel. For these earlier reviewers such considerations did not figure. References above to tone and charm indicate a different center—as usual, that of interest. By making the main character narrate his or her own story, the novelist invested a more exclusive interest in that character and allowed the character a more intense presence than where the character was distanced from the reader by the intervention of a noncharacter narrator. "The interest of the story," a *Harper's* reviewer wrote in April 1857 about *The Days of My Life*, is "chiefly concentrated on the heroine, whose frank and artless relation of her history secures a sympathy with her fortunes, and compels the reader to listen to her naive recital as to an account of private experience." Similarly, a review in *Peterson's* observed that "the autobiographical form" in *The Heiress of Greenhurst* "affords a better play to the delineation of high passion than any other style" (August 1857). Closing the gap between reader and character, the autobiographical mode permits, indeed "compels," a closer involvement and a more intense reading experience.

On the other hand, the autobiographical mode imposes a new distance between the reader and story events, since one is restricted to the knowledge of the narrating character. The increasing separation of character from plot, and the increasing interest in the inner life as the locus of action, both find expression in the growth of the autobiographical mode, which confines attention to one character. "The autobiographical style of narration," observed the *Literary World*, "except in very skillful hands, fetters plot and restrains freedom of description" (March 9, 1850). A sacrifice of breadth for intensity was thus the bargain struck by the autobiographical novel, and only a handful were noting its potential to change the terms of novel reading.

One author who induced such perception was Hawthorne, as a *Graham's* reviewer reported of *The Blithedale Romance* in September 1852. The "interest" of that work centers in the characters of Hollingsworth, Zenobia, and Priscilla, who are "represented as they appear through the medium of an imagined mind, that of Miles Coverdale, the narrator of the story." He "only tells us his own discoveries; and there is a wonderful originality and power displayed in thus representing the characters. What is lost by this mode, in definite views, is more than made up in the stimulus given both to our acuteness and curiosity, and its manifold suggestiveness. We are just watchers with Miles himself, and sometimes find ourselves disagreeing with him in his interpretation of an act or expression of the persons he is observing." *Blithedale* is unique in its use of a subsidiary character as narrator rather than the main character; because of this it really does not fit the acknowledged category of autobiography, and it thus emerges as one of the most "advanced" works of the era. Unlike the other autobiographies reviewed, it was concerned with limitations—on knowledge and interpretation of events—rather than with enhancement of affect.

There is no mention in these discussions of the narrator of the device of the limited third-person narration. If the novel was not recited by one of its characters, then it was recited by the novelist, who, as we have seen, was fettered only by the limits of his own character and certainly not by lack of knowledge about the story or its agents. The only serious criticism of narrator deployment, besides the frequent complaints about authorial tone, involved intrusions—or more properly speaking extrusions—which were identified as one of the chief defects of the old-style novel. As early as July 1825 the *North American* credited Scott with overturning the convention of the authorial intrusion: "the writer's aim is to keep himself out of sight, or to appear only like the ancient chorus, to connect the parts of his story." From our vantage point Scott seems a highly intrusive author; since reflections and other forms of authorial commentary were well accepted, we realize that the criticism applied to a limited category of rhetorical strategies, specifically those in which the author reminded readers of his presence as author, consequently pointing out that the work was only a novel, as in this March 1845 comment on Fielding in the *Democratic Review:* "the frequent communings of the author with his readers produce a disagreeable effect. They do away the illusion by bringing too often the writer, instead of the actor, before the reader." "There is one thing in the work which we consider a fault, though we regret to say it is a very common one. . . . We mean that of speaking in the person of the author. . . . The manager who pulls the wires should never be seen by the spectators" (*Mirror*, July 7, 1838).

The *American Review* voiced the same objection about Longfellow's *Kavanagh:* "we voluntarily give ourselves to the perusal of a fiction, and losing that consciousness as we proceed, should never be permitted for a moment to recall it; for the time the imaginary must stand for the real, and no inconsiderate assertion of the author should dispel the illusion" (July 1849). "The novelist should never do anything to cause a recognition of his personal existence" (*Tribune*, November 13, 1850). "He is the invisible agent that moves the magic machinery by which you are transported into a region of illusory enchantments. . . . The moment you perceive the finger of a man the fond deception vanishes." "The illusion of the story is sometimes impaired by the introduction of the novelist in the first person, a blemish which we should hardly have looked for in a writer who is so obviously well acquainted with the resources of artistic composition as the author of this volume" (*Harper's* on Mayo's *The Berber*, October 1850).

The narrowness of the category of authorial intrusion, compared with our post-Jamesian distinctions, points to a different sense of the way the novelistic illusion is maintained from that operative in contemporary criticism. The difference lies again in our epistemological, as opposed to their affective, approach to the novel. Modernism, believing the authorial presumption of omniscience to be hypocritical, decries the very stance of the narrator as illusory. But this objection posits a narrator commenting about real people, knowledgeable about the real world rather than presiding over an artifical region; in a curious sense it is more naive than the view that assumes from the first that one is dealing with a story referring to real life rather than with real life directly and accepts the narrator or author as the chronicler of a story. From this view the narrator has a set of appropriate activities to carry out, and his assumption of knowledge about the story he is telling is nothing but the simple reflection of a fact. The only inappropriate activity is that of stopping his narration to remind auditors (or readers) that he is narrating, that his story is no more than a story. While all in the audience know perfectly well that the novel is no more than a story, the rhetorical act of reminding them of this breaches convention, since everybody is engaged in a transaction that involves pretending the events narrated are real. To point out the pretense changes the status of the characters from pretended real beings to real fakes; and it also undermines the reader's trust that the game's rules are being observed.

Simply, authorial intrusions make a reader seem foolish. The only reason for revealing himself as author, from the author's point of view, would be to gloat in his power over the reader; as he does that, the author loses that power, since the reader's participation is entirely voluntary. Once again we are in the presence of the self-displaying author, as opposed to one who directs his energies toward the characters he has created, the story he is telling, and the readers who receive it. The tendency of mind that might erupt in an authorial intrusion was precisely the one that would be morbid in tone, and for the same reason: putting oneself ahead of obligations. Egotism. "The characters, if they can be so called, in a fiction like *Ernest Maltravers*, are all shallow. Most energetic and various are they in deed, and copious in speech, but they act and speak at the command of that most potent and arbitrary of powers, the will of their literary father; they are not endowed with independent life. The character, therefore, into which in the course of a volume we get the most insight, is that of the author" (*New York Review*, January 1838).

"He is the best novelist who describes men with perfect fidelity, and yet leaves upon the mind the impression which the best men have in contemplating life," *Harper's* explained in August 1859. There is inevitably an author in the novel and the more exemplary a human being he or she appears to be, the better the novel. Crude authorial self-absorption impeded narration and was a formal defect wherever it appeared; but the demand that a novelist represent objective reality, or life as it is, goes much further. Criticism of the novel becomes a criticism of the author's human grasp rather than of artistic skill.

8

The Novel as a Picture of Nature

"He is the best novelist who *describes* men with perfect fidelity," the *Harper's* reviewer had written. Description, as I noted in
chapter 6, has a different textual force from narration. Its subject
is static, and to conceive of the novel as descriptive is to remove
the emphasis from story and the dynamic, emotional, immediate
involvement that story creates in readers. To equate the achievement of something static with the better novel meant that story-
telling, though remaining the defining formal characteristic of
the novel, was less and less admired as its reason for being.
Novels that were purely story, no matter how well done, were
not seen as striving for the highest reaches of novelistic art, and
novels that were superior were judged so on the basis of something other than their stories. This distinction remains in force
today, just as reading for story rather than meaning is still considered a less admirable kind of activity. In effect, the critic is
looking for novels that are moral statements, for novelists who
are moralists. Evidently pure story is thought to be childish,
frivolous, and—above all—lacking in moral weight. But defining
the better novel in such a way as to ignore or downplay its
fundamental formal feature does not merely modify the form, it
undercuts it; and the critics' effort (along with the novelists who
also wanted to make the novel a weighty moral achievement) was
in essence a co-optation of the popular form for less popular uses.

The language in which reviewers wrote about and praised the
novel as a form representing static reality was, perforce, taken

from a nonliterary artistic form. It was the language of painting.
There is nothing new, or specific to the novel, in the alliance of
painting (or, more generally, pictures) with literature. But this
alliance has different results when its literary subject is the plot-
generated novel as opposed, say, to lyric poetry, because it en-
hances the spatial at the expense of the dynamic. One of the
impulses behind this behavior, an impulse common to intellectual discourse in many fields, is the emphasizing of sight over
other senses. For literature generally the practice drops out the
appeal to sound and severs the tie between writing and speech.
Among many ramifications where the novel is concerned, the
practice erases the temporal field, overwrites the novel as a form
that unfolds itself inevitably in time, and permits the reviewer to
reconstitute it as a complete, framed object that he and the reader
can step back from and examine in a spatial totality. Insofar as
this routine makes the work seem more representational than it
would appear if a temporal, voice-centered model were used, it
can only be because reality itself is thought of as something
complete and fixed from which the observer can be abstracted.
The stance implied here is opposed to that implied in formal
notions of the novel as plot, because it is the essence of plot, and
the reader response connected with it, interest, to be engaged,
caught up—not to be standing back, not to be an observer. To
view the novel as a picture implies ideas about reality and how to
encompass it that are basically different from those implied when
one views the novel as a plot.

Besides downplaying plot and the emotional responses it engendered, talking about novels as though they were pictures obscured or mystified such other elements of fiction as style and
characterization, producing criticism that praised a novel for representational fidelity without providing any clue to how that
fidelity had been achieved. To some degree this was a useful
strategy in that it enabled reviewers to avoid grappling with the
basic question of how nonlinguistic experience or existence (putting aside for the moment the matter of whether anything can be
experienced without language) can fairly be represented through
it. Language in a play was clearly representational, in that it
represented characters talking. Dialogue in a novel was mimetic
in the same way. But for all other aspects of the novel language
was representational only by virtue of a set of mediating conven-

tions that the American Victorian left unexamined. The use of a painterly rhetoric for discussing novels allowed reviewers to leap over a gap that, as the history of criticism in the twentieth century shows, could only threaten the status of the novel as a vehicle for representation. Of course, if the reviewers had not wanted to make the novel a vehicle for representing the human condition, the gap would not have been there to leap over. The problem is a direct result of the paradigm. The paradigm in turn is a response to two differently oriented reviewer desires: first, to separate novels from their powerful emotional affect in favor of a more measured, intellectual response; second, to enforce through the novel a particular idea of reality and the human situation within it.

More innocently, the use of a painterly rhetoric left the novel's lifelike illusion undisturbed. Representational authenticity, from a formal point of view, is useful because when characters and events seem real to readers they become more interesting, thanks to the basic psychological principle of sympathy. To the extent that one understood how they were made to seem real, however, they became less real: art was unmasked as artifice. A vocabulary of painting terms permitted the reviewer to discourse knowingly about the art form without uncovering any of its actual rules of production. The pleasurable experience of novel reading remained undisturbed, and the reviewer, rather than taking pleasure in undermining the novel's achievement, cooperated with it by use of a complicitous discourse. *Harper's* reviewers said that characters in *The House of the Seven Gables* were "drawn" in "sharp and vigorous perspective. They stand out from the canvas as living realities," and of *Villette* that "the plot is simple, almost to bareness. But the personages of the story stand out from this plain canvas with a truly marvelous distinctness, showing the miraculous skill of the writer in the art of dramatic perspective" (May 1851, April 1853). The reviewer can call attention to skill without having to expose its methods, leaving it miraculous. The technical achievement of making a character stand out from the canvas is not analyzed; indeed it cannot be, since characters in a novel are not figures on a canvas to begin with. Thus, anything we might hypothesize about why figures in a painting who stand out from the canvas seem real is beside the point in the instance of the novel, where canvas is a metaphor.

Pictures

Picture language is present in all the journals over the years. The *North American* in a review of Cooper said that the novelist, in comparison to the dramatist, must "paint at full length," that "novels are pictures of life" (January 1838). The *New York Review* wound up a review of Balzac by observing that he "has been before us wholly as an artist, and as such, we have endeavored to give some idea of his magic pencil. . . . He who draws from the wide range of human nature, in whatever land he may find the original of his copies, must fill his gallery with many a revolting picture" (April 1839). *Peterson's* thought Fredrika Bremer "the most exact delineator of character now living; her pictures are finished with all the elaborate nicety of a French painting," and said of Julia Kavanagh that "her minute painting gives a reality to her fictions, which makes them more interesting than those of most other novelists" (October 1843, June 1855). The *Democratic Review* noted in Lippard's *Blanche of Brandywine* "two or three portraits very skillfully drawn" (October 1846).

The *Christian Examiner* said that in *Mary Barton* the characters were "painted by a master's hand," but in Longfellow's *Kavanagh* "the characters are outlined rather than painted" (March 1849, July 1849). In *The Lamplighter*, according to a review in *Knicker-bocker*, "every character is a finished portrait. Very artist-like are the pictures drawn of the scenery of our glorious Hudson," and it observed of Chesebro's *Getting Along* that "the canvas, though full, is not crowded" (May 1854, May 1855). A *Tribune* reviewer, however, thought the effect of *Getting Along* "diminished by the attempt to introduce too many conspicuous personages crowding the foreground of the picture, and impairing the proportions essential to the harmony of the whole" (March 30, 1855). The *Tribune* had also praised Mayo's achievement in *The Berber* for "the subtle lights and shades of passions, and the distinctive individuality which he is thus enabled to give to the prominent figures of his canvas" (November 11, 1850).

Taking the novel as a static spatial form, this commentary concerns itself with a separation of figures from ground that achieves a vividness and concentration making them seem real. Another important and related metaphor concerns the disposition of light and shade, implying both an idea of artistic skill and an idea of the real that the novelist was supposed to represent. When I write "idea of the real" I mean to point to two significant issues: first, the general question of what is taken to be real, and second, a specific cultural concern with the ideal and the real. "Sometimes," a critic in *Peterson's* wrote of Alice Carey's *Married Not Mated*, "she paints her pictures too much in shadow. To us, this seems a mistake, artistically, as well as otherwise" (June 1856). The novelist makes an artistic mistake when she paints "too much" in shadow because objects cannot be seen in the dark. She makes a mistake "otherwise" because life is really made up of lights as well as shadows. "The attempt to delineate the lights and shades of character with the truthfulness of nature seems not to have occurred to the writer, as belonging to the task of the novelist," a *Tribune* review objected on March 21, 1854. "We do not know where to look in the whole range of contemporary fictitious literature, for pictures in which the sober and the brilliant tones of Nature blend with more exquisite harmony" than in *Adam Bede* (*Atlantic*, October 1859).

The advent of daguerreotypy in the 1840s strengthened the notion of art as transcription and encouraged the certainty that there was a real world out there sitting for its portrait. "We commend *Hawkstone*," the *Literary World* said, "for to the charm of an exciting narrative it adds a kind of daguerreotype of existent religious opinions"; "Dickens daguerreotyped life at the King's Bench prison, in his *Pickwick Papers*" (March 11, 1848; December 9, 1848). *Harper's* found in Anna Warner's *Dollars and Sense* "a transcript from the world about us, whose charm lies in its almost daguerreotype exactness to the original" (September 1852). The *Ladies' Repository* commended Elizabeth Stuart Phelps's *A Peep at Number Five* "to those who would have a faithful daguerreotype of a city preacher's trials and enjoyments" (July 1853). *Ten Nights in a Bar-Room*, according to *Godey's*, "exhibits the actualities of bar-room life, and the consequences flowing therefrom, with a severe simplicity and adherence to truth that gives to every picture a Daguerrean vividness" (August 1854).

In other instances, artistic deployment of light and shade meant adding something to reality, and this addition might be viewed in different ways. "Though every scene in the story is to the reader, if New England born, as plain as the way to church, and true as the catechism, yet the lights and shadows in this picture of home life are so artistically arranged, that we seem walking in Fairyland," *Godey's* rhapsodized about *Kavanagh* (July 1849). "It is not enough for an author of fiction to represent society exactly as it is," a long essay on novels in the *Christian Examiner* stressed (January 1847). "There is a far loftier art. It is, departing from the general truthfulness of nature and life in no single feature, violating no essential probability, so to collocate the figures and dispose the groups, so to distribute light and shade, as to produce a certain whole more richly suggestive than any serviceable copy could be. . . . Real life is not to be departed from, not contradicted; it is to be idealized." Adding to reality by artistic arrangement meant, in these cases, to represent a higher, a truer, truth than that attainable by simple representation of what appears. The ideal, artistically speaking, is translated into the activity of the artist-observer who arranges and intensifies what is perceived: the link between American transcendentalism and normal American Victorianism is evident.

In other instances, describing the specific quality of a book or author, the reviewer considered the artist's additions to or departures from reality in more purely aesthetic terms. In *Henry Esmond*, the *Tribune* remarked, "the painting does not, indeed, exhibit such broad contrasts of light and shade—there is no character which starts so prominently from the canvas" as in *Vanity Fair* or *Pendennis*, yet "the characters are portrayed with more delicacy and naturalness of finish" (November 30, 1852). *Little Dorrit*, according to *Putnam's*, "has the usual bright lights and dark shadows; it is, as usual, a little more grotesque than the life of the day. . . . It has the old extravagance of portraiture" (August 1857). "In spite of these defects," the *Atlantic* commented on an Italian novel, "Guerrazzi has succeeded in so intensifying the high lights and deep shadows of passion, pathos, and horror in the story, as to make a very effective picture, of the Caravaggio school" (March 1858).

Reviewers also borrowed the metaphor of outline and filling from painting. In *The House of the Seven Gables*, "the general outline is well conceived, but the filling up is not of equal excellence" (*Christian Examiner*, May 1851); the journal complained that "the first outlines of character are never filled up" in the Baroness Tautphaeus's *Quits* (January 1858). *Harper's* found that in Mary Jane Holmes's *Tempest and Sunshine* "the outlines of the leading personages are admirably given, demanding only a more thorough elaboration to make a superior work" (July 1854). "The actors are drawn in bold outlines, which it does not appear to have been the purpose of the author to fill up in the delicate manner usually deemed necessary for the development of character in fiction," the *Atlantic* said of *Sword and Gown* (December 1859). The notion of light and shade, like that of standing out from the canvas, relates to the perceptual categories of foreground and background and to the illusion of three-dimensionality that is associated in turn with the illusion of life; the category of outline and filling is related to the perceptual categories of first and subsequent impressions. Here the activity alluded to is at last temporal; the outline, the first impression, is later modified or completed by filling. Having more opportunities to observe, one gets more and more information, and the figure consequently becomes more and more detailed. (Here is the difference between the sketch and the novel, as well as the painterly genesis of the term "sketch" for the shorter work that never goes beyond its outline.) The temporality invoked here, however, is different from that involved in following out a plot line, since it is cumulative rather than sequential. The figure was really as much there, in the real world, the first time as the tenth; the time involved is the real time it takes the perceiver to assimilate material rather than the time required for the plot to transpire.

A third important painting metaphor is coloration. "We think the style of *Deerslayer* more polished, and the descriptions of natural scenery traced with greater grace of outline, and freshness, and transparency of coloring, than in any of Mr. Cooper's previous works" (*New York Review*, October 1841). "The substance of the book illustrates in vivid colors, the evils of the manufacturing system," the *Democratic Review* observed of *North and South*; in her historical novels Agnes Strickland "may heighten the colors of her picture, and that, indeed, is the artist's privilege; but she neither distorts the facts nor falsifies the general accuracy of tradition"; "the colors used" in A. S. Roe's *A Long Look Ahead*, "though heightened here and there, are generally true to our common experience of the world" (February 1849, February 1855, April 1855).

This metaphor, with its implicit contrast of pale and bright, looks like the contrast between light and shade, but actually refers to a different aspect of painting and of reality. The contrast of light and shade is essentially monochromatic and alludes to such associated categories of experience as cheer and gloom, good and evil, joy and sorrow. The contrast implicit in coloration has to do with intensity, richness, and depth. The *North American*, reviewing Balzac, praised the "extraordinary richness and delicacy in his coloring" (July 1847). The *Literary World* complained that *Lonz Powers* by James Weir "reminds us of some life-like engraving, ruined by daubing it over with glaring water colors" (October 5, 1850). The *Southern Literary Messenger* warned its readers about Southworth's novels: "there could be few greater evils, in our estimation, than the introduction of these warm, highly colored, 'artist' productions . . . into a Virginia family of young girls and boys" (June 1851). *Tribune* reviewers faulted William Henry Herbert's *The Roman Traitor* for "excessive warmth of coloring"; found that *The Lamplighter* "bears the stamp of genuine truthfulness—nothing is overdrawn, or too intensely colored"; thought that in *The Old Homestead* Ann Stephens's "pictures of scenes in the city, though often drawn in too high colors, are on the whole effective"; and decided that Alice Carey's *Married Not Mated* was "free from the excess of coloring which vitiated the effect of *Hagar*" (September 24, 1853; May 28, 1854; December 6, 1855; May 3, 1856).

Each of the various painterly metaphors utilized by reviewers of novels implied certain proper judgments. It was good art when characters stood out from the canvas and occupied a relatively uncluttered foreground. The picture should contain balanced contrasts of light and shade. It should fill up its outlines. It should be delicately, not excessively colored. As categories for talking about novels, these metaphors' function is substitutive, replacing plot with picture and the engaged, enchained, and excited reader with the contemplative, detached observer. In this way the judgments enjoined an interaction with the novel quite different from that which was inferable from reviewer discussion of the popularity of the novel and the reasons for that popularity. In addition, these putatively aesthetic statements carried with them important normative implications about the real world, not the least of which were that such a world existed independent of observation, could be known through observation, and was representable. Reviewers were frequently more certain about the nature of the real world as pictured in the novel than about the art by which the picture was achieved. And truth to nature became a criterion by which superior novels were known.

Nature

It became commonplace for reviews of the 1850s to see the novel progressing historically toward ever more truthful works of art, and to identify fictional superiority in particular instances with such truthfulness. This, indeed, more than the clever concealment of a moral, was the accepted criterion, but of course truthfulness had an inalienable moral aspect. We recognize familiar nineteenth-century assumptions here: history as progress, the human being as improvable and perhaps perfectible; less familiar, perhaps, is an equation of the improved human being with one who prefers instruction to enjoyment. "What is wanted to constitute a good modern novel," a *Putnam's* critic expatiated in an essay entitled "Novels: Their Meaning and Mission," "is not a monstrous assemblage of grotesquely illusive pictures of life and nature, interlarded with inconceivable sentiments, unheard-of-adventures, and impossible exploits. Not at all. We demand that they be veritable and veracious segments of the great life-drama, displaying Nature and Man as they are, sentiments as they are felt, and deeds as they are done" (October 1854). The construction of a literary history, and of a supporting canon of major authors, went forward under the aegis of this demand, which imagined novels to have a "mission." In this project the reviewers exacerbated, if they did not create, a division between better and popular novels, simply because popularity has always been based on the capacity of a form to give pleasure to the greatest numbers.

Obliterating or denigrating the pleasure-producing function of the novel and distrusting novels that give great pleasure to great numbers remain characteristics of academic criticism and theory to this day, reminding us of the middle-class Victorian origins of our own habits of literary criticism. "Novelists recognize that Nature is a better romance-maker than the fancy," *Harper's* commented in a favorable review of Eliot's *Scenes of Clerical Life*, "and the public is learning that men and women are better than heroes and heroines, not only to live with, but also to read of" (May

1858). The taste for better novels had to be learned, which meant it had to be taught, and the novel thus became enmeshed in an interaction of instruction rather than entertainment.

The criterion of truthfulness, the emphasis on nature and the real, is much stronger in some journals than in others—indeed it becomes a means of classifying them—and is found much more commonly toward the end of the period, especially in the later fifties. Certain journals were aligning themselves with and to some extent had become advocates of the poetics of a given group of novelists, those whom we now call "realistic" (though the word does not appear in the American reviews of the day) and who still constitute, so far as the English canon is concerned, the major figures for literary study. *Harper's* and the *Atlantic* were both important organs in the ultimately successful advocacy of these authors and their works. But I would qualify these comments by acknowledging that it *was* advocacy—that truthful works and the criterion of truth had by no means achieved the dominance they have now, even as we imagine ourselves to have progressed far beyond Victorian ideology. A debate was in progress; the situation was in flux. I would also note—though the point may be obvious—that even where reviewers agreed that novels should be true to nature, their ideas of that truth were inevitably conventional.

The opposition, if it may be called that, to elevating truthfulness to nature as the means of identifying the superior novel falls into two camps—the idealists who maintained that truth was not enough, and the formalists who insisted that novels were stories, not essays. Both these camps came together in a sense that the novel ministered to desire, whose rules were not necessarily congruent with observed reality. From the point of view of the self-proclaimed idealist, a mere representation of reality—granting it could be attained, which for the most part this contingent did—was insufficient to the needs and demands of that very human nature that the advocates of the novel of the real claimed to be representing.

"In the details of daily life, especially in the ruder forms under which it appears in the wilderness and on the frontiers of civilization, there is much which no skill can make poetical, much which no light of imagination can clothe with the radiance of artistic beauty, much which cannot, by any possible magic of literary genius, be raised out of the region of squalid, groveling, repulsive vice and barbarism. This sadly unpoetic side of American life should not, indeed, be kept wholly out of sight in fictitious delineation; but it cannot be brought prominently forward without violating the laws of ideal beauty, under which all the works of imagination must necessarily arrange themselves," the *North American* commented in a review of the works of Simms (October 1846). "The rule, that fiction must always copy nature, must, obviously, be adopted with some little restriction. To represent man as he is with perfect fidelity would not, in many cases, be desirable. Where the imitation is so exact, the canvas often reflects forms, loathsome, hideous, and repulsive. Would the interest or utility of fiction be increased by such grotesque portraitures?" asked a reviewer in the *Southern Literary Messenger* (September 1849).

On January 18, 1851, the *Literary World* wrote that it would not "quarrel" with Thackeray (who for all these reviewers was the ultimate realist) "provided he does not insist upon any exclusive theory in regard to the construction of the novel. He would not tell us that his art must be always imitative, and never creative. He would not surely shut out the ideal from its province. Whether he wills it or not, the world will laugh with Dalgetty and Pickwick, and weep with Little Nell and Jeanie Deans. The experience of this world will never supply us with the humor of one or the pathos of the other. Scott, and Dickens, by the immortal power of genius, have filled that void in the human heart." On June 7 of the same year the journal identified two "schools" of novel writing, one epitomized by Thackeray and the other by Dickens: "Thackeray is essentially an artist of the real school. . . . Dickens, on the other hand, works more in the ideal. It is nonsense to say of his characters generally, intending the observation for praise, that they are life-like. They are nothing of the kind." A slight change in perspective would produce a different sense of the opposition between real and ideal, for Scott and Dickens before 1850 were usually praised for the powerful lifelikeness of their characters, and thereafter as exponents of the ideal.

"We object to the employment of materials like this in a fictitious work, as hostile to the true purposes of art. . . . Granting that their prototypes are to be found in nature, it does not follow that they are legitimate subjects for art. A depraved taste may delight in loathsome natural scenes, but no true artist will give them preference over the revelations of beauty with which the Universe is filled" (*Tribune*, January 1, 1853). *Godey's* (December 1855) praised the virtuous sentiments interspersed in the melancholy narrative of *The Old Homestead:* "were it not for such gems as these to brighten the way, and to solace the hopes of the reader, all such narratives would, however true to life and society, become in a measure intolerable." *Graham's*, reviewing *The Newcomes*, allowed that "Thackeray aims to give the truth, and the whole truth," and that "it is through no fault of his that the world is not what the philanthropist and the sentimentalist desires it to be," but it still preferred writers who "are delineators, not of actual, but of possible life and character," who "not only look into life" but "look through it . . . creating a new world of beings, having its roots and principles in the actual world" (December 1855). According to this description, actuality is not so much the ground as the embellishment of the satisfying fiction, which originates in and is responsive to desire. The *Christian Examiner* took a similar approach to Thackeray: "the key-note is too monotonous, the scene too dreary, the *dramatis personae* too repulsive for renewed acquaintance. . . . It is not healthful, then, to dwell upon and fraternize with even the truest pictures of life, if they exclusively tend to keep in view its mechanical level, and to strip it of heaven-born illusions" (January 1856). The *Home Journal* reviewer reported in the novel *Berenice* "a faithfulness which would be often painful from its startling truthfulness to nature, were it not for that ray of hope, slender though it be, with which even the darkest shades in the picture are illumined" (May 31, 1856).

The *New York Ledger* for October 30, 1858, the nation's most popular fiction weekly, attributed the advanced state of contemporary civilization to poets and romance writers, "mainly owing to their prominent principle of keeping the mind dissatisfied with commonplace things, their power of creating images superior in every respect to reality, which we admire and would fain imitate, and the admiration they infuse for what is good and excellent, or sublime and daring. . . . By making us discontented [they] spur us to pursue things beyond our reach, and keep us in progression." "One of the great advantages of fiction, as compared with history," observed a reviewer in the *Ladies' Repository*, is "that it may avoid these hum-drum everyday realities, and realize in imagination the ideal excellences which 'life' so seldom affords. Hence it often happens that the greater the number of facts, the less perfect and truthful the story" (May 1859).

Fiction merely truthful to nature, idealists complained, was incommensurate with the human spirit regardless of whether spiritual longings guaranteed the existence of an unseen reality. (Of course they preferred to think it did, but this question was muted in reviews.) The ground of the "formalist" complaint with such fiction was that truthfulness to nature did not make an interesting novel. Because the argument of real versus ideal was more general, and that of nature versus interest more specific to the novel, it is this latter concern that we find more frequently argued in reviews, argued because the proponents of the truthful novel could not afford to allow that the type of novel they advocated was not interesting.

As early as July 1816 the *North American*, reviewing a work called *Rhoda*, remarked on the "numerous and constantly increasing class of productions, in which fiction is brought home to daily occurrences and observations" and added that "readers are apt to complain of such that they are monotonous and ordinary." Reviewers for the sober *North American* constantly advocated the truthful novel but could not deny the significance of the complaint. Even domestic novels, one wrote in April 1825, should not comprise "the dull diary of ordinary occupations, or amusements" but rather "some event, or at least a series of events, of unusual importance, standing out in strong relief from the rest of the biography of [the] principal characters." The *American Review* commented on a work of Eugene Sue that "so much are we interested in its startling details, that we absolutely lose sight of all the monstrous incongruities and absurdities with which the book is stuffed from beginning to end" (April 1846). "Those fond of the improbable and the unnatural," *Godey's* grumbled over a Dumas novel, "will, as usual, be gratified to their heart's content" (May 1848). "Actual life, with the element of romance expelled, is dull and depressing," a reviewer for the *Literary World* admitted on November 14, 1849. "There is so much namby-pamby fiction about, that when one meets with a novel that rises, like this, to the heights of tragic passion, one can excuse many faults of style and even some improbabilities of incident," *Peterson's* wrote of Southworth's *Retribution*. "No one equals her in variety of incident, or surpasses her in the interest she imparts to her narrative" (October 1856).

The most acute discussion of the dilemma I have found occurs in a signed essay called "Reading for Amusement" by Caroline Kirkland in *Sartain's* for March 1850, part of which seems worth quoting at length. "Though we profess to relish most those fictions which are like transcripts of life, we in reality covet a certain exaggeration, and an artful veiling of the more vulgar truths," she wrote. We would not be interested or excited by direct contemplation of "the actual occurrences which the writer of fiction describes," and accordingly it *cannot* be life transcripts that we desire in fiction.

> It is the repose and refreshment of a little illusion that we long for, although this illusion be thrown over the very subjects of all others about which we feel most anxious to discover truth. Yet we persuade ourselves that we accept fiction only as a substitute for truth. This is one of the unavoidable inconsistencies of a condition full of blunders. . . . If the truth be familiar, we despise it, no matter how well presented. "Where's the use of putting all that into a book?" said a plain-spoken western woman, on reading some sketches of the life she saw about her. She did not want suggestions of the homely, though they might suit well enough the child of luxury and wearisome convention. When she selected a book for her own reading, it would be one of the wildest and most exciting romances, perhaps a harrowing ghost-story, or the impossible adventures of some pirate or highwayman. . . . Indeed, distance, either of time, place, or circumstance, from the scene of our own knowledge or recollection, seems to be one of the requisites for fascination in fiction, although if this distance be *too* great it precludes interest by chilling sympathy.

Since the requirement that readers be interested could not be put aside in a context where reading was voluntary, those critics concerned to forward the cause of the truthful novel had to argue, or insist, or claim, or *decree* that the natural was interesting. In many instances we see this claim advanced with a becoming tentativeness, which acknowledges implicitly that the natural is not naturally interesting but is made so as an artistic achievement. "No novelist has at all approached her in the interest with which she invests home-scenes and incidents of every day life, which, in her hand, assume an interest rivalling the more romantic and dignified events of Scott's romances" (*Peterson's* on Fredrika Bremer, October 1843). "It is a picture of real life, without the least exaggeration, and yet intensely thrilling" (*Peterson's*, May 1849). These days, the *Literary World* found, readers demand "a little more nature, not so milk and watery as the nature Mr. Arthur deals us, but in its vigorous state as mixed by Thackeray and Dickens" (August 31, 1850). *Arthur's* praised a novel by Mary Andrews Denison as excelling "in the art of throwing around every-day life and every-day scenes a humanitary aspect that elevates the seeming common-place into interest and importance" (July 1854).

His "characters are natural without being commonplace," the *American Review* said of Thackeray, "and to represent characters in this manner is, we think, the perfection of writing" (May 1851). "The dull conventionalities of life become instinct with interest in her hands" (*Democratic Review* on Jane Austen, March 1855). "The incidents and characters are, indeed, striking, but, at the same time, probable, natural, and truthful"; "with all her bold limning, the incidents are natural"; "but, with all this trueness to nature, the work abounds with interest almost to *piquancy*" (*Home Journal*, March 24, 1855; March 15, 1856; March 29, 1856). "The various characters, and the domestic occurrences introduced, are natural and probable, and will, though quietly introduced, be found sufficiently impressive to sustain the interest, and to reward the curiosity of the reader" (*Godey's*, June 1857). "Without indulging in extravagance of plot or sentiment, the author throws a vital human interest about his narrative, and produces a deep impression by fidelity to nature and force of illustration" (*Harper's* on *Adam Bede*, April 1859).

The more aggressive move was to claim that fidelity to nature became interesting not thanks to authorial skill but simply because nature was interesting in itself. "Her personages," ruminated *Knickerbocker*, "are, without an exception such as have fallen or might fall within the knowledge of every one; and there is not an incident in the whole progress of the story that almost any one could not match from the stories of his own experience. What is it, then, that makes *Allen Prescott* a most delightful book to read?" It answered, "the very fidelity to nature" (March 1835). Similarly, the *Mirror* observed that "without the ostentation of profound plot, it is a perfect transcript of some of the most interesting and ludicrous scenes and persons of ordinary life. A strong interest in reality carries you through to the close. No mystery is unfolded, but actions probable in their nature and delightful in their descriptions, become important by their just consequences" (January 9, 1836). Catharine Sedgwick, the *North American* noted, "writes of minds and hearts, as they muse and beat, not in ancient Rome, nor modern Cumberland, but in the streets of our marts, and the retirement of our villages. So her own mind obtains the excitement, which nothing gives, like the sense of dealing with realities . . . and her readers are wrought to a warm interest by seeing themselves reflected, as in a glass" (October 1837). "Mrs. Haven delineates with ease and skill the characters of everyday life, and invests them with the charms that only fidelity to nature can impart," *Godey's* editorialized in February 1856.

An Easy Chair in *Harper's* for June 1859 summed it up in considering Thackeray: his novels "delineate the play of daily life, and of common, but not uninteresting, characters. They deal in no surprises, no scenes, no melodrama and red lights of any kind. And hence they address the highest faculties and the best audience; for their interest springs from their fidelity to nature, and the genial skill with which that fidelity is carried into the minutest details." The summation is important because in referring to the "highest faculties and the best audience" *Harper's* in effect admits that the appeal of the novel it espouses is limited because nature is by no means universally or inevitably interesting.

"What is a novel?" the Easy Chair asked again in February 1860. "It is a picture of life. Just in the degree that it is a true novel, it is an accurate representation—within such limits of space and time and mutual relation as to make it effective and real in its impression and influences—of the characters and circumstances which surround us all, and with which we are most familiar." The insertion of the normative adjective "true" here is accompanied by an equally telling parenthetical clause admitting that the "accurate representation" is really an artful structure. And we must not overlook the equation of life as it really is with characters and circumstances that surround "us all," with which "we" are most familiar. Here the *Harper's* reviewer betrays another gap in his argument, showing that the reality with which this accurate novel deals is simply conventional. He takes for granted that its "we" speaks for "us all," and that what we-all see around us every day is the real. This is not the same as saying that people are interested in books about people like themselves, a statement that would recognize experiential pluralism and the gap between human perception and the constitution of reality. It is a far more arrogant assertion, advocating, albeit unawares, the truthful novel as an agent of cultural indoctrination, of instruction.

Nature and Convention

Of course the practice of identifying what one believes to be the state of things, or wishes to claim as the state of things, as "nature" or the "real" is hardly limited to novel reviews in antebellum America. But its prevalence in such reviews shows that the novel had become established by 1850 as a significant site for debates about reality—whether or not novels actually contained views of reality, whether these views were implicit or explicit, reviewers discussed them as though they did and as though these views mattered. Such discussions inevitably recreated the novel as the expository form that reviews took it to be. The novel had become an occasion for a specific kind of cultural discourse, and as such an occasion it lost its formal integrity and coherence, ceased to be "itself," and was dissolved into the stream of culture. From this perspective—the perspective of how it was talked about, what it was used for—the novel, as soon as it became an important cultural phenomenon, was literally translated into a cultural document (which it still remains and indeed now often self-consciously, internally, formally strives to be), although the word used by our commentators was not culture but nature. Because novels were important to so many people, it was important to reviewers that they contain views of nature, and that these views be "right."

There was striking, though perhaps not surprising, accord in these reviews on what were the most important elements of the

right view of nature. Nature had design, its design was ap-
prehensible by human beings, it centered on and provided a field
for human action, and it had an inherent moral dimension; in the
long run good predominated over bad and joy over sorrow. In a
word: Victorianism, though not the competitive variety that encourages entrepreneurship and individual achievement. Just the
reverse, one which concentrates on modest expectations, the
presence of powerful external controls and the need for equally
powerful internal ones, and the pleasure of duty rather than the
pleasure of pleasure. "Our author never separates the tie that
unites virtue and happiness, vice and misery, which succeed each
other as invariably as thunder follows lightning or as spring
comes after winter" (*North American* on Sedgwick, January 1831).
In *The Scarlet Letter*, according to *Graham's*, Hawthorne "has
made his guilty parties end not as his own fancy or his own
benevolent sympathies might dictate, but as the spiritual laws,
lying back of all persons, dictated to him. In this respect there is
hardly a novel in English literature more purely objective" (May
1850).

Ann Stephens's "novels are transcripts of life, not mere ideal
pictures. . . . Her men and women are the men and women we
meet every day in our streets, with loves, hatred, vanity, generosity, and all other human qualities at war in their bosoms: men
and women, who become good or bad, as they strive, or neglect,
to work out their progress to a better life, to a higher spiritual
condition" (*Peterson's*, August 1854). As for *Peter Gott, the Cape
Ann Fisherman*, by Joseph Reynolds: "when so many highly
wrought and over-colored pictures are sent forth from the press,
it is well to have one of these sober, truthful delineations to show
us life as it really is—a serious and toilsome march from one duty
performed to another yet to be done; and not a fierce battle with
fate, from which we come off either victors and triumphant for
the rest of our days, or else are left a useless corpse on the field of
the struggle" (*Godey's*, August 1856).

Why is it "well" to have such a novel? And would we be
surprised if a novel like this should turn out to be less popular,
and its type less common, than the "highly wrought and over-
colored pictures" *Godey's* deplores? If interest, even to excitement, is the principle by which novels enchain their readers and
according to which their form must be designed, we can see that

the reviewers' ideal undermines the novel's formal base. If they are right about nature, then the novel is inherently an unnatural form. To simplify somewhat, the novel, which appears historically as an occasion for self-gratification and pleasure, is being conscripted by the reviewing establishment as an agent of social control. When we remember that the great population of novel readers was thought to consist of the less educated, and to be concentrated among the young and especially the female, we might interpret all these gestures as support for a stable patriarchy.

The class struggle here seems to me less significant than the generational struggle and, above all, the gender struggle. The view of nature set out in these reviews is especially concerned to assert that woman's place is decreed by natural or divine laws and therefore immutable. In March 1846 the *American Review* castigated George Sand for preaching the "injustice, inequality, and absurdity of the marriage tie, which she admits springs from the dependence of woman upon man, based on a natural law—which law, however, she stigmatizes as unjust—attempting, with shrill outcries, to mar the majestic harmony of nature" (even then feminists were "shrill"). "It is disagreeable to the fancy," the same journal remarked of McIntosh's *Charms and Counter-Charms*, "to picture a passionate couple, such as these are represented to have been, living in that manner for a long space of time, neither *married* nor bound in duty *to be married*. The thing is against nature and reason, and therefore to contemplate it tends to corrupt and unrefine" (October 1848). It complained revealingly about Chesebro's *Isa*, where an unconventional couple moves to Europe and lives happily ever after without marrying: "would not their 'experiment' have exerted a more healthful influence" on the public mind and "on individual morality, and consequently, security, if the result had shown in its true, its life-light, the consequences of this, as every other violation of that domestic law which cannot be violated with impunity?" (July 1852). The *American Review* was a Whig journal, deeply conservative; the three works it attacked here were written by women.

The *Literary World* excoriated Brontë's *The Tenant of Wildfell Hall* for its depiction of an abusive husband: "one of the chief improbabilities of the book consists in the absurdity of supposing any community or family in England would tolerate such a husband as Mr. Huntingdon among them. In this world men do not maltreat their wives, seduce openly other men's, and beat their brothers-in-law with impunity. The same natural law that decrees the dependence of women guarantees their happiness and safety in the arrangement" (August 12, 1848). It complained about *Lady Alice; or, The New Una*, in which the heroine spends some time passing as a man, that there is no way "of abolishing the immutable distinction between petticoats and pantaloons"; it approved of Bremer's novels because in them "woman plays the important part nature has assigned her" (July 21, 1849; December 1, 1849). *Graham's* liked *Edith Kinnaird* because it was "a fiction which the most artistic mind will feel delight in perusing, yet one which the humblest will understand, and from which both may derive improvement. The heroine is neither a saint nor a fool, but a living woman; her sufferings spring from her errors, and are redeemed by her repentance; all is natural, beautiful, refreshing, and noble. . . . Instead of rendering its readers dissatisfied with themselves, and their lot in life, with society, with everything, this novel makes them feel that life is a battle, yet that victory is sure to reward all who combat aright" (May 1848). And a reviewer for the *Atlantic* praised *Out of the Depths* despite its sensitive subject (it was the "autobiography" of a prostitute) because the heroine accurately attributed her "fall" to "her vanity and unrestrained passion" (November 1859).

These reviews reveal a social context wherein those who read novels were thought of as discontented, or as easily becoming so; behind the static, perhaps stodgy issue of truth to nature lies the more volatile issue of social unrest, and especially the unrest of the young and the female. The very attraction of the novel-reading population to "untrue" novels—that is, novels encouraging discontent—suggested as much and also suggested the advisability of neutralizing the novel's perceived threat. "Recreative books disarm criticism," the *Christian Examiner* reflected in a long essay on Thackeray in January 1856. "Yet, if there is one class of works more than another which it is specially desirable to estimate correctly, it is that included under the generic name of popular fiction. If this department of literature does not reflect, it in a degree moulds the age. . . . It is through vivid and fascinating pictures of human life, through the adventures of some hero or the sentiment of some heroine [*sic*], that we usually image our own career, or, at least, first shape our ideal of what it should be. . . . It is on account of this enduring and personal agency of the gifted novelist, that it becomes requisite to examine his claims by a more comprehensive test than the direct moral of his story, or the degree of cleverness it manifests." The essay continued: "there is often a perverse mood in genius that leads to the choice of subjects which it only irritates or revolts the mind to contemplate, or to such a treatment of more legitimate themes as distorts and renders grotesque the facts of nature"; and it concluded, despite its own counterexamples, that art "is essentially conservative, and aims to keep alive sentiments which the world too often blasts." As the descriptive gives way to the normative here, one wonders whether the real perversity was not in the reviewer, determined to ignore the inextricable psychological linkage of excitement and interest with dissatisfaction. If art *were* essentially conservative, it would not be necessary to insist that it ought to be.

Apart from the question whether novelists were or were not radical in the particularities of their social, sexual, or personal world views—quite apart from the question whether they wrote to situate those views in an authenticating fiction—lies the possibility that the form of the novel assumes discontent as the psychological ground from which it springs. The essence of plot, after all, is that something is wrong; there is a disturbance that needs correcting. Because women and youth mostly read novels, it was thought, their discontents in particular would be ministered to and hence exacerbated. The conviction of many contemporary students of popular culture that popular forms sedate discontent was not held by this earlier group of critics. If, as many feminist critics have argued, the "better novel" appears regularly to be instinct with misogyny, this may not be an accident. Novels putting women in their place may well have been selected by reviewers as better than—more true to nature than—novels that legitimated their discontents.

9

Morality and Moral Tendency

Since the American Victorian reviewer believed that nature and the real possessed an inalienable moral character, discussion of morality in novels was inevitable as soon as truthfulness became a criterion of novelistic value. Indeed, reviewers appear interested in nature mainly as a channel to morality and were far more concerned with morality than philosophy in their criticism (although to some degree they did not distinguish morality *from* philosophy). Talk about morality is so characteristic of and so widely prevalent in novel reviewing in the 1840s and 1850s as to indicate that it was taken as part of the reviewer's job. In the more than two thousand reviews that underlie this discussion, only one reviewer stated that in principle the morality of the books he wrote about was not his business. This was Edgar Allan Poe, who, when reviewing for *Graham's* in the early 1840s, savaged (among other novels) Harrison Ainsworth's *Guy Fawkes* "as a work of art, and without reference to any supposed moral or immoral tendencies (things with which the critic has nothing to do)" (November 1841). In May 1848 *Graham's*, whose staff Poe had long since left, reversed his position (though it did not mention him by name): "in criticizing a novel, it becomes important to examine the tendency of the work. We utterly repudiate the idea that a reviewer has nothing to do with the morality of a book. . . . There can be no medium. A fiction which does not do good does harm. There never was a romance written, which had not its purpose, either open or concealed, from that of *Waverley*, which inculcated loyalty, to that of *Oliver Twist*, which teaches the brotherhood of man."

The closest any other reviewer came to Poe's position was this in *Peterson's* for April 1856, on Southworth's *India:* "we speak of it, of course, entirely from a literary stand-point. Of late, it has become too common to praise or censure novels, on other grounds; whereas a critic, so long as a fiction is not immoral, has nothing to do except with the literary merits and demerits of a work." So long as a fiction is not immoral. The first responsibility of the critic, accordingly, is to determine whether a novel is immoral; only after that determination is made may one proceed to examine the work's literary merits and demerits. The morality of the novel is not a function of the quantity of overt moralizing it contains, nor of its membership in the category of didactic novels or novels of practical morality. All novels without exception have—must have—moral or immoral tendencies, often operating independently of any inferable purpose of the author. "Here," a *Godey's* reviewer said, "is a volume written with evident pretensions to taste and refinement of language, but which, unwittingly to its author, perhaps, is lamentably deficient and deceptive in its moral tone" (August 1856).

Every journal, even in brief reviews, mentions and assesses "tendency." "We cannot but doubt the tendency of tales of such unmitigated horror," *Knickerbocker* wrote of *Martin Faber* (October 1833). "We confess that we never could see the injurious tendency of these transcripts of life," it commented on Bulwer's works in an Editor's Table for February 1835, but it later changed its mind in a review of *Ernest Maltravers:* "we can no longer concede that which we have hitherto claimed for him, a purpose to hold up to the world the rewards of virtue and the consequences of vice. On the contrary, the tendency of his morality seems to be, that we are the victims of destiny, and that circumstances alone determine the phases of character, and prescribe the paths of virtue and vice" (December 1837). A *Southern Literary Messenger* review agreed: "The tendency of Bulwer's novels is of an evil kind" (November 1842).

Maria McIntosh's *Woman an Enigma* did better with the *Southern Literary Messenger:* "its tendency is decidedly moral," it reported (October 1843). "Novels," the *Ladies' Repository* declared, "are, generally, bad in their tendency, it is true, yet some have redeeming qualities" (July 1847). It commented that the "moral tendency" of Scott's novels "may not be altogether pernicious;

but we doubt much whether that tendency can be said to be beneficial" (September 1848). "Well written, and, of course, full of interest to those fond of tales of this character, though there can be but one opinion as to their tendency" (*Godey's* on Henry Miles's *Dick Turpin, the Bold Highwayman*, August 1848); "of course, the moral tendency of the work is unexceptionable" (*Godey's* on a work by Timothy Shay Arthur, February 1851). *Harper's* said that in *The Two Families* "the moral tendency . . . is pure and elevated," and a later review commented more generally, "if novels and romances, of which the tone is low, and the taste bad, and the coloring voluptuous, and the morality questionable, are among the subtlest and deadliest poisons cast forth into the world, those of a purer spirit and a higher tendency are, we honestly believe, among the most effective agencies of good" (July 1852, June 1853).

A January 1851 review in the *North American* explained that "tendency" in novels derived from the sympathetic instinct. "The appetite for narrative has a solid foundation in the social nature, and must endure. Works of imagination will ever find hearts eager to be made to throb with sympathy for the joys and woes, the physical and moral struggles, of humanity. . . . In man's eagerness to know his fellow-man, even imaginary characters and situations are interesting to him; and he is strongly moved by the common fears inseparable from a state of bodily and moral weakness, the common hopes which the very emptiness of the world suggests, the desire to alleviate misery and uphold justice, to return or reward kindness, and all the other emotions and impulses, which, like wheels within wheels, actuate the moving figures offered to his imagination." Then, if sympathy—which this review sees as an outgrowth of self-love—is called out for immoral characters, the novel's tendency is immoral also; if sympathy is created for good characters the tendency is good.

As its broadest, most diffuse effect, the novel of good tendency would bring about a love of virtue. A *Mirror* review for February 9, 1839, approvingly quoted from a preface by G. P. R. James where the novelist claimed that good fiction

excites our good passions to high and noble aspirations; depicts our
bad passions so as to teach us to abhor and govern them; arrays our

sympathies on the side of virtue, benevolence, and right; expands our hearts, and makes the circle of our feelings and affections more comprehensive; stores our imaginations with images bright and sweet and beautiful; makes us more intimately and philosophically acquainted with the characters of our fellow-men; and, in short, causes the reader to rise wiser and with a higher appreciation of all that is good and great.

The good novelist, according to another comment in *Knicker-bocker,* "enforces a healthier moral tone, awakens a deeper de-testation of worldliness and hypocrisy" and "inspires a warmer love for genuine unaffected worth" (October 1855).

More narrowly, the novel of good moral tendency created love and esteem for one's fellow human beings; one of bad tendency made for misanthropy. Dickens "sees the divine image, where others beheld only squalidness and rags"; he "is doing more than any other living or recent writer, to open the fountains of kindly feeling" (*Christian Examiner,* March 1843, May 1843). "The heart warms with the narrative as it progresses, and at its close we feel our admiration of virtue increased, and our faith in human nature strengthened" (*Democratic Review* retrospectively on *Waverley,* September 1853). Conversely, a *Knickerbocker* review found *Rich-ard Hurdis* "vicious in its tendency. . . . It presents the most hideous distortions of character, and is enough to make a man sick of his humanity" (October 1838). *Sartain's* assailed novelists "who, with contempt in their hearts, and bitterness and sarcasm on their lips, go through the world . . . only to sneer." Such works "lower the standard of human excellence, they unsettle our faith in human nature" (September 1850). The *Christian Ex-aminer,* whose reviewers steadfastly resisted the vogue for Thackeray, objected that he "indulged in a skeptical spirit" and "held up to the jeers of the superficial our weak, spotted, per-verse, but inexpressively deep human nature; and *woman* nature especially, which is its redeeming half" (May 1856).

Misanthropic novels had an unhealthy tone, symptomatic of disease or morbidity. The *North American* in October 1848 at-tacked the (then anonymous) author of *The Tenant of Wildfell Hall,* who, if "he" continues to write novels, "will introduce into the land of romance a larger number of hateful men and women than any other writer of the day. . . . The reader of Acton Bell gains no enlarged view of mankind, giving a healthy action to his sympathies, but is confined to a narrow space of life, and held down, as it were, by main force, to witness the wolfish side of his nature literally and logically set forth." This was also *Peterson's* objection to *The House of the Seven Gables;* it was morbid because it had no sympathetic characters. "The fault of the book, indeed of all Hawthorne's books, in a moral aspect, is the sombre coloring which pervades them, and which leaves an effect more or less morbid on even healthy minds. The only really lovable character in the book is Phoebe" (June 1851).

The earliest theoretical argument on behalf of the moral tendency of novels had risen from a sort of Shaftesburian view of human benevolence. If sympathy is a good emotion and novels always promote it, then all novels were good in tendency. That had been, in the earlier part of the century, a common argument in favor of the claims of fiction against those who were hostile to it. "No fiction can delight, but as it interests; nor can it excite interest, but as it exercises sympathy; nor can it excite sympathy, without increasing the disposition to sympathize, and, consequently, without strengthening benevolence," a *Mirror* review rehearsed the argument (June 2, 1838). As the novel's presence and popularity became ever more pronounced, rendering defense superfluous, it became clear that this argument was too simple. Some novels did not operate on the principle of sympathy so much as its opposite, repulsion. Worse still, many very popular novels aroused sympathy for bad people. A novel operating on the principle of repulsion was, though morbid, still morally correct; a novel making bad people sympathetic confounded morality altogether.

Reviewers therefore assessed the morality of novels according to whether bad characters were made sympathetic; and the complaints were frequent indeed. This example from the *Christian Examiner* for May 1845 (in an essay on cheap literature) conveys the tone: "vapid and silly romances . . . appeal to all the baser elements in our nature. They minister to a depraved curiosity. They suggest no elevating conceptions, call forth no generous resolves, prompt to no disinterested deeds, instill no right principles, awaken no holy aspirations. A group of unworthy characters are set forth to utter sickly sentiments, and practice detestable vices. . . . Villainy is represented as successful, sin garnished and clothed in fine raiment, knaves pictured as happy fellows,

debauchees as gentlemen, and treachery and blackest guilt un-
visited by any adequate chastisement. . . . All the novelist has to
do is to go on dressing up pollution and publishing the arts of vile
rascality!"

And so on throughout the period, chiefly with reference to
"cheap" books designed for the populace. "Vice and illicit indul-
gences are made to assume the garb, appearance, and language of
virtue and innocence, and, when the former have produced their
natural and inevitable consequences, the sympathies of the reader are awakened, his pity enlisted on the wrong side, and his
notions of right and wrong confounded" (*Mirror*, April 23, 1836).
"We find in the work no glossing over of vicious principles, no
depravity dressed up in a fascinating garb, which constitutes the
greatest objection to books otherwise delightful and useful, for
their spirit, taste, and talent"; Bulwer had "lent his fine genius to
the sanctification of what the world must deem vice and crime,
however gilded" and had ignored "the extreme danger of suggesting a false sympathy with crime" (*Knickerbocker*, February 1839,
March 1841). There are novelists, fulminated a critic in the *North
American* in July 1843, "whose whole employment seems to be to
turn vice into virtue, and shame into glory . . . to represent
human nature, when defiled, degraded, and passion-stained, as
more elevated than before its fall. . . . The delusion contami-
nates the heart that gives it welcome; it conducts many a youth to
a wretched life, a lonely prison, an untimely grave, or, perhaps,
to the pirate's doom." Another critic in the journal wrote somewhat more temperately that "the writer who colors too warmly
the degrading scenes through which his immaculate hero passes
is rightly held as an equivocal teacher of purity" (October 1848).

Bulwer was one such equivocal teacher, as we have already
seen. A *Graham's* critic for April 1843 announced a preference for
The Last of the Barons over his other novels because of "the entire
absence of that pandering to corrupt or vitiated tastes—that palliation of sensuality, and that straining effort to undermine our
most sacred institutions and to subvert the morality of marriage."
"He never fails to render vice agreeable when it can possibly be
done," the *Southern Literary Messenger* stated, "by connecting it
with agreeable characters" (January 1847). French novelists were
also dangerous. "Under the tinsel decorations of a sickly sentimentality are hidden the pitfalls of vice and iniquity," the *Ameri-*

can Review wrote of Sue's novels; the author "literally revels in the fires of burning passion" (March 1846). When vice is made to charm in French novels, "and vicious people to dazzle, harm must needs be done, especially among the young and inexperienced" (*Literary World*, February 13, 1847). The *Literary World* also described "the common error of novelists" as "enlisting the compassion due only to suffering virtue, for frailty and crime, exciting sympathy for objects unworthy, and giving to positive wrongs the gloss of palliation or the support of laborious apology" (July 21, 1849).

Sartain's complained that in *Wuthering Heights* there was "no attempt at placing the evil in its true deformity . . . no apparent shrinking of the writer from the fiends whom he has conjured up from a morbid, though powerful imagination" (June 1848). It praised Mathews's *Moneypenny* because, "though introducing to our notice, as must necessarily be done by one endeavoring to illustrate miscellaneous society, the vicious and depraved, care is taken that their view shall not seem attractive." According to the *Tribune*, Alice Carey's *Hagar* was unworthy of her: "not only does it luxuriate over the records of foul and festering sin, but it throws such a lurid and unnatural glare on the page, that the moral lesson, which is the sole apology for such delineations of perverted passion, is completely neutralized" (January 1, 1853). A *Godey's* reviewer faulted Henry William Herbert's historical novel *The Roman Traitor* for "describing, so carefully, so repeatedly, and in such glowing sentences, the most revolting scenes of debauchery and shameless profligacy that have ever met our eyes even on paper" (November 1853). "Books—whether fictitious or not," according to the *New York Ledger*, "which glorify vice, which make silly girls and sillier boys in love with handsome, dashing villainy,—which make it seem a noble and heroic thing to discard the rules of morality and follow the worst impulses of human nature,—are bad books and cannot be read without damaging the heart and degrading the character" (March 19, 1859).

More extreme reviewers stated that merely to come into contact with vicious scenes, no matter how portrayed, would inevitably corrupt the reader. "A grave reproach to which fiction is too often obnoxious, of stimulating the passions with images of superhuman depravity, and poisoning the moral sense by familiarity with unthought-of guilt" (*New York Review*, July 1840). "Hearts that ought to remain as pure and uncontaminated as the Alpine snows, are stained with impurity of thought and unholy imaginations" (*Ladies' Repository*, April 1843). "This thrilling work must produce something of the evil, that would flow from keeping company with the characters described," the *Southern Literary Messenger* said about Sue's *Mysteries of Paris;* "its moral tendency can only be sustained upon the principle, which would introduce the young, the pure and the virtuous into all the haunts of vice, debauchery and infamy with which the world abounds" (December 1843). "What good effect, either for warning or example," the *American Review* asked about George Sand's fiction, "is to be drawn from familiarity with characters or scenes such as those above alluded to? There are some things, with which the very contact is an abomination" (March 1846). A September 1854 editorial in *Godey's* pointed out that many women temperance novelists, "of refined sentiments and delicate nerves—are employing their talents in describing minutely the scenes of drunkenness which are said to occur at public hotels, and in bringing to light the secret sins of individuals, which, for all the good that can be anticipated from their exposure, might well be left in the darkness and privacy in which they were committed. The object which these good and gifted ladies have in view, as understood, is to teach morality. But would it be safe, think you, for a prudent mother, in order to impress upon the still pure heart of her daughter a warmer regard for the beauty and dignity of virtue, to introduce her to the companionship of the vulgar, the obscene, and vicious, even admitting that she kept her guarded by the presentation of the most vivid contrasts? Would not the experiment be dangerous, we ask, the end and good effect doubtful, to say the least?"

The more moderate view held that the attractiveness of vice in novels derived from its handling by the author; the other suggested that it resided in the scenes or events themselves. Both views, however, implicitly acknowledged that the reader's imagination was not inherently prepared to defend itself against "vice." The only reader who can withstand the appeal of vice is an experienced reader; yet the whole effort of the critic is to protect or shield the inexperienced reader from contact with experience, which alone can give one the power to discriminate vice from virtue and choose the latter. The critical shield, clearly, is highly ineffective, since so many novels, even as they are criticized, are acknowledged to be popular. Not the least of the contradictions and conundrums in which the issue of morality involved reviewers was its undercutting of the claim that the best novels were pictures of life as it is. Faced with the idea of a novel of dangerous tendency, reviewers withdrew that claim even as they were in the process of advancing it as the highest justification of novelistic art, in favor of preserving the vulnerable innocence of novel readers—young and female novel readers.

Indeed, though the vices made so dangerously attractive in fiction of immoral tendency are usually left unspecified, it is clear enough that they are those with particular pertinence to the young woman. "Surely, a glowing picture of virtue appeals far more powerfully to our feelings," *Knickerbocker* wrote wistfully in November 1836, "excites more agreeable sensations, and offers a finer moral, than those daring freebooters, magnanimous outlaws, heroic highwaymen, and unhappy wives, who, having sacrificed their virgin affections on the altar of wealth and rank, end with immolating their own honor, and the happiness of their offspring, at the shrine of adulterous love." Note the different rhetoric and emphasis as the reviewer describes male and female vices. Note that the woman's rather than the man's adultery concerns him. The locus of distress is the glorification of adulterous love; the chief issue hence the suppression or disciplining of female sexuality, on which the happiness of society depends.

A long review of Fredrika Bremer's novels in the *Christian Examiner* took exception to the universal approbation of her books, complaining that they presented and condoned many instances of "unlawful" love. "In *The Neighbors*, a young man, whom the author evidently intends that we shall like, becomes attached to a married woman. His love is rejected; but there it is; the love is one of the incidents of the work." In another, "a blind girl falls in love with her Uncle" who "acknowledges that he has loved this niece,—acknowledges it to *her*! . . . For what good purpose can such a passion have been introduced at all?" In *The Home* one is "confounded" by "love entertained unlawfully, for a being consecrated by marriage, and by one in whom the author evidently wishes to interest us. . . . The whole affair . . . is not calculated to excite sufficient horror. . . . Could we believe that such trials often entered the sanctuaries of virtuous homes, and tested the principles of good wives and mothers, we should still think Miss Bremer's management of this particular illustration injudicious" (July 1843). In the novels referred to no unlawful loves are consummated, nor do any of Bremer's "good wives and mothers" feel any unlawful emotion: but the *Christian Examiner* reviewer finds the subject so sensitive that he must deplore the depiction of any situations that test the "principles of good wives and mothers." The critic must have believed that women readers were likely to be excited by such situations, and that their real-life principles would be weakened by exposure. "The institution of marriage," according to another review in the journal, this one of George Sand, "is by no hyperbole called divine. . . . It should remain to be made one of the last objects of public reformatory movements of all the great departments of civilized life" (March 1847). Sand is culpable for making it the first object of reform, for presenting "meretricious pictures of domestic discord and inconstancy," and for "harping continually, in Parisian dialect and voluptuous touches, on the solicitations and suggestions of animal nature."

Reviewers in other journals felt the same way. The *American Review* contrasted *Wuthering Heights* and *Jane Eyre:* in the former, "the frenzied love, too, so powerfully pictured in these volumes, fresh and undefiled, free alike from sensuality and sentiment, such as men might have felt when the world is young, is un-hallowed; and this leads our noblest impulses to sympathize with crime"; while in the latter, "when the mystery is cleared up that makes it crime for Jane, or the reader, to listen to words of love, she flees from its pollution; and its voice is no more heard, till punishment frees the man's hands, and purifies his soul" (April 1850). "A story of guilty love," the *Southern Literary Messenger* reported of *Light and Darkness*, whose "effect is all the more injurious because, while conducting the charming criminals to the retribution of the catastrophe, the author seeks always to enlist our sympathies in their behalf. . . . No amount of genius, no display of literary and dramatic skill, can atone for the palliation of vice or the inculcation of spurious morality" (October 1855). In *Berenice* "the whole effect of the story is bad in enlisting our sympathies for a woman who loves one man while married to another, and this is all the more to be regretted because the book is so readable"; *Household Mysteries* is "highly objectionable. Near-ly all the incidents on which the book is founded are those of real or supposed guilty love. . . . The author seems by some strange fascination to prefer walking on the verges of the forbidden" (*Southern Literary Messenger*, June 1856, September 1856).

In these innumerable moralizing comments, sexual attraction is never considered apart from the institution designed to contain it or (to put it more accurately) the institution that depends on its containment—that is, marriage; and it is invariably considered with reference to the feelings and acts of the woman rather than the man. Marriage is "the root from which society springs, the groundwork upon which it stands" (*Sartain's*, September 1850); it demands female sexual fidelity. Whether or not reviewers valued female chastity, fidelity, and monogamy as virtues in themselves, they treated them exclusively in terms of their social utility. And they must have devoted so much space to marriage in their re-views because they thought that women, either eligible for mar-riage or married, composed most of the novel-reading popula-tion. In doing so, however, they clearly took it on themselves to write as preceptors, making novel reviewing the occasion for instructing women on their sexual duties and sexual natures, an activity a certain sort of pedagogue always delights in. The re-viewing transaction had an erotic dimension of its own.

What also cannot be overlooked is that, evidently, novels provoking this response by reviewers were numerous and popu-lar. The novelist's "strange fascination" with "walking on the verges of the forbidden" looks not in the least strange, being nothing more than knowing and responding to what women readers wanted to read about: exciting sex and passionate feeling, which, the reviews all too clearly imply, were not likely to be found in marriage. Two basic Victorian assumptions about female character—that women do not experience sexual desire and that they are naturally suited to monogamous marriage where they are the servants of their husbands, their children, and society at large—are here exposed as cultural constructions whose maintenance requires constant surveillance, even to the supervision of novel reading.

"The object of the writer is, to enlist the reader's sympathies on the side of Benedict and Valentine, on the side of criminal and misplaced affection, and against the bond of marriage," the *North*

American said of George Sand's *Lélia* (July 1841). The moral tendency of Dickens, *Putnam's* noted, is "unobjectionable," because "his subjects are out of the range of a prurient and luxurious fancy. His loves are the pure loves of marriage, or that lead to marriage. He is *English*, and not *French*, in his love of home" (March 1855). "Let us be thankful," *Godey's* said, for a novel like Southworth's *The Deserted Wife*, "combining, as it does, the strongest incentives to purity and forbearance, with the most elevated sentiments of love and constancy" (December 1855). As its title implies, *The Deserted Wife* praised the purity and constancy of the deserted woman who remains a "wife" in the situation of abandonment. A relaxing of attitudes toward fidelity in marriage, a greater tolerance of divorce, suggests, *Godey's* added, "that there is something radically wrong in American female education, in public sentiment, and even, to a fatal extent, in religious sentiment." Similarly, the *New York Ledger* for May 15, 1858, noted with horror that divorces in New York City were running at three a week, a number representing a serious threat to social stability.

"It will hardly do to say that the object of the book is only to amuse," the *Atlantic* wrote about *Sword and Gown* in December 1859. "Dealing with the subjects it does, it must work good or evil. . . . The moral of the book is not a good one. The author does his best, by various arts, to make the reader look kindly upon a guilty love, and to regard with admiration those who are animated by it. . . . And such is his undeniable power, that with many readers he will be too likely to carry his point." It is important to note how sexual passion is automatically defined as extramarital; for these Victorian Americans marriage, whatever aspects of the (female) character it answered to, was not an enabler of sexual expression or an enclave for its satisfaction, but its grave. The reviews were telling woman, as clearly as or more clearly than the novels she read, not to anticipate passion or romance in marriage. They were also attempting to dissuade her from reading novels that located it outside marriage, because they feared she would be stimulated to follow the example such novels presented. What did they fear would follow from this?

The most offending novels in their eyes were the French, which flooded this country in cheap translations during the 1840s. In the *North American* for April 1843 a reviewer wrote that the novels of Paul de Kock were, "in respect to morality and true refinement, more than half a century behind the English." But the popularity of the novels in the United States was precisely the issue. Less than a year later—January 1844—a reviewer in the *Southern Literary Messenger* announced that "during the last two years we have visited almost every section of our Union, and the books which met our view more often than any other, were the pestilent French novels." In November 1846 a *Peterson's* reviewer said "the country is deluged with reprints of French novels, many of them openly, and all covertly injurious to morals."

In March 1846 the conservative *American Review* complained that Hugo's novels show "courtesans exemplifying the duties of maternal fondness—strumpets testifying disinterested attachments—thieves and murderers actuated by the most generous and noble impulses—and the whole foundations of the social system uprooted and overturned, to carry out an idle and absurd theory. . . . Those who search in the French novelists generally for any traces of a high and pure morality, will lose both their time and their labor." *Sartain's* noted that "Sue describes Fleur de Marie as the purest of human angels, though he gives us to understand, at the same time, that she has lived a life which the experience of all times has shown to be the most thoroughly degrading and destroying to heart and soul, mind and body, of all the varieties of sin and shame. . . . These impossible pictures we call French, because they are at least nothing else, and they are drawn by people of unmistakable ability. But we cannot consider them edifying, to say the least" (November 1847). *Knickerbocker* for June 1848 praised a novel by contrasting it to those of Sue and Sand; here "there are no luscious descriptions of brothels, no abortions procured by dissolute ladies, no scenes of madness from rampant lust."

In a review for February 1854 *Sartain's* complained that *The Hunchback of Notre Dame* and *The Wandering Jew* were "the plainest and most undeniable prostitutions of Art to the cause of impurity" and asserted that "Sue is, in all his views of life, essentially false and corrupt; and Hugo is fond of exploring those moral sinks which exhale the most offensive odors." A *Putnam's* reviewer agreed: "the books of Sue, Dumas, Balzac, and a crowd of lesser names, contain, under the form of fiction, nothing but the history of the corrupt and false social state in which they live and move." *La Dame aux Camelias* "is simply the biography of a courtesan, and is objectionable as being calculated to throw around the life of vice, degradation, and misery ineffable, the halo of sentiment, and the interest of beauty, wit, and unperverted nobleness." *La Dame aux Perles* "is simply an uninteresting tale of marital baseness and wifely deception, adulterous love being represented as universal and natural, and the art of society as consisting in keeping a veil of external decency over the corruption which prevails in every sphere of life" (December 1853).

Interestingly, the reviewers agree that the virtues praised in these novels are indeed virtues, but they think it is immoral to associate them with persons who live sexually licentious lives. This association puts in question the claim that virtue is a product of the monogamous bourgeois marriage. "Home, just as it is, is about as effective an institution as we have for human salvation. It is the fountain of what is purest and noblest in character" (*Christian Examiner*, March 1847). If this connection did not exist, on what grounds could women be persuaded to so confining and obliterating a way of life, especially in an era of individualism? The French novels stated what the reviewers' rhetoric only implied: that women had sexual desires incompatible with marriage as it was then constituted; accepting this, they went on to legitimize passionate extramarital love. "It seems impossible for a Frenchman, however brilliant, to make at the same time a tale of deep interest and preserve a pure moral. The nationality will break out, and that always to the distaste of an American reader," *Peterson's* commented on Dumas (February 1849). But if American readers felt this distaste, their buying habits did not show it. Again, the *North American*, surveying recent French literature in a series of review essays, commented, "it has been our lot . . . to read many books which shocked our moral sense and appeared to us as the sign of a moral inferiority in the nation that could crown such works with popularity" (January 1859). But his own nation had so crowned these works.

These reviews provide an interesting context for the reception of *The Scarlet Letter*, which appeared soon after the revolution of 1848 had reduced the number of French works, but while those written before the revolution were still in wide circulation. "Then for the moral," a *Literary World* review concluded: "though severe, it is wholesome. . . . We hardly know another writer who has lived so much among the new school who would have handled this delicate subject without an infusion of George Sand" (March 30, 1850). "Hawthorne, in *The Scarlet Letter*, has utterly undermined the whole philosophy on which the French novels rest, by seeing farther and deeper into the essence both of conventional and moral laws," *Graham's* commented. "He has made his guilty parties end, not as his own benevolent sympathies might dictate, but as the spiritual laws, lying back of all persons, dictated to him" (May 1850). It repeated this assessment in a review of *The Blithedale Romance:* "as an illustration of the Divine order on which our conventional order rests, [*The Scarlet Letter*] is the most moral book of the age, and is especially valuable as demonstrating the super-ficiality of that code of ethics, predominant in the French school of romance, which teaches obedience to individual instinct and im-pulse, regardless of all moral truths which contain the generalized experience of the race" (September 1852). If we have here an explanation, beyond his artistic merits, for Hawthorne's favorable reception among critics, we may also have an explanation for his lack of popular success.

Dealing with the question of morality for women, reviewers involved themselves in various incompatible preachments: mo-nogamous marriage was the relation divinely designed for the fullest human satisfactions; sexual satisfaction was animal, hence not included in the design; marriage might more likely than not turn out unsatisfactorily but still compelled fealty, and so on. Tellingly, the idealistic novels of George Sand, which attacked marriage for failing to provide for women's sexual enjoyment, fared worse with reviewers than novels by Sue, Balzac, and Paul de Kock, which pragmatically accepted marriage for other pur-poses than sex and looked for an equilibrium of marriage and extramarital sexuality. I wish the reviewers in this instance were all men, but not so. *Sartain's* carried a particularly virulent attack on George Sand, by a Miss Maria J. B. Browne, in October 1851: "domestic infidelity and consequent wretchedness, is a theme on which she delights to ring interminable changes. Herself, an unbeliever in connubial love, and the victim of connubial misery, her teachings scatter the winged seeds of moral contagion and with woman's fair and gentle hand, level malicious thrusts at the very buttresses of social order, by battering against that great God-instituted necessity, marriage." And other American wom-en also went on record as dissociating their sex from Sand's ideas.

In a March 1846 review the *American Review* expatiated on

George Sand's habitual exercise, in her own life, of "the privileged vices which custom and society have restricted to the sex
who wear the pantaloons," thus clarifying the double standard
underlying this morality. "We love and revere the female character too much to accept [Sand] either as a fit exponent or advocate
of the feelings or sentiments of refined and virtuous women—
those intermediate links between men and the angels who, kept
apart and above the contaminating influences to which the ruder
sex are exposed, preserve inviolate that purity of heart and feeling, which makes a modest and true-hearted wife the best and
highest good attainable here below." The woman's task is to be
good, the man's to "attain" her, and the task of all society is to
keep her above and apart from contaminating influence—in
short, to manufacture "woman" from the materials of a varie-
gated human field. Novels were getting in the way of this social
regulating. "We would not think of putting the novels of George
Sand in the hands of a young female friend," the *Southern Literary
Messenger* wrote in November 1851.

That novels could have seemed so dangerous testifies to the
fragile nature of this enterprise, which is also evident whenever
reviewers address it directly, as in this excerpt from the *American
Review* for June 1845 on George Sand, which moved immediately
from consideration of her writings to the issue of women's rights.
"By the 'equality of rights' thus claimed for women, is meant, we
conceive, that the wife should enjoy the *same* rights civil and
political—same in extent and in subject—as the husband. But an
equality of this sort is clearly incompatible with the very existence of the social, or even the family, association. No association, domestic or political, possible, without a government. No
government without the right in some one to command. No right
of command without the duty to obey, without subordination.
But subordination and the equality contended for are a contradiction even in the terms. We need not dwell upon the practical
objections, which are sufficiently obvious—the consequence of
admitting woman upon the arena of politics; the diversion from
domestic avocations, the depravation of those qualities that
chiefly ennoble her nature and endear her to man; the capricious
disregard of the husband's wishes or weaknesses, with which an
independent right of property would not fail to inspire her." If
woman was to any significant extent the being that men claimed,

then clearly the independent right of property would not lead so inexorably and immediately to a "capricious disregard" of the husband, or to the other terrible results that are envisaged if she were given equality: making "the fireside a scene of anarchy, the state a system of intrigue."

It might be an anachronistic mistake to see control of female sexuality as the only preoccupation of reviewers considering moral tendency in novels; it might be more accurate to say that the control of women in all ways was their concern. (Perhaps control of men *through* women was also an indirect goal.) The "animal nature" of woman was just one quality calling for regulation, receiving particular attention in novel reviews because it was so much in evidence in popular fiction. In fact, throughout the era reviewers were looking for novels featuring heroines who exemplified such virtues as self-sacrifice, self-control, and self-discipline. In the same *American Review* that excoriated George Sand and descanted on the horrible results of equal rights for women and men, another essayist saw novels as the source of feminine inspiration. "Who ever read a romance that inculcated listless, shapeless idleness? It encourages action and endurance," the writer claimed. "Among all the young women I have been acquainted with, I should say that the novel-readers are not only the best informed, but of the best nature, and some capable of setting examples of a sublime fortitude—the more sublime because shown in secret and all-enduring patience. . . . Love, it is said, is the only subject all novels are constructed upon, and such reading encourages extravagant thoughts, and gives rise to dangerous feelings. And why dangerous? Are they not such as are requisite for wife and mother to hold, and best for the destiny of woman? . . . For the great mark of such an education is endurance—a power to create a high duty, and energy and patience, where both are wanted." Endurance, fortitude, energy represent the active ideal of true womanhood that is more characteristic of mid-nineteenth-century American ideology than the passive, submissive creature we have sometimes heard about, though perhaps it is no less oppressive. It represents an attempt to persuade women to control themselves, in a social atmosphere where control by main force is less and less possible. And the purpose of the control is to fit a woman to be "wife and mother," a prospect the writer does not make at all attractive.

"Designed to illustrate the strength of woman's attachment; the holiness of her zeal; her unselfish labours; her deep and enduring fortitude"; "praise to the young author for her efforts to restrain the blighting influences of a cold and sordid selfishness, which, in her own sex, under the new idea of proprieties in the married life, are destroying all the generous, noble, and refined impulses of love, confidence, and duty" (*Godey's*, August 1840, November 1857). "We shall consider Madame George Sand as doing a far better work for her sex and for her race if she will show us a woman, or a married pair, suffering under the miseries which belong to an ill-assorted marriage, with a true and generous *forgetfulness of self*, a lowly spirit of pious submission" (*Sartain's*, November 1847). "The sacrifice of her own happiness, which the heroine makes . . . is a trait conceived from a profound knowledge of the nobleness and devotion of a true woman's heart" (*Peterson's*, May 1851).

The question of female sexual morality, then, figures in the larger context of feminine character, which in turn is linked to the issue of social stability and specifically the maintenance of a patriarchy. When reviewers touch on non-sexual moral issues, which they do only occasionally, they preach necessity and resignation. The *New York Review* praised *Three Experiments of Living*, a novel based on the Panic of 1837 detailing the successful efforts of a young woman to retrieve the shattered fortunes of her family, "because its influence is so likely to be salutary. . . . It teaches, so emphatically, that happiness is chiefly dependent on ourselves, and not on our outward circumstances" (March 1837). *Constance* is about "the losses of a pious family in the late commercial reverses, and the Christian resignation with which the change from riches to poverty is submitted to. The moral of the book is very good" (*Mirror*, January 30, 1841). In our country, the *North American* noted complacently, "the tales which will be remembered have been intended to show life as in reality it is, and thus to point out the way of preparation for its business and its duties. . . . They endeavor to reconcile men and women to the condition in which Providence has placed them, and teach them to accomplish that for which they were designed by Providence" (October 1844).

The *Democratic Review* praised Bremer's novels because "we rise from the perusal of one of them with gentler feelings, better satisfied with the world, better pleased with our friends and neighbors, better content with our lot in life, and more sensible of and grateful to our Heavenly father, for the innumerable blessings that we daily and hourly receive at this hand" (June 1843). *Peterson's* complained of Geraldine Jewsbury's *Zoe* that "its tendency is to unsettle the mind; it points out evils in society, and neglects the remedy" (June 1845). "Irregularities and caprices of passion in the married are not the uncontrollable giants that George Sand and her associates represent them to be, but things that *can* be controlled, and must be, under penalty of social and personal ruin," the *Christian Examiner* wrote in March 1846, "things not to be cured by the detestable, mean, debauching doctrine of a 'change of object,' but by a small portion—every strong-minded man and woman knows how little and how attainable,—of self-command, by useful occupation, temperate living, and a Christian culture of the thoughts and affections of the upright soul."

Though *Sartain's* was not sure the matter was so simple, it agreed with the *Christian Examiner* that self-control was the only answer to marital misery. In its long review of George Sand in November 1847, the journal asserted that "marriages are every day contracted with a thoughtlessness, a forgetfulness of the principles that should actuate rational beings in an affair of life-long importance"; but "to make it easy for such marriages to be dissolved would—to say nothing of the direct prohibition of our Saviour, who 'knew what was in man,'—practically nullify the institution of marriage, and throw society into a confusion and horror which in the worst days of the worst marriages, or even among the most barbarous nations, has never yet been equalled." Novels "attacking thus any of the institutions which have been adopted by common consent for the well-being of society" are particularly culpable, "since the darts which, if wrapt in dull essays, would fall harmless to the ground, will find their way, winged with fancy and pointed by wit, directly to the susceptible young heart." The review concluded that "George Sand is the unsuspected flatterer of all who are discontented with their own lot, and who find gratification in shifting the responsibility from themselves to society and its institutions and abuses. As such we cannot consider her a safe companion for youthful or excitable minds."

Evidently in every instance of a conflict between people and institutions, the institutions needed buttressing. "Away with this mawkish sentimentality, which undermines human responsibility," declaimed the *Literary World* in a long general complaint about novels, "and leaves men in that vapid state of nonentity more humiliating, more destructive to a sound morality, than a thousand errors of practice, recognized as errors, and heartily repented" (June 24, 1848). A book subtitled *Trials of the Heart*, it assured readers, is not about love's trials but about "a sensitive mind thrown, by the sudden death of an improvident father, on the cold charities of the world, and the trials of that same heart, although aided by a strong and resolute will, to bear the misfortunes of that lot with resignation, patience, and cheerfulness" (October 12, 1850). (We need hardly observe that the "sensitive mind" was a woman's.) "We gratefully acknowledge" that *The Blithedale Romance* "has offered to us wise and good lessons which ought to make us strong for truth and duty" (*Christian Examiner*, September 1852). Concerning Chesebro's *Isa*, the *American Review* observed, "we, every-day mortals as we are, must sorrow to see the bulwarks of our purity and faith levelled without so much as an acknowledgement of wrong. What we prize is dear to us. What has protected us during our whole lives, what we have learned to love with every lesson we have ever taken, must not be discarded" (July 1852).

The *Southern Literary Messenger* stated that works like A. S. Roe's *Time and Tide* "will forever be popular. . . . And this is as it should be. The writer who purifies in any degree one human heart, or reconciles that heart to its earthly state of probation, has done more for humanity than many a celebrated philosopher and man of science" (August 1852). In a rage over the success of *Uncle Tom's Cabin*, it claimed that the book's moral stance was "absolutely fatal to all human society," that "it is the very evangel of insubordination, sedition, and anarchy. . . . In the complicated weave of trials, difficulties and temptations, with which Providence in its wisdom has thought proper to intertwine the threads of human existence, an unbroken career of happiness or prosperity is not to be found. . . . The very aptitude of this life for that state of probation which it was designed to be, depends upon the alternation and juxtaposition of weakness and virtue, or joy and misery." Reviewing works by Timothy Shay Arthur, its favorite author, *Godey's* announced: he "is a good man. He puts no idea upon paper, he adopts no precept, he advocates no maxim, he favors no theory that may not safely be connected with the highest and purest interest of society" (March 1853).

"It will encourage many a fainting heart to be not weary in well-doing," *Knickerbocker* extolled Jenny Marsh's *Toiling and Hoping* (May 1856). "A novel devoted to the virtue of self-renunciation, and the spiritual compensations for worldly disappointment and wretchedness," *Graham's* noted approvingly of Jewsbury's *Constance Herbert* (August 1855). "The aim of the author," *Godey's* explained of *The Belle of Washington*, "is to portray in attractive colors the strength, beauty, and commanding influence of the Christian and domestic virtues in the midst of severe trials"—a woman's trials, compensated for by virtues it defined as "love, obedience, discipline, and self-control" (May 1858). In *Vernon Grove*, which "truly deserves to be ranked with the highest of our works of sentimental fiction," the theme is love, "not love the guilty passion, but that love which, however ardent it may be, elevates and refines the heart, and finds, even amidst the torments of self-sacrifice, those pleasures and those rewards which ever attend upon the consciousness of duties fulfilled" (*Godey's*, January 1859). "We feel that the hard discipline of her men and women is like that which we make for ourselves, and the process by which they struggle into greater freedom is that by which we must ourselves emerge from bondage" (*North American* on Charlotte Brontë, October 1857). The author of *Sword and Gown*, it said critically, "looks at life from a very low standpoint. . . . The charms of moral beauty, the dignity of self-denial, the power of discipline, have no place in our author's thought" (January 1860).

If this is an ideology of individualism, it is advanced in the cause of stability rather than progress, on behalf of duty rather than self-enhancement. It is antagonistic to any kind of change other than the internal reconstitution of the individual in a way that makes her or him—chiefly her—accept full responsibility for her life circumstances. Though the reviews assure readers that institutions help them, their demand is for individuals to help the institutions. Society appears extremely fragile. The only reward for self-discipline and self-sacrifice is, apparently, the consciousness of duty well done. Not one of these reviewers proposes that there is any fun involved in the morality advocated. Or excitement. Or interest. Quite apart from what this morality meant in terms of reader behavior in life, we need to think of what it implied in terms of the reading of novels themselves. Books grounded in this sort of moral expectation could not have been the source of that pleasure, interest, or excitement that reviewers had always identified as the reason for the novel's popularity. There is an attempt under way here fundamentally to change the novel. If the "serious novel" is thought to be better because of its incorporation of a "serious" morality, with consequent diminishment of the novel's capacity for giving pleasure and for enchaining and enchanting the reader, how are post-Victorians to assess this claim? And how are women to view the assertion that the better novel is one that contains a view of women's nature as high and noble when those qualities imply willing subordination to a social system that, while granting her an independent self, demands its sublimation in the cause of other, more faulty beings?

Two issues with respect to our own, later age concern me here. First, though Victorian morality is now out of date, the notion of the serious novel with which it was originally confounded is not. "Serious" is itself a Victorian concept of value. And it is worth considering by whom, and for whom, seriousness is defined; it is clear to me that assessments of the novel still often involve the intention to suppress, or direct, or improve, the female reader. If anything, those novelists elevated to "serious" status these days are more severe, more brutal, and more crude in their sexual ideologies than the earlier fictions, and the reviewers are a good deal more strident. The "woman's novel" for even the most liberated anti-Victorian is an object of scorn and contempt as it never was earlier—indeed, the concept did not really exist in the fully detached form it now takes. The critic seeking to name a deplorable novelist will inevitably come up with Jacqueline Susann or Judith Krantz rather than Irving Wallace or Mickey Spillane; the wonderful author who can't sell is invariably a William Faulkner rather than a Willa Cather. Blatantly misogynist novels by authors like Norman Mailer, John Barth, or Philip Roth get high praise; the same respect is not accorded the occasional example of misandry. The matter would be different if distinctions were made on formal or aesthetic grounds—if, for example, John Updike (his males all soul, his women all body) were praised as a fine prose stylist rather than a serious explorer of spiritual values. But no.

Feminist critics seem to constitute an exception to this generality, and of course feminists are keenly sensitive to the misogynist portrayals and ideologies in so many so-called major contemporary novelists. But there is in this group as in the others a powerful desire to teach women, improve them, deluge them with "serious" depictions of their own opportunities. In a word, the didactic impulse directed toward the female sex continues very strong in novels and in novel criticism alike.

A second issue is the unexamined assumption in earlier reviews that persists into the contemporary scene: that the moral tendency of a novel really exists, and that it affects people's actions. Sophisticated as critics claim to be today, they do not seem to consider it possible that women (or men) might read popular novels for the formally and emotionally pleasurable experience of reading novels. This is to ignore the genre as a formal entity with its own pleasures and rules. The contemporary critic, journalistic or academic, is no less naive here than Victorian predecessors. Indeed, many critics who have the most severe definitions of literary language as only self-referential cannot imagine that the reader of a female gothic might be seeking a self-contained—a literary—experience. This is, I think, because they equate naively pleasurable literary experiences with a naive sense of literature or, differently put, because the only "literary" experience they accept as such is the experience of the most sophisticated, advanced, difficult, reflexive texts or those that are made so through classroom or scholarly exegesis.

10

Classes of Novels

The critics' project of demanding philosophies, moralities, or statements about life from the novel involved them and their descendants in the continuing problem of how to distinguish a serious from a nonserious novel, or a better from a worse one, when idea content or morality formed the only basis for judgment. Searching for some objective, formally discernible features to which their judgments might appeal, they developed the odd criterion of story *in reverse:* the more the novel at hand was merely, or only, a story, the less it could be a work of importance. The good way of reading a novel came to be reading beyond the story for something else: its meaning. And hence the novel was transformed into a text to be interpreted. This approach imposed a formal paradox or impossibility at the novel's core, because it was as narrated story that the genre was identified. And since, apparently, the popular audience continued to read novels for their stories, the work defined as insignificant by critics was more often popular than the one they praised for seriousness. Here, then, is the source of the break between critics and readers that has plagued the history and development of the novel from the mid-nineteenth century on.

As novels proliferated during the period, reviewers took on a less problematic task: ordering them into subclasses. This enterprise was not theoretical or ethical; it rose from the practical desire to impart more information about the particular novel than merely calling the work a novel could convey.

It would be of great service to criticism, or at least to critics, if some judicious classification of books could be made, by which a more minute discrimination should be effected, than at present exists. The fact is, there is too much generalization. Works are included under one general head, which ought properly to be arranged under half a dozen; and the consequence is, a great increase of labor and perplexity to us, whose vocation it is to write, not books but *of* books, by reason of the necessity to which we are put, in almost every instance, of prefacing our opinions with a description, more or less elaborate, of the work to which they apply. Take the head of novels, for example; we have but two recognized divisions,—namely, the novel, properly so called, and the historical romance. Yet there are a multitude of fictions which require something more definite to express their peculiar qualities; and each of the two species includes almost an infinite of varieties. We feel the want of that more particular classification to which we have referred, in noticing the work whereof the title appears at the beginning of these observations. It is nothing like *Ivanhoe*, or *Tom Jones* or *Gil Blas*, or Mr. Cooper's *Monikins;* it is not a historical novel, a religious novel, a political novel, a descriptive novel, or a satirical novel. Neither is it metaphysical, like Godwin's *Caleb Williams*, or Mrs. Shelley's *Frankenstein;* nor yet fashionable, (Heaven save the mark!) like the frothy nothings of my lady Blessington. Of its kind it is excellent; but what is its kind?

This witty complaint in *Knickerbocker* for August 1835 shows that many terms for classifying novels existed early on; it also shows that the subsequently all-important distinction between novel and romance was already obfuscated; and it shows that the project of classifying novels, though helpful and necessary, was also an endless one, given the formally unparalleled flexibility and freedom of the genre.

Many years later (in November 1859) a *Knickerbocker* reviewer said more directly that no totalizing system of classifying novels was possible. Reviewing an academic work called *British Novelists, and Their Styles*, by David Masson, in November 1859, the magazine described his system and dismissed it:

from the time of Scott he reckons thirteen great classes. . . . This classification is hardly more useful or scientific than that of Bulwer into the three classes of the familiar, the picturesque, and the intellectual novel, which might be sub-divided till every purpose of theory would be satisfied, though possibly it would be impossible to decide in which of a dozen classes to range any particular novel. Of all departments of literature the novel is that which embodies the elements of real or ideal life with the least attempt to transfigure them; it lies the nearest to the extemporaneous and shifting phenomena of life as distinguished from the abstract principles and forms, the pure results of wide generalizations, which constitute the vital organism of productions of high art or exhaustive thought. To classify novels, therefore, is very much such an undertaking as it would be to classify men and women, to classify the seemingly fortuitous occurrences of an hour, a day, or a season, to classify the variations of the weather, or write the law of individual moods. The lectures of Professor Masson are nearly the first attempt to weigh in the critical balance the most peculiar and distinctive class of books in the literature of the present century, regarded comprehensively, but probably it is as yet impossible either to assign to past novels their proper comparative place in literature, or to predict what new forms the prose romance may assume in its future developments.

Classifying, then, was helpful if its limitations were recognized. Grouping novels remained pragmatic, ad hoc, ongoing.

The earliest distinction in use discriminated the modern from the older novel; but by about 1850 that approach had lost its usefulness on account of the great number of new novels. Old novels were invoked merely as a means of congratulating the current age on the superiority of modern works. For some the novel itself was so new a genre that it was appropriately contrasted not with older forms of itself, but with fictions that were not novels. "Beautiful as are the tales of the Arabian nights, and perennial in the delight which they have afforded to successive generations, yet they lack many of the elements which are now deemed indispensable in fictitious composition; such, for instance, as the close discrimination of character, the ingenious complication of plot, and above all, the close adherence to the realities of life and achievement" (*Mirror*, May 20, 1837). In another place the same journal called the novel "a fiction copied from common life," a type "not above a century old" (June 2, 1838). Reviewers who distinguished modern from old-style *novels* assigned to the old-style novel the very features that the *Mirror* had given to nonnovelistic fiction. So, for example, the *North American*, reviewing Cooper, defined "machinery" as "all that answers in the modern novel as a substitute for mythological divinities, fairies, giants . . . within the narrowed limits of modern probability" (July 1826). "Where is the *Children of the Abbey?*" asked a critic for the *New York Review*, "where the *Scottish Chiefs?* where the *Three Spaniards?* where the *Mysteries of Udolpho*, and a dozen others? Aye, where is *Tom Jones?* where is *Peregrine Pickle?* where *Roderick Random* even? . . . The public taste has left them. Some were too coarse, some too silly, some too extravagant, some too ridiculous" (January 1842). A *Literary World* reviewer described two forms of early novel, one centering on "the graceful profligate or gentlemanly highwayman," the other on "the pattern hero or heroine" (July 1, 1848). The *North American* opposed the modern novel to the earlier sentimental novel, which had "a hero, whose duty it was to suffer impossible things and say foolish ones; a heroine, oscillating between elegant miseries and genteel ecstacies; a testy old father . . . a talkative maiden aunt, who imagines the hero to be in love with herself; a pert chambermaid . . . and a deep villain, who is the only sensible person in the book:—these shadows of character, which the author has the impertinence to call men and women, joined to an unlimited power to create and demolish fortunes, constitute about all the matter we have been able to find in some scores of these novels" (October 1849).

The point that critics were making in these contrasts had to do with the fantastic nature of the story and characters in early fiction. In the modern novel beginning with *Waverley* (which until about 1850 was accepted as the first example of the new form), all agreed, "fiction is brought home to daily occurrences and observations," at "home among natural objects and real persons" (*North American*, July 1816), "a tale of our own times" in which "every body knew the characters" (*North American*, April 1833). "What could, to a great extent, be very well predicated of novels fifty years ago, is totally false in its sweeping application to our present species" of novel; "we have now no desire for the extravagances of sentiment and action, that, with a few brilliant exceptions, characterized English novels of former times. . . . What is wanted to constitute a good modern novel" is that such works be "veritable and veracious segments of the great life-drama, displaying Nature and Man as they are, sentiments as they are felt, and deeds as they are done" (*Putnam's*, October

1854). The novel has not lost its form as narrated invented fiction, but that form is now embedded in what represent themselves as representations of the real world. These representations permit a much greater novelty of story and character than in the old, repetitive form. Nothing is said in these distinctions about greater decency or more elevated morality in the modern novel: form remains the essence.

If the *first* characteristic of the modern novel was its greater fidelity to everyday life, the *second* was precisely its proliferation and fragmentation into subgenres treating different segments of the social field. The earlier novel, not taking the social field for its domain, had no particular responsibility to locale; the modern novel, given the complexity of modern life and its responsibility to that life, had to specify and specialize. Thus the emergence of classes of novels was itself an aspect of the modern novel that those classes exemplified: the older novel had no subclasses. Where, then, at the advent of *Waverley* the label of modernity had seemed sufficient characterization of a novel, new novels called for more subtle description. And the trend accelerated in the 1850s. "Modern fictions, we know, are expected to do, not only their own legitimate work, but also that of the hard, dry, voluminous treatises on philosophy and morals of former times; they are expected to supply the place of legislators and divines, to obviate the necessity for polemical essays and political pamphlets, in short, to perform all the functions which the several departments of literature could scarcely accomplish half a century ago" (*North American*, April 1856). At first, critics believed, the modern novel had supplanted other fictional modes, creating and uniting a vast readership through its appeal. Now, as its very popularity led to expanded scope, this community of readers might again be fragmented, the modern novel fall victim to its own success.

Modern novels were most commonly distinguished from each other by subject matter—the area of the real world from which they ostensibly derived and to which they referred. Masson's categories, for example, included the novel of Irish life and manners, of English life and manners, the fashionable novel, the illustrious criminal novel, and so on. Subject matter, in turn, broke down geographically (where it took place) and vertically (among what social class it was set). Since the modern novel was presumably a story of the present day, the historical novel—sometimes called a historical romance—presented itself as another subgenre (see chapter 11). It was also common to categorize books by pointing to other novels or other authors who presumably had supplied the model: the school of Dickens, the school of Scott. A novel whose purpose was other than storytelling—religious, didactic, political, reformist—appeared in a separate, somewhat problematic class of novels, each kind of purpose defining a subclass of the subclass. The "domestic novel" was much written about, defined partly by subject matter (the everyday doings of ordinary, usually rural or small-town people), partly by setting (mostly indoors, in the home), and partly by its low-key, quiet style. Though associated with women writers, it was not confined to them, nor they to it. Reviewers struggled throughout the era with the question whether there was such a thing as women's fiction but were unable to find a way consistently to distinguish works by women from works by men. Women read, wrote, and appeared as characters in every class of novel. Opposed to the domestic novel was the highly wrought fiction dealing with extraordinary personages, unlikely events, and unfamiliar settings, and composed in an intense, flowery style; this evolved into the "sensation novel" of the late 1850s and after, a genre much written about in criticism of the English novel but hardly noticed in American literary histories.

One term—amazingly—that never appears is "gothic," and this is because, so far as I can see, the very idea of the gothic at this time seemed incompatible with the idea of the novel. Conversely, since it is the characteristic of modern fiction that it uses the real world as its source of story, the word "realistic" had no particular defining utility and does not appear. Yet another concept, as already noted, that has come to occupy an important place in discussions of the American novel but had no force at the time is that of the romance as distinct from the novel; although the distinction appears in a variety of contexts, these subvert one another (see chapter 11).

Given that the novel was recognized as a genre of unprecedented literary freedom and possibility, it is surprising that reviewers had so little trouble telling what was, and was not, an instance of the novel itself. Perhaps the very scope of the subcategories allowed them to assimilate problematic instances, but in general we see only a few criteria, and these of no particular subtlety, used to tell the novel from other forms: length, prose, fictionality. If short, the work was a tale or sketch; if in verse, it was a poem; if not fiction, then history or philosophy or essay; if a fiction whose agents were abstractions, then an allegory.

Along with the sketch, reviewers recognized the book of sketches as a form in its own right, a collection connected by various possible threads but without the unifying, complex plot of a novel. This absence relieved the writer of a serious artistic challenge and made both the individual sketch and the sketch-book as a whole minor forms in comparison to the novel. "Why, with all her successful experience, Mrs. Embury has not yet tried her hand upon a two-volume novel, we really cannot understand. . . . The desire again returns that a gifted writer of such acknowledged ability should give full play to her powers in a novel"; "defective in plot . . . rather a series of sketches" (*Literary World*, May 26, 1849). "Not a novel. It is but a series of sketches wired together. Looked upon as sketches, they are capital, and furnish decidedly some of the most amusing and racy reading of the season"; "not a novel, but a slight sketch of modern habits, manners, and conversation" (*Literary World*, August 18, 1849; February 9, 1850). Before Hawthorne published *The Scarlet Letter* he was not taken seriously as a candidate for high art, though at least one reviewer found his sketches unusually weighty: "we are startled in the class of composition chosen by Hawthorne with these revelations" (*Democratic Review*, April 1845).

The most interesting question of this sort was, When did a long prose fiction, by virtue of incremental nonfictional additions, cease to be a novel? Sylvester Judd's *Margaret*, Longfellow's *Kavanagh*, and Kimbell's *St. Leger* were all novellike works that reviewers did not accept as novels, chiefly because of sparseness of plot. Melville's problem works—*Mardi* and *Moby-Dick*—were not problems to these reviewers, who agreed that they were not novels, though they also agreed that it was hard to say what they were.

Domestic Novels

The use of the term "domestic" to describe a type of novel became common in reviews of the 1830s and continued to the end of the period. *Allen Prescott* was a "natural domestic story" (*Knickerbocker*, March 1835). Caroline Norton's *The Wife* was "a tale of the domestic class," giving "a picture of every-day life and manners, which, after all, are the most interesting, and come home more closely to our bosoms and business" (*Mirror*, July 25, 1835). Fredrika Bremer's novels were "quiet, simple tales of domestic life" (*Democratic Review*, April 1843). *Mary Grover* was "of a domestic cast" and *The Elder Sister* "a story of domestic life" (*Peterson's*, September 1848, November 1855). Mrs. Ellis was "an excellent domestic writer" (*Home Journal*, February 8, 1851). The *Tribune* took note of a "popular school of novel-writing, of which *The Wide, Wide World* was the pioneer," which it called "domestic novels" (June 26, 1852), but a month earlier *Godey's* called Jane Austen's reissued *Sense and Sensibility* "a domestic story," thereby endowing the form with a pedigree (May 1852). Marion Harland's *Alone* was a "domestic story" (*Putnam's*, October 1855). *Cora and the Doctor* was "an unpretending narrative of domestic life," *Sea-Spray* "a new novel of American domestic life," Catharine Sedgwick an author "particularly at home" in the "quiet, domestic sphere," and *Walter Thornley* a "charming domestic story" (*Harper's*, November 1855, April 1857, September 1857, August 1859).

In one sense the domestic was simply the novel's ultimate modern manifestation; "novels (we use the word in the sense it now expresses) are the epics of private, domestic life" (*Democratic Review*, March 1845). But for most reviewers the term had a more specialized sense, implying a setting chiefly within ordinary people's homes and a plot made up of incidents that were appropriate to such a setting. The *North American* identified a "class of domestic novels . . . describing minutely and faithfully the interior of households in our own times" (April 1843). "No novelist has approached [Fredrika Bremer] in the interest with which she invests home-scenes and incidents of every day life"; the scenes of *Angela*, by Mrs. Marsh, "are principally laid in the quiet of home" (*Peterson's*, October 1843, September 1848). *Harper's* described Eliza Buckminster Lee's *Florence* as "filled with charming pictures of domestic life in the interior of New England" (January 1852). "Whatsoever Emilie Carlen writes is true and affectionate," *Knickerbocker* observed. "She loves home-hearths and firesides like a cricket, and wherever you hear the crackling of the logs; wherever you see the cheerful blaze, and the genial faces gathered around it, you may be sure that every sound she utters will find some quiet human heart for its home and resting-place" (June 1853). *Toiling and Hoping* was, for *Knickerbocker*, "a narrative of *home*, and its characters are such as are met around the fireside" (May 1856). This approach permitted the reviewer to identify a domestic novel simply by its content.

Although the domestic novel was not confounded with—it was usually distinguished from—the sentimental novel, an outmoded form dealing with "pattern" heroes and heroines and impossible situations, the concept did carry expectations about tone, attitude, sentiment, and beliefs. Simply, domestic fiction was presumed to be written not only to depict but also to celebrate home as haven. References recur to calm, quiet, the unpretending. Bremer's novels were "quiet simple tales of domestic life" possessing an "indescribable charm" such as "one rarely meets" in "more elaborate novels" (*Democratic Review*, April 1843). In *The Diary of Lady Willoughby* "domestic life, with its quiet scenes and deep, silent enjoyments, is here painted in the master-strokes of nature" (*American Review*, May 1845). *Katherine Ashton* was notable for its "quiet domestic scenes" (*Southern Literary Messenger*, September 1854). In *Kathie Brande* "the quiet routine of domestic life is wrought up into a delightful narrative remarkable for its simplicity and pathos" (*Harper's*, February 1857). *Godey's* classified Trollope's early *Doctor Thorne* among the "quiet narratives" and *Isabella Grey* as a "quiet, unpretending story" (October 1858, December 1858). As with the western or the New England tale (see chapter 6), the reality of the depicted social field was thought to require a specific kind of treatment. Decorum, a match between matter and manner, is anticipated. Such anticipation had, of course, no necessary relation to objective truth, and it might be supposed that the rhetorical purpose of the domestic novel was precisely to imagine home as a quiet place no matter what the truth might be. In due time this literature generated its antithesis, as other writers exploded the home's claim to "deep, silent enjoyments" by presenting another sort of domestic literature where home is the setting of misery and melodrama.

A second aspect of domestic fiction, to judge by the praise it won from reviewers, involves its conception and control of the reading experience itself. The reader of a domestic novel has a calm, soothing time: home *and* the reader alike are domesticated. *Agnes Morris; or, The Heroine of Domestic Life* "will be considered tame by readers whose taste has been accustomed to the spiced wine of popular modern fiction, but its quiet pictures of domestic life . . . will gain for it many admirers" (*Tribune*, April 28, 1849). "For the 'fast' taste that is now so much the rage, this quiet domestic story [*My Brother's Keeper*] will be too tame"; *The School of Life* "is a quiet, domestic story" that contains "numerous passages of graceful vivacity, and inculcates a pure and noble moral aim; but it is destitute of the exciting scenes which are demanded by the taste of modern novel readers" (*Tribune*, May 16, 1855; June 26, 1855). Clearly, the domestic novel had to compete with more exciting fictions and was appreciated by reviewers for the reading alternative it provided.

But though appreciative, the very reviewers who praised domestic fiction all admitted, sooner or later, that the heights of literary art were inherently beyond the reach of this subgenre. The art of domestic novels, as the *North American* explained, lay in "describing minutely and faithfully the interior of households in our own times . . . without aspiring to touch the higher chords of passion and sentiment" (April 1843). Bremer, noted the *Southern Literary Messenger*, "writes of Homes and Neighbors, the Strife and Peace of the Household and the Diary of Domestic Life. These subjects can soon be exhausted, not of their purity and loveliness, nor of their importance; but of all originality" (April 1844). *Agnes Morris*, according to *Knickerbocker*, "without laying any great claim to originality of plot, brilliancy of style, depth of thought and observation, or new delineations of character" is still "a winning book," one that "comes under the list of *pleasant books*" (August 1849). While granting that Caroline Lee Hentz's *Linda* and *Rena* were "models of graceful domestic fiction," the *Democratic Review* thought that in her political and prosouthern *Marcus Warland* the author "has chosen a higher path" (April 3, 1852). And *Graham's* reported that *Peace; or, The Stolen Will* was "a spirited, genial, and original novel" representing "a move out of the circle of the thousand and one commonplace stories of domestic life with which editors' tables groan—all very well written, but all intolerably stupid" (December 1857).

Since reviewers thought that most novel readers were women

and knew that many novel writers were women, logically they should have associated *every* kind of novel with women; in fact they especially associated the domestic novel with women writers. *Margaret Capel* is "evidently a lady's production. It is one of those simple narratives of everyday life, which your concocters and devourers of raw-head-and-bloody-bones stories despise" (*Literary World,* March 17, 1847). This association obtains for obvious reasons. First, home was seen as woman's particular province, and therefore to celebrate the home was especially in her interest. *Godey's* made the connection overtly and continuously throughout its long life as the voice of the domestic American woman; we do not think, it wrote in describing its own aims in an editorial of June 1841, that "scientific researches or literary criticism, though of such elevated standards as to give the highest reputation for learning to our periodical, are so much to be desired as pictures of domestic life, which will convey to the young of our own sex, a vivid impression of their home duties and their moral obligation to perform them; also impressing on their minds the power which intellectual attainments, when united with moral excellence and just views of the female character, give to woman to promote the refinement, the purity and happiness of society, and even decide, as it were, the destiny of our country." While domestic ideology aimed to persuade men as well as women to acknowledge the female character as higher than the male, the immediate appeal of this ideology would naturally be stronger for women than for men.

Domestic fiction was also associated with women because they were supposed to have the finer powers of observation and discrimination that the minute chronicling of domestic detail required for interest or notice. The *North American* observed of domestic novels that "women have labored most successfully in this department, as might be expected from their finer tact, and power of keen and delicate observation"; reviewing the novels of Charlotte Yonge it commented that "in one of the most fascinating department of literature, that of the novel of domestic life, we think the gentler sex, if not unequalled, quite unsurpassed" (April 1843, April 1855). The type was also associated with women, of course, because they spent so much of their lives within the home's confines and therefore knew more about it than men did and also knew more about it than they knew about anything else. "There is something in the department of polite learning, and especially of the novel, dwelling as it does, or should do, chiefly on the scenes and characters of domestic life, that renders it a field particularly fitted for the graceful genius of the sex. When a man sits down to write a novel, he is apt to consider it as a means of effecting some, as he supposes, more important end, and you find with dismay, before you have finished the first volume, that you are perusing, under this seductive form, a treatise on metaphysics, or an inquiry into the antiquities of Italy, Egypt, or China" (*North American* on Sedgwick's *The Linwoods*, January 1836). In Mary Jane Holmes's *Tempest and Sunshine*, "the domestic scenes are written as only a woman could write. In this department there is no comparison between male and female writers. The former always fail,—the latter nearly always succeed" (*Southern Literary Messenger*, August 1854).

Though they knew the home, women were supposed to know little of anything else. "Restricted as [women] are to a much inferior knowledge of life and the world, the choice of subjects is much more limited, their style and expressions must be much more guarded, and their delineations of the more hidden passions of human nature must, in many instances, be much more feeble and imperfect" (*Mirror*, September 3, 1842); this view, though not usually expressed so bluntly, was widely shared. The domestic women writers did not disagree but responded that what women did not know was not *fit* to be known, so that their novels, if not able to show life as it really was, were of the unexceptionable moral tendency that reviewers were everywhere looking for and praising in fiction. Given the dilemma in which moralist criticism of fiction had enmeshed critics, this argument had to be accepted. The domestic novel was therefore both advanced as better than, and patronized as feebler than, other sorts of fiction—precisely as women were better and yet weaker than the other sort of human being: men.

Highly Wrought Novels

Though women were believed to be the chief, if not the only, composers of domestic novels, they were also seen as the major

perpetrators of something called "high-wrought fiction," which
was the domestic novel's antithesis: a feverish, florid, improbable, melodramatic, exciting genre whose emergence was closely
linked to female ignorance (knowing little about life, women
produced these improbabilities) and susceptibilities (out of the
same ignorance, women enjoyed them). "Novels of passion,
which try to 'pile up the agony' of our poor human nature,"
Putnam's complainingly called them (June 1855). Three extremely successful American practitioners were E. D. E. N.
Southworth (at first called the American George Sand), Ann
Stephens, and Eliza Dupuy. Indeed, these writers ultimately
were more successful than such "domestic" authors as Susan and
Anna Warner or Maria Cummins, though sales of individual
books may not have equaled those of *The Wide, Wide World* or *The
Lamplighter*. In Southworth's *The Discarded Daughter*, *Harper's*
found "an intolerable glare of gas-light; truth is sacrificed to
melodramatic effect"; Dupuy's *The Country Neighborhood* contains
"high-wrought language . . . several situations of exciting interest," and "lurid exhibitions of unbridled passion" (October
1852, April 1855). *Peterson's*, describing Southworth's *The Curse of
Clifton*, said she would take "very high rank as a novelist" if only
she "intensified less," and it identified Ann Stephens (one of its
editors) as one who had no rival "in American literature, in the
higher walks of passionate fiction" (June 1854, August 1854).
Putnam's also saw Stephens's works as "belong[ing] properly to
the melo-dramatic and sensation schools" (July 1857).

Many other highly wrought works were written by women.
According to reviews in *Harper's*, Mrs. Martin Bell's *Julia Howard*
was a "story of exciting interest, which, by its powerful delineation of passion, its bright daguerreotypes of character, and the
wild intensity of its plot, must become a favorite with the lovers
of high-wrought fiction"; *Hagar the Martyr* by Mrs. H. Marion
Stephens was "a story belonging to the school of melodramatic
intensity . . . more adapted to charm the lovers of 'fast literature'
than to gain the approval of discreet readers"; Mrs. Marsh's
"highly dramatic" *The Heiress of Houghton* was "distinguished for
its intensity of conception, its almost masculine vigor of style";
and *The Heart of Mabel Ware*, anonymous but assumed to have
been written by a woman, was "a romance portraying the darker
passions of the human heart in lurid and terrific colors. Written

with a singular power of expression, it unfolds a terrible domestic tragedy" (September 1850, February 1855, August 1855, February 1856). Many more women read this sort of fiction than wrote it, of course, so that the reviews reveal the woman reader escaping domesticity as much as, or more than, accepting and celebrating it, at least so far as favorite books were concerned. The reviewers completely failed to integrate their two types of woman reader, the lovers of domestic and of high-wrought fiction, into one gender. (As I have proposed elsewhere—in *Woman's Fiction* [Cornell University Press, 1978]—what might have united the readers and writers of domestic and high-wrought fiction was their deployment of an essentially similar plot, the story of female trials and triumph. The high-pitched agonies of a Southworth or Stephens heroine were intensifications of the quiet sufferings of a Cummins or Warner protagonist, a similarity the rhetorical differences may have obscured for reviewers.)

Metropolitan Novels

Domestic tragedies did not exhaust the scope of highly wrought fiction, nor were women the only writers of these exciting books. Another significant variant of the mode, more congenial to men though not exclusively written by them, was the "metropolitan novel" or the "novel of low life." Characters in such works were drawn from the bottom of the social heap, and the novels took place mostly on city streets or in public places. This was the domestic space, so to speak, of the urban poor. The metropolitan novel was the novel of ordinary life among the lower classes and, considering the middle-class orientation of most American readers, a sort of exotica. Reviewers frequently placed the metropolitan novel, or novel of low life, at an extreme from the fashionable novel, or novel of high life, with the domestic novel occupying the normative middle ground. Though domestic fiction embodied an ideology we can properly call bourgeois, it was seldom set in the city; placed in rural or suburban space, the domestic fiction complicated its celebration of middle-class values by a nostalgic setting that made it oddly unrealistic even as fidelity to daily life was its announced achievement.

The metropolitan novel is then, paradoxically, both a variant of the domestic novel (when that novel is thought of as representing the lives of ordinary folk) and the antithesis of that form (in that its ordinary folk's lives are virtually devoid of domesticity). This important paradox was most remarkably embodied, for reviewers of the age, in the brilliant work of Charles Dickens, which might be seen either as ethically salutary or as socially dangerous. For the *North American*, in Dickens "the native beauty of the human soul has been drawn from under the coarse disguises of want, hardship, and woe, and clothed with living light" (January 1843). For the *Christian Examiner* his books "breathe a tender sympathy with man as man, in whatever garb, under whatever culture. He is doing more than any other living or recent writer, to open the fountains of kindly feeling, and diffusive world-embracing charity, and to inspire deep compassion, earnest prayer, faithful effort for the toiling, suffering, and neglected of our race" (March 1843). To *Graham's*, "the tendency of Dickens' work is irresistibly democratic. . . . Shakespeare has degraded the lower classes in every picture he drew of them. Dickens has degraded the upper classes in just the same way. . . . In the hands of a man of less genius, the same undertaking has often degenerated into vile demagogism. But, so to speak, Dickens is the statesman of the masses, while the scribblers to whom we allude are but the grovelling stump orators. His works are to us great studies" (November 1856). The *Graham's* review conveys a characteristic uneasiness at the possibility that an approach like Dickens's might encourage social unrest. The metropolitan novel always made reviewers uncomfortable, all the more because it tended to be so exciting and hence so attractive, and they were relieved when novelists who chose the genre studied, rather than agitated on behalf of, the social group on which they concentrated.

To a journal like *Godey's*, programmatically dedicated to advancing the middle class and its values, espousing the middle way, and addressing an audience of women whose leisure to read the journal depended on a degree of financial comfort, the city novel's emphasis on the worth of poor people, especially the permanently poor, could be quite overdone. *Helen Leeson* will "correct some erroneous impressions in regard to a class against whom an envious and unsparing warfare, as malignant as it was undiscriminating, has been kept up for years, the only effect of which has been to widen the social breach between honest wealth and honest poverty" (January 1856). It complained about *Glen-wood*, a novel describing the appalling conditions in a New England poor house: "Books of this description have become very popular of late, and, whether exaggerations or the relations of simple facts, they add but little to the moral or literary reputation of the country" (February 1856). Reviewing a novel called *Hampton Heights*, it objected that "there has been, as we humbly conceive, quite enough written for the present, about rag-pickers, lamp-lighters, foundlings, beggars, rogues, pirates, murderers, etc., to allow that particular species of literature to rest for a season, or at least until the details of mendacity and vice can be reproduced with some pretence to originality" (April 1856). It praised a novel called *Blonde and Brunette* because it was not "an olla podrida of all kinds of crime, licentiousness, and horror . . . but a natural picture of such personages, scenes, and events as are to be met with in what is most usually called 'good society'" (February 1859). Note how *Godey's* reviewers slide from the honest to the criminal poor and associate virtue with the higher social classes.

The other side of the metropolitan novel was its possible encouragement of sympathy for crime and the criminal, and more generally of an attitude that saw the poor—criminal and virtuous alike—as victims of society rather than of their own shortcomings or of an inscrutable yet eventually proper divine plan in which some won and others lost in order to validate the necessity of struggle and self-reliance. Not everyone had Dickens's balance. "The brilliant success of Mr. Dickens, in his incidental but matchless pictures of metropolitan degradation and crime, undoubtedly prompted our author to attempt the feeble imitation before us; but instead of employing these themes as final accessories to a good purpose, Mr. Ainsworth adopts them as the very staple of a work whose lessons are of the worst description. Crime is the one source of every interesting situation" (*Knickerbocker*, December 1839). Another offender was Victor Hugo, "the first who dared to descend from courts and palaces, for heroes and heroines, to the walks of lower life; and like most daring innovators, he rushed from one extreme into another. His characters are literally picked up out of the street" (*American Review*, March 1846). The error, however, was not in choosing such characters, but in making them virtuous. "That moral purity might possibly be found to exist in the breast of one whose earliest associations had all been connected with scenes of vice and low debauchery, is but within the extreme verge of possibility—a kind of special miracle, to be met with in possibly one instance out of ten thousand," it explained. "However good may be the intention of authors whose pens trifle with the lower and disgusting phases of metropolitan life, we fear the results of their labors are not always rewarded with the desired effect" (*Literary World* on Cornelius Mathews's New York novel, *Moneypenny; or, The Heart of the World*, December 9, 1848). Since the source of all virtue is the home, street characters cannot be virtuous.

The author of *Hot Corn; or, Life Scenes in New York* "has long been familiar with the pauper classes of New York, as well as with the haunts of misery and vice in which the destitute and inebriated harbor in that great city; and in this volume he has described them with a fidelity only equalled by its power, and with a power only surpassed by its pathos. Few more absorbing books, perhaps, have ever been issued from the press" (*Peterson's*, February 1854). But the *Southern Literary Messenger* complained of that book in the same month: "if we ever wish for a censorship of the press, it is when we see works like that now before us. . . . It may be a very efficient agent of bringing about a moral revolution, but that revolution will only bring down the rest of the community to the level of the Five Points—not elevate the degraded wretches of that locality to decency and virtue." Emerson Bennett's *The Forged Will* was a work "containing many elements of popular success. The scene is laid among the haunts of crime, poverty, and wretchedness in New York describing situations which always challenge the interest of the reader" (*Harper's*, November 1853); Bennett's *Ellen Norbury* was "another of those melancholy pictures of the sin, shame, and misery of city life" (*Godey's*, July 1855). *Fashion and Famine*, by Ann Stephens, was "a story of geniune power, founded on the hideous contrasts of social life in an overgrown city. The staple of the work, of course, is the misery, desperation, and crime which are always festering at the heart of a great metropolis" (*Harper's*, July 1854). In this context the appearance of Maria Cummins's *The Lamplighter*, a work that domesticated lowlife scenes and elevated all the characters to middle-class prosperity at the conclusion, was welcome. "Devoted to the delineation of scenes in lowly life, without aiming at melodramatic effect by high-wrought pictures of depravity and crime" (*Harper's*, April 1854). *The Lamplighter* was followed by *The Watchman* and *Old Haun, the Pawnbroker*, imitations that were also favorably reviewed by a press disturbed about the metropolitan novel's appeal "to an imaginative craving for unnatural excitement" (*Harper's*, September 1855).

Perhaps the most dangerous of all these metropolitan writers was Eugene Sue, whose *The Mysteries of Paris* was a phenomenal best-seller throughout the 1840s. At least one translation of this work eliminated all the passages in which Sue advocated socialism as a cure for the appalling conditions he depicted so thrillingly, to the relief of several reviewers but the outrage of Horace Greeley's *Tribune:* "to chronicle the horrors and suppress their moral—omit the very passages that can alone excuse such exhibitions—is the wrong way entirely" (November 24, 1843). The next month it recommended an uncensored translation of the work, commenting that "no work of the age has made a more vivid impression than this, and though its exhibitions of human depravity and villainy are horrible, almost beyond belief and endurance, yet we believe more good than evil will result from its publication" (December 28, 1843).

Advocacy Novels

The kind of novel that reviewers thought the best, as we have seen in earlier chapters, was one in which the world was detachedly contemplated and hence presented to the reader as an object from which detachment was possible; such a novel was itself rather an object of contemplation than a source of excitement. When novelists like Eugene Sue or George Sand wrote novels advocating socialism or attacking marriage, they went even further in what most reviewers thought to be the wrong direction: not only did they ground their works in an interactive rather than a contemplative model of the relation between reader and text, but they aimed for specific social change as the result of such interactions. Reviewers almost unanimously felt that this use of the novel form was both inartistic and unfair: social advocacy was supposed to issue from reasoned or rhetorical argument, not from attachment to attractive characters and their exciting adventures. Yet the novel of advocacy became an increasingly prevalent, and increasingly powerful, form during the era. Where critics were usually ready to argue that a novel was improved by having more to it than its form of narrated story, now they objected to the political or religious novel as a hybrid. In no other aspect of their reviewing were critics as purely formal as in their discussions of the novel of advocacy, and in no other was their formalism as suspect.

Among their other faults, French novels contained passages of improper political and social advocacy, but the earliest noted novel of advocacy was *The Monikins*, by James Fenimore Cooper. *Knickerbocker* grumbled over the book that "it is the unhappiest idea possible, to suppose that politics can be associated, in any effective way, with romance or fiction" (August 1835). The *Mirror* faulted *Home as Found* as "an imposition upon the public, put forth, as it is, in the form of a novel, when it has about as much claim to be ranked under that head as a fourth of July oration, or a book of travels" (December 8, 1839). They, like today's literary historians, preferred Cooper's mythic—unthreatening—stories of the forest and the Leatherstocking.

But complaints, as so often in this chronicle of reviewing, were to no avail; by April 1844 the *North American* was writing that "the novel has become an essay on morals, on political economy, on the condition of women, on the vices and defects of social life" and (July 1847) that "this is the age of lectures. . . . The novel has become a quack advertisement in three volumes. . . . Everywhere pure literature seems defunct. Art for the sake of art is no more." Again, in a review of "Novels of the Season" (October 1848—a review commenting on *Jane Eyre, Wuthering Heights, The Tenant of Wildfell Hall, Hawkstone, The Bachelor of the Albany, Harold, the Last of the Saxon Kings, Grantley Manor,* and *Vanity Fair*): "opinions have nearly supplanted characters. We look for men, and discern propositions,—for women, and are favored with women's rights. . . . The march-of-intellect boys in a solid phalanx, have nearly pushed the novelist aside." "There is yet another class of novels that has sprung up within a few years past, those which aim at great political reform, or theological exposition" (*Southern Literary Messenger,* November 1849). "The novel is now almost recognized with the newspaper and the pamphlet as a legitimate mode of influencing public opinion, an indispensable organ in the discussion of any party question or set of opinions"; "every sect and every cause must now have its novels" (*Literary World*, November 30, 1850; October 29, 1853). Kingsley, *Graham's* observed, "is not singular in this selection of the novel for a purpose apart from the general subject of novel writing. The tendency of the age is to present every thing in this form. Thus we have political novels, representing every variety of political opinion—religious novels, to push the doctrines of every religious sect—philanthropic novels, devoted to the championship of every reform—socialist novels, philosophic novels, metaphysical novels" (April 1854).

The reviewers maintained that this subgenre was a formal hybrid, whose argumentation cut across and spoiled the story, and whose story cheapened the argument. *Sartain's* reviewer called Cooper's *The Ways of the Hour* "a political novel . . . a style of writing to which we bear no partiality. We do not like argument in the shape of a love story. . . . When we read politics, or metaphysics, or any other *ics*, let us have it in its own proper shape. But pray deliver us from all nauseous mixtures of love and logic" (August 1850). "A novel is not an appropriate vehicle for the exposition of doctrine, at the best" (*Putnam's*, May 1854); its object "should be to represent life and manners as they are, and not to advance the cause of a party or sect."

Although the putative criterion reviewers brought to discussion of this sort of novel was formal, their estimate of a given instance was closely tied to the degree to which it advocated controversial positions or enjoyed controversy itself. Public peace was the paramount issue. Accordingly, the didactic novel per se—that is, the novel of what was called "practical morality" —though seldom thought to be artistic, was yet not perceived as highly objectionable and indeed was considered appropriate for the undeveloped aesthetic tastes of the reader for whom it was designed. "Mr. Arthur writes very unexceptionable tales illustrative of American and domestic life, and adapted to the capabilities of the young and uneducated classes. All his stories inculcate a moral, and some of them are pleasing specimens of invention, and very true reflections of manners in the sphere for which they are designed" (*Literary World*, October 2, 1847). "Mrs. Ellis belongs to the class of utilitarian novelists, which are, we are happy to say, gaining ground rapidly" (*Southern Literary*

Messenger, March 1843). "A work of much more practical value than cheap novels generally possess. . . . Another of Mr. Arthur's plain, unromantic, commonsense, practical stories" (*Sartain's*, June 1848). "This tale is eminently practical in its character, tending to show the rewards of enterprise and industry when combined with religious principle" (*Literary World*, February 2, 1850). "A charming and instructive book, and none can peruse it without learning wholesome lessons as to the conditions of their own happiness, and the connection of that with the happiness of others, through duty faithfully performed" (*Christian Examiner*, September 1852). "A practical story of real life, full of warning, instruction, and high moral teaching. . . . The writer is well known as the author of some of our most practically useful tales"; "a work of practical common sense . . . in which the author has connectedly and steadily illustrated sound principles"; "in this as in all his previous stories, the author has presented a practical lesson of life, from the relations of which the reader will be able to draw the most salutary admonitions" (*Godey's*, March 1853, December 1854, July 1858).

Knickerbocker praised the author of a didactic fiction in October 1846 by asserting that "no one can rise from her pages without being deeply entertained and as sensibly improved" (October 1846) and generalized that "no work of fiction can retain a reputation worth a just ambition that has not for its end the inculcation of virtuous principles" (March 1848). But how different this language is from what the same journal accorded to, for example, Thackeray, "this consummate master" (October 1855). Or Dickens; or Hawthorne; or Cooper. A mixed form, designed primarily for the less subtle intellect and the less skilled reader, the didactic novel was welcomed politely by the reviewer, who saw it as a wholesome alternative to the highly wrought fiction that such a reader tended to prefer. It was especially celebrated by reviews in those journals—*Godey's*, the *Home Journal*, and (of course) Timothy Shay Arthur's own *Arthur's Home Magazine*—with didactic aims themselves.

But perhaps the chief virtue of the didactic novel was negative: its lessons of practical morality, self-control, duty, and the like were uncontroversial and politically and socially safe. This was not the case with the religious novel, which was defined by these reviewers as a work either advocating or attacking the doctrines of a particular religious sect—"A religious novel, in which one form of religious belief is inculcated, as the only one in which safety may be found" (*Literary World*, March 6, 1847). It was a popular form, especially in the 1850s, and may well have been responsible for making novel readers out of numerous evangelical Protestants for whom the novel had before been anathema. "This class of religious novels has many admirers, and form[s], doubtless, an agreeable mode of disseminating what are conceived to be the truths of religious teaching," the *Democratic Review* observed cautiously in a review of *The Earl's Daughter* in September 1852; the next month, writing on *Margaret Percival in America*, it commented less favorably that "the class of religious novels seems to be spreading and multiplying through the jealousy of sects as to the usages detailed in those most popular."

As examples of the form became more numerous and prevalent, reviewer objections crystallized: the partisan nature of such books would exacerbate controversy: "there is little difficulty in getting the better of an argument, both sides of which are carried on by the same disputant" (*Southern Literary Messenger*, October 1851); the affective and highly biased nature of the arguments would lead to religious irrationalism: "throughout this book, the opponents of the author's religious creed are made to utter not only sentiments open to attack, but sentiments which no one possessing common sense can for a moment tolerate. Fiction is not a legitimate means by which to argue or enforce doctrines" (*American Review*, December 1851).

"It is perhaps too late in the day to discuss the expediency of wrapping up religion in a novel," said a *Literary World* reviewer. "When the hybrid first made its appearance, many worthy and straightforward critics spent their strength in grave dissertations on the subject, and probably flattered themselves that they had weeded the literary garden of a mongrel that could never produce good fruit. But preaching (rather than practice) seems to be the mania of the day. . . . To attempt now to bring this class of literary anomalies into disuse, would be to try stemming Niagara with a straw." But the critic tried: "the vocations of the novelist and the polemic are so at variance, that it is not to be expected that they can ever be united in one person, and we do wish those excellent people who think they can make the world better by the inculcation of doctrine, would offer it pure, leaving the personal application to the sagacity of the reader; while the few who are gifted with the power of interesting the imagination and the heart by the delineation of character, may safely be trusted to draw pictures of real life, from which the most obtuse reader can derive abundant lessons of virtue and religion, if he chooses" (March 6, 1847).

"'Religious' and 'novel' are not merely paradoxical but directly antagonistical," according to a *Knickerbocker* review of the popular *Hawkstone* (May 1848). The *Literary World* objected to *Lady Alice; or, The New Una:* "this book has strengthened our conviction that the practical Christian moralities of life are very feebly enforced, if they are not positively weakened, by the prevailing style of modern religious fictions" (July 21, 1849). The *Christian Examiner* said *Alban* "is one of the religious (?) [*sic*] novels of our day,—for the most part, an unhallowed and mischievious class of publication" (January 1852). Some reviewers found the religious novel boring. In January 1846, for example, a *North American* critic asserted that "the doctrine is sure to crush down the narrative with its weight. The sable fleet of religious novels, oppressed with their leaden cargo, have shown marvellous alacrity in sinking where they were never heard of more; and the whole history of these experiments proves, that there is an inherent unfitness in this form of communication for any such purpose." Since the greatest vogue of the religious novel still lay a few years ahead, the *North American* cannot be congratulated for its foresight.

Other reviewers, claiming that the presentation of competing religious doctrines was unfair, worried that these novels would increase controversy. "We confess that we are not partial to this kind of fiction," *Godey's* editorialized. "We do not go to novels to learn our religion, nor have we ever found in such works, any real aid to devotional feelings. Faith in the novel-writer is not faith in the Saviour; nor can the illustrations of a religious life found in novels, except on rare occasions, be useful, or even possible in the every-day duties of this working-day world" (March 1857). The editorial also complained of the "unfairness and bitterness" of the "satirical representation" found in most such novels; to this, in a review of a Southworth novel, it contrasted such lessons of faith, hope, and charity as "may have a tendency to soften the asperities of religious controversy, and to foster in many hearts purer and more amiable feelings than now find a place in them" (June 1857). "We do not, we confess, approve of the practice adhered to by many of our popular writers, of choosing their characters from sects of religion or sections of the country, and, after making them as odious as possible, leaving them to be viewed as fair representatives of classes or bodies of men" (*Godey's*, January 1858).

Only a few entertained the idea that a partisan, quarrelsome spirit might be the precise attraction of religious works. "Under the guise of a novel," a *Southern Literary Messenger* review said of *Hawkstone*, it "unfolds the present condition of religious opinion among a large body of Christians. All are more or less interested in the points at issue; to those who are actually partisans, we can imagine no recent volume half so attractive" (April 1848). "Apart from its controversial interest, which cannot fail to attract a numerous class of readers at the present day, the story is constructed with remarkable skill" (*Tribune* on *Beatrice* by Catherine Sinclair, March 24, 1853). *Inez*, by Augusta Evans, "will doubtless have a good run during the present excited state of the public mind on the vexed questions of religious faith and observance" (*Godey's*, April 1855).

The reviewers' response to political novels depended to a great extent on how pertinent the social analysis seemed to the American scene and how revolutionary was the proposed solution to existing ills. The socialism of Sue's novels, and the attacks on marriage in George Sand's works, were both severely criticized, but reviewers were much more worried that such books would lead to individual acts of rebellion than to widespread, methodical social disruption. Socialist hope in the United States "is not so warmly outspoken as in other lands," the *Tribune* acknowledged in a review of Sue, "both because no pervasive ills as yet call loudly for redress, and because private conservatism is here great, in proportion to the absence of authorized despotism" (February 1, 1845).

They looked at the novels of Dickens, Gaskell, and others attacking the factory system as containing wholesome advice for England but having little pertinence for the United States. "The American reader will shudder oftentimes in perusing *Mary Barton*, and wonder at the extent and intensity of human misery, of which he had entertained no adequate conception," the *Democratic Review* wrote in February 1849. "That such a state of things cannot for ever last, that sooner or later, the thousands who have long suffered in silence must be aroused to active despair, with some such war cry as 'La propriété est un vol,'—lamentable experience teaches us to believe. Long may such a result be averted, even for England; and may the system that leads to such a result, never obtain upon our native soil!" In no less oratorical fashion, the *Literary World* reviewed Kingsley's *Alton Locke:* "the Charter must eventually be the law of the land in England, all of its dreaded six points are as common and unquestioned to us of America as the air we breathe, but no charter, no republic, no Fourierite dreams, will ever thoroughly eradicate these evils. 'The poor ye have always with you,' said the Great Reformer, and with the poor must be always more or less of misery to be alleviated. Woe to us, as individuals and as nations, if we do not set our shoulders to the wheel and do what in us lieth for its amelioration!" (November 30, 1850).

The matter is altogether different, however, with respect to slavery and North-South relations. Reviewers would have gladly avoided this subject, but the phenomenal success of *Uncle Tom's Cabin* forced it into their professional domain. "How to treat her book is our difficulty at present," wrote an uneasy reviewer in the *Literary World*, "for as a lengthy abolition tract, we desire no acquaintance with it, as a political affair it is entirely out of our province. . . . We must regard the work as a whole, as rather an odd one, being neither fish nor flesh, nor yet good red herring." But it acknowledged before concluding that this was "a book capable of producing infinite mischief" (April 24, 1852). The mischief to which it alluded was less the abolition of slavery than the exacerbation of hostilities between the regions and the consequent jeopardizing of the Union. There is no way to account for the tone of those reviews that grappled with *Uncle Tom's Cabin* and other books, pro- and antislavery, that followed it, other than to assume that the fragility of the Union was very much a recognized fact of the national life in the 1850s. This the *Literary World* made clear when it gave the book a second review, on December 4, 1852. "We are not prepared to deny that the motive of Mrs. Stowe in writing her book has been good, but we are ready to assert that its influence is bad. The social evils of slavery have been exaggerated and presented in a form calculated to excite an inconsiderate popular feeling. A subject which involves the happiness and life of many of our countrymen . . . has been tricked off . . . and displayed with a boldness that knows no reserve and cares for no consequences, to a pernicious and unthinking multitude. . . . What the common sense, the statesmanship, the religion, and the humanity of our country have by unanimous consent agreed to allay, Mrs. Stowe has been reckless enough to do her best to excite."

Judgments of *Uncle Tom's Cabin* invariably accorded with the particular journal's political orientation. Critics who favored it were open in acknowledging their political bias. The *Tribune*, of course, was most commendatory, noting the "high moral purpose of this tragic story" and maintaining that it "cannot fail to produce a strong and healthful effect on public opinion" (April 9, 1852). The *Christian Examiner*, too, said "we know of no publication which promises to be more effective in the service of a holy but perilous work than this" (May 1852); the *Ladies' Repository* said that both *Dred* and *Uncle Tom's Cabin* "develop, in clear and strong light, some phases of that monstrous iniquity, which has long challenged the exertions of humanity and the judgments of God, and is now causing our very national fabric to totter as by the throes of a pent-up volcano" (November 1856). Only *Harper's*, which did not formally review it, considered it as a work of art, editorializing: "more than a partisan, or even humane tract, it was a work of high literary art . . . an addition to the literature of the world" with characters "typical and individual . . . incidents and dialogue, which constantly rose in interest and dignity" and other "qualities of permanent literary value" (May 1855).

Opponents of the book were much more strongly political. The *Southern Literary Messenger* reviewed it twice in frantic rhetoric; among its milder comments was this: "the whole tenor of this pathetic tale derives most of its significance and coloring from a distorted representation or a false conception of the sentiments and feelings of the slave. It presupposes an identity of sensibilities between the races of the free and the negroes"; in fact, "the joys and sorrows of the slave are in harmony with his position, and are entirely dissimilar from what would make the happiness, or misery, of another class" (December 1852). A long angry essay entitled "Black Letters" condemning *Uncle Tom's Cabin* and all the other books inspired by it appeared in *Graham's*, asking, "what would the negroes do, if they were free among us?

Nothing at all, or next to nothing. They have not the muscle or the mind of the European races" (February 1853).

But *Uncle Tom's Cabin* also inspired an aesthetic criticism that denied the work's literary value and tried to make those who had been moved by it reconceive their enthusiasm as overreaction. This criticism could not gainsay the work's success. "The popularity of Uncle Tom is a phenomenon in the literary world, one of those phenomena which set at naught all previous experience and baffle all established and recognised principles. No literary work of any character or merit, whether of poetry or prose, of imagination or observation, fancy or fact, truth or fiction, that has ever been written since there have been writers or readers, has ever commanded so great a popular success. . . . Was there never a book before? . . . How is it to be accounted for?" asked the *Literary World* (December 4, 1852). It could not be literary merit; it could only be the coincidence of a strong antislavery feeling in the population with the larger human response to "the description of such terrible sufferings as never fail to awaken sympathy, and of such cruelties as are always sure to arouse indignation." This was humanly commendable, perhaps, but not sufficient to validate the novel as a work of art.

The reviewer for the *Literary World* also invoked the criterion of probability: "atrocities that may have been committed by some depraved wretch devoid of human feelings, are here set down and pictured forth, as if such things were of common and daily occurrence." Other journals reviewing pro- and antislavery novels following *Uncle Tom's Cabin* commented on probability and, at the same time, on discretion and decorum as desirable in works dealing with such a sensitive subject. *Godey's*, for example, called the prosouthern *The Cabin and the Parlor* "among the best and most feeling of the several productions that have appeared in relation to the delicate questions of which it treats. The author has shown himself to be not only an inimitable sketcher, but a writer of sound judgment and discretion, especially in relation to the mutual duties of the States under the confederation" (March 1853). And of another work of the same sort: "here we have still another generous effort in mitigation of the strong and odious contrasts of American life and character, as drawn by some of our native writers. . . . The author seems to have scrupulously avoided every expression that could, or ought to give offence to any honorable or conscientious person who has taken a part on either side of the question naturally involved in the development of her plot" (*Godey's*, April 1853). "Great care seems to have been taken . . . to abstain from introducing offensively any of those 'vexed questions' which have lately been made the basis of similar works of fiction"; "happily for the reader, the author has taken care not to introduce any of those modern devices to obtain an ephemeral popularity which has rendered so many works, north and south, eminently untruthful and ridiculous, and, we may add, destructive to those fraternal feelings which should knit together all sections of our common country" (*Godey's*, July 1854, January 1858). The "moderate" novels were invariably those written in mitigation of slavery, presenting favorable views of the South. Many more pro- than antislavery novels were reviewed.

Again, as with the question of the relation between a novel's moral tendency and its effect on reader behavior, it is difficult to know what really happened to the reader of an advocacy novel. Abraham Lincoln is said to have credited Stowe with the Civil War, but that was gallantry: there is no reason to believe that an unthinking multitude was ready to take up arms to abolish slavery, as the *Literary World's* rhetoric suggested; indeed, the anti-draft riots in New York City after war was declared suggest the opposite. *The Jungle* is held directly responsible by some scholars for regulation of the content of processed meats, but not for ameliorating the wage slavery that was Upton Sinclair's target. The persecution of dissident writers in totalitarian countries represents a clear conviction on the part of social authorities that novels (or poems) are dangerous; but Aristotle's theory of catharsis seems to see narrative literature as safety valve rather than incitement. The subject needs careful study and attention of a sort it has never received. The point for our study of the novel climate in antebellum America is that reviewers distinguished sharply between ethicomoral content, which they thought to be transcendent, and sociopolitical content including religious advocacy. The former represented the perfection of the genre, the latter a troubling and troublesome hybrid.

I I

Romances, Historical Novels, National Novels

The three classification terms discussed in this chapter have had special importance in the twentieth century for those writing American literary history and selecting a supporting canon. For many scholars, as the editors of the *Literary History of the United States* put it in their "Address to the Reader," ours is "a literature which is most revealing when studied as a by-product of American experience" (New York, 1959, xix). In finding the right works for this view, critics have more often than not approached novels (and other literary works) with firm convictions about what constitutes the American experience and have chosen works that they construe to back up these ideas. Although the specific content of Americanness varies from critic to critic, most have agreed that literature displaying it must involve a degree of conscious reflection on national identity.

The circularity of this enterprise has led to neglect or devaluation of a great many literary works written in America, not on account of aesthetic inferiority (though in some instances aesthetic superiority has been equated with the desired Americanness of content) so much as their lack of the requisite American essence. Some critics have felt that as a nation uniquely related to time—both the past and future—we express ourselves characteristically in a special sort of historical fiction. Others have felt, on the contrary, that in the absence of history as well as a social field our literature is characterized by an ahistorical, mythical form that they have called the "romance." Although the three terms—

historical novel, romance, and national or "American" novel—functioned in American novel reviewing around the middle of the nineteenth century and before, they had quite different applications from those in present-day study of American literature.

The Romance

The single most powerful theoretical concept in modern American literary history and criticism is that of the "romance" as a distinct and defining American fictional form. It is thought of as emerging in the works of Charles Brockden Brown—who, according to the *North American*, could not be said "to have produced an American novel. So far from exhibiting any thing of our native character and manners, his agents are not beings of this world; but those dark monsters of the imagination, which the will of the master may conjure up with an equal horror in the shadows of an American forest, or amidst the gloom of long galleries and vaulted aisles. His works have nothing American but American topography about them" (July 1824). This review is interested in the specific nature of Americanness as it might be manifested in novels; but it implies that the "romance" (if that is what Brown was writing—the review did not use the term) was not especially American; and it also hints that Brown's form (whatever it was appropriately called) was not the novel. We can read the review as suggesting that Brown wrote novels that were not American, or that he wrote works that were not novels. In any case, the critical frame was quite different from that which subsequent literary history has retroactively imposed.

In all the material I examined, I found only one comment prefiguring the notion of the American imagination as particularly well suited to something like what we now call the romance, and it is a reprint in *Harper's* for April 1852 of a criticism originating in a British journal, the *London Leader*. The magazine saw in "such genuine outcoming of the American intellect as can safely be called national"—an "outcoming" that included Poe, Hawthorne, Melville, and Emerson—"a wild and mystic love of the super-sensual, peculiarly their own. To move a horror skillfully, with something of the earnest faith in the Unseen, and with weird imagery to shape these phantasms so vividly that the most incredulous mind is hushed, absorbed—to do this no European pen has any longer the power—to do this American literature is without a rival. What *romance* writer can be named with Hawthorne? Who knows the horrors of the sea like Herman Melville?" The fact that this is a *British* perception does not, of course, necessarily make it wrong. But it is worth noting that the defining quality of the American imagination in this approach is something the European writer believed his continent to have outgrown; the imagination of the uniquely American writer is atavistic, simple, primitive, superstitious, of earnest faith. The novel is beyond this kind of writer because it is so advanced, so modern.

I will consider shortly how reviewers thought a national aspect might enter into the *novel* as they understood the genre. First I want to discuss the term "romance" in novel criticism of the era. If, in my sample, only one essay associated something *called* romance with American literature, the idea could not have been a common one. The term romance was certainly used in novel reviewing, but with no national reference; in fact it was used so broadly and inconsistently that in any given instance of trying to fix its meaning the critic (then and now) was evidently indulging in a creative rather than a descriptive activity. But mainly the term romance was deployed as no more than a synonym for the term novel.

The *North American* said that Cooper "has laid the foundations of American romance, and is really the first who has deserved the appellation of a distinguished novel writer" (July 1822); wrote both "historical novel" and "historical romance" in a discussion of Italian "romances" (April 1838); began a review of new popular "novels" "with the romance which stands at the head of our list" and ended, "we have selected these three novels from the multitude about us" (October 1856); and commented with reference to a novel by Bulwer that "there are so many different ways of doing one or the other of these things through the medium of a good romance, that the novel which fails of them all cannot redeem itself" (April 1859).

From the *New York Review:* "the common prejudice of sober men against novels is well founded. . . . But romance may become, and often is, an impressive medium for the transmission of truth" (April 1839). From the *Literary World: Lady Alice* is "considerably above the common level of modern Romances. . . . It is a genuine novel, with a plot and a catastrophe" (July 21, 1849); "it is very hard work nowadays for the novelist to construct an effective romance out of those meagre materials which, fifty years ago, were considered all-sufficient" (August 17, 1850). From *Graham's:* "some of the most deleterious books we have are romances. . . . Hence, in criticising a novel, it becomes important to examine the tendency of the work" (May 1848); *Vanity Fair* is "one of the most striking novels of the season. It bears little resemblance in tone, spirit, and object, to the other popular romances of the day" (November 1848). *The Scarlet Letter* is "a beautiful and touching romance"; readers "will hardly be prepared for a novel of so much tragic interest and tragic power" (May 1858). A review of *Westward Ho!* referred to "the evident intention of the novelist" that "the romance evinces" (July 1855).

From the *Mirror:* a new "novel" was "happily" not "executed in the worst style of modern romances" (June 2, 1838). From *Knickerbocker:* "we live in such a novel-reading age, that every work of romance, possessing more than ordinary excellence, is seized on with avidity, and made popular at once" (October 1838); "in the romance before us, as in his previous novels . . ." (June 1843). From *Peterson's:* "the author of this novel is favorably known to the public. . . . The present story is exceedingly well told; and, like all the author's romances, teaches a moral lesson" (July 1846); "one of the very best works of romance that has appeared since Christmas, a period, it must be remembered, fertile in superior novels" (August 1851); "a new romance by Hawthorne is always an event. . . . The novel [*The Marble Faun*] is, in one sense, an art-novel" (May 1860).

From the *Christian Examiner:* "a little more of human imperfection would have made her more interesting to all but thorough-bred novel readers, who expect, as a matter of course, to pursue one such 'faultless monster' through the mazes of romance" (July 1843). From *Harper's:* "a new romance by the author of *Talbot and Vernon.* . . . Like the previous work of the same author, the novel is intended . . ." (November 1850); a work's "interest as a novel . . . is guaranteed by a plot of high wrought romance" (June 1854). From the *Atlantic:* "novelists recognize that Nature is a better romance-maker than the fancy. . . . Sometimes, indeed, a daring romance-writer ventures . . ." (May 1858).

Examples could be greatly multiplied, but these will show how the terms were used interchangeably in all the journals throughout the period. There were reviews and essays that did make an effort to distinguish the two terms, but definitions varied from review to review, and whatever was established was often abandoned even within the individual reviews. In many cases the distinction appears to be entirely ad hoc; the reviewer is developing an idiosyncratic scheme and calls on these two words to make a point in a classification not duplicated in other critical writings.

For example, a *Knickerbocker* review said that under "the head of novels" there are "but two recognized divisions,—namely, the novel, properly so called, and the historical romance"; it later explained that the novel implied "only fiction," whereas the historical romance was bound by fidelity to events and personages that had actually existed or taken place (August 1838, October 1838). The *Southern Literary Messenger* similarly distinguished between the novel and the *historical* romance: "in the *novel*, all this is bad enough, but it becomes intolerable in those *romances* which, blending history with fiction, aim to portray the renowned characters of other ages" (June 1847).

A critic in the *Southern Literary Messenger*, in a long essay on Hawthorne, distinguished "two distinct kinds of fiction, or narrative literature, which for want of more apt terms, we may call the melodramatic and the meditative; the former is in a great degree mechanical, and deals chiefly with incidents and adventure; a few types of character . . . approved scenic materials and what are called effective situations, make up the story; the other species, on the contrary, is modelled upon no external pattern, but seems evolved from the author's mind" (June 1851). The terms novel and romance do not appear in this essay, which distinguishes outer and inner fiction but fails to mention the form contemporary fictitious narrative was usually thought to take, the unmelodramatic narrative of everyday life.

In March 1842, a review of Dickens in the *Christian Examiner* began with a long general disquisition on fiction, defining epic, pastoral, novel, and romance. The novel "deals primarily with events, and makes character subsidiary. Its aim is to replace the lost thread of cause and effect, to bind actions to their legitimate consequences." The romance mingles all the other forms of fiction, combining "the stately epic tread of heroes on an elevated stage, with the passion and sentiment of the tragic muse. It borrows the tenderness of the pastoral . . . while with the novel its plot turns on the principle of retributive justive." This is not a particularly useful or acute distinction; indeed, it is difficult to know just what works the reviewer might have had in mind to exemplify his description of the romance. The comment shows how reviewers setting out to distinguish romance from novel were likely to invent their distinction on the spot. This means that a later critic or student looking for a distinction between novel and romance that was current and widely shared in this era should probably avoid precisely those essays which feature such a distinction.

In September 1850 the *American Review,* writing on Bulwer, also expatiated on the general nature of fiction, stating that "as a preliminary step" to a criticism "it will be necessary to set forth briefly the recognized ideal of a Novel, and to distinguish it from the Romance. This is a task demanded by the present scheme of criticism, and not out of place in correcting a prevailing error of the day, which tends to call every fiction a novel." It described the novel as "a picture of society, a delineation of manners, increased in interest and effect by the aid of plot and incident. . . . Vastly more than other fiction it requires to be philosophic and scrutinizing." In contrast, the romance was "a panorama of outward life" that "surveys men and manners in mass, avoids all analytic investigations of character, and deals for the most part in broad and free strokes," with plots that are "rarely complicated," thoughts that are "never above the comprehension of the most ordinary minds." The romance is "vivid, startling, and fond of effect," the romancer "essentially objective. Nothing that he relates conveys the bias of his own mind." The novel is a more descriptive, more analytic, and more subjective mode than the romance. This distinction is not a true contrast; different and unrelated qualities are discussed for the two genres. But insofar as it might be related to our current distinction, it reverses the application of the terms. It is the romance that we see as the inward form, the novel as the outward.

Putnam's in October 1854 featured a long essay entitled "Novels: Their Meaning and Mission," which also merits quoting at length: "There is no more unfortunate circumstance than the lack of an appropriate and experienced name for that kind of composition to which we are necessitated in lieu of a better, to affix the appellation, Novels, Romances, etc. They are total misnomers, every one of them. The fact is, that the thing has repeatedly changed, while the name has not, and thus thing and name are mutual contradictions. . . . The terms novel and romance, though often confounded, are, in a general signification, analogous to the philosophico-metaphysical divisions, '*imagination*,' and '*fancy*.' . . . The term Romance is an indication of a *combination* of wonderful deeds and daring," while Novel "carries the idea of an Art-creation; not an accretion of circumstances and particulars from without, but an inly production of the mind in its highest imagining or *poetic* moods." Again, novel rather than romance is identified with an inward creation, but the association of the novel with poetry is unique.

Another instance appears in an Easy Chair in the June 1858 *Harper's*, distinguishing "novels of society," where "it is the picture of life and the development of character that interest us, and not the fate of the people," from "a love story, or a proper romance," whose "point is the concurrence of every circumstance to the union or separation of the lovers. They may be, in themselves, but names and shades, but the description of where they were and what they did must be very absolute and distinct." The *Harper's* editorial uses romance to mean love story and also equates it with plot. Novel is related to character and description. In other words, the romance is the more dynamic and superficial form, the novel more static and reflective. A year later *Harper's* repeated its definition in inconsistent if not incoherent phrasing: "the novel is interesting, philosophically, as illustrating completely the style of romance which depends upon the delineation of character for its interest rather than on the progress and development of a story. It is unquestionably the higher kind of novel—but equally without question it is less popular" (June 1859). This passage notably twice makes a distinction and twice erases it within the confines of two sentences: the novel is a form of romance, the romance a form of novel, and the two modes are distinct. Interesting, too, is the perception that insofar as the two forms can be distinguished, the romance is the more popular. This subgenre is certainly not the one today's critics are writing about when they describe the romance as a genre developing in response to American hostility to fiction.

In this context, Simms's distinction in the preface to a revised version of *The Yemassee* in 1853 and Hawthorne's in his preface to *The House of the Seven Gables* in 1851 should probably be seen as two more attempts (and perhaps less disinterested ones than those appearing in the journals) to fix terms in flux at the time. That Hawthorne pretended to be using a distinction known to all his readers ("When a writer calls his work a Romance, it need hardly be observed that he wishes to claim a certain latitude, both as to its fashion and material, which he would not have felt himself entitled to assume, had he professed to be writing a Novel") has permitted later students to believe—as Hawthorne no doubt intended—that a fixed definition was in use at the time, and that people knew that some novels were romances and some were novels and also knew which were which. If, indeed, the romance was thought to be more popular, we have an explanation for his strategy, as well as for Simms's attempt to renew his reputation by affixing the term to an early book.

To complicate matters still further, the literary discourse on romance and novels, though at one extreme characterized by total interchangeability of the terms and at the other by total definitional anarchy, also contains two "mainstream" definitions. That is, in a preponderance of essays and reviews where one can see an operative distinction, one or the other of these usages obtains. One of these definitions incorporates a history of fiction (is diachronic) while the other schematizes existing fiction (is synchronic). In the diachronic mode of writing, the novel is seen as a modern form of romance, which is the overform, the generic name for narrative fiction over time. In the synchronic mode, the generic name for narrative fiction is the novel, and the romance is one type of the genre. If we put these two modes together we come up with a discourse where romance is a type of novel, which is in turn a modern type of romance. No doubt a great deal of confusion can be attributed to this merging of two different approaches to fiction.

Authority for both these typifying schemes stems from a single source, Walter Scott's long essay on romance in volume 6 of the 1824 supplement to the *Encyclopaedia Britannica*. Scott began his survey by deconstructing a prior authority, Samuel Johnson, who had defined romance as "a military fable of the middle ages; a tale of wild adventures in love and chivalry." Scott wrote that "the 'wild adventures' is almost the only absolutely essential ingredient in Johnson's definition. We would be rather inclined to describe a *Romance* as 'a fictitious narrative in prose or verse; the interest of which turns upon marvellous and uncommon incidents.'" Scott's purpose in making this new definition, he openly allowed, was to facilitate a contrast "to the kindred term *Novel*, which Johnson has described as 'a smooth tale, generally of love'; but which we would rather define as 'a fictitious narrative, differing from the romance, because accommodated to the ordinary train of human events, and the modern state of society.'" Scott then produced an elaborate history of the romance, not the novel—this edition of the encyclopedia has no separate entry for novel—and his essay shows that he regarded the novel as a modern form of the romance *even though* he had described them as contrasting modes. Thus Scott simultaneously posits romance as an overarching historical and generic term and as one term in an atemporal opposition. To confuse matters further, the eighth edition of the *Britannica*, published in America in 1859, used Scott's essay (in volume 19), and added a postscript on "modern romance and novel," identifying the novel as a modern form that superceded not the old romance, but the *drama*.

Following Scott, when reviewers before 1860 laid out a history of prose fiction, they generally used the term romance to refer to the form throughout the ages and the term novel to imply a modern type distinguished by its concentration on the ordinary and the contemporary. Then they slid into using the term romance to mean premodern types of novel, those produced in the past century that had depended on supernatural and marvelous events to resolve their plots and to achieve their effects. What they did *not* do in this approach was use the term romance to refer to any contemporary work at all; inevitably, the word was associated with older works. As a *Harper's* critic observed in a notice in July 1857, "Derby and Jackson have tempted the throng of novel-readers to fall back on the ancient favorites of their grandmothers by the publication of a neat edition of the world-famous romances of Mrs. Radcliffe, and Jane Porter's *Thaddeus of Warsaw* and *Scottish Chiefs*. It is a curious experiment to try the effect of these high-spiced productions of a past age on readers who have been trained in the school of nature and reality, as successfully illustrated by Scott and Cooper."

At the same time, when the term was used to refer to a contemporary work in a way that singled that work out from the
overclass of novels, then it referred to works of fiction that were
especially exciting, stirring, dramatic, action-packed, thrilling.
The highly wrought modern fiction, the sensation novel, and the
painfully exciting story were described as romances to suggest
that the reader would find passion, intensity, and thrilling interest. (This synchronic distinction may be thought of as derived
from the diachronic one, but there is no evidence that it actually
was.) For example, in a review of *The Heirs of Derwentwater* by E.
L. Blanchard, a critic for the *Literary World* said, "the book possesses much of the *materiel* of a true romance. An intricate plot
skillfully developed; an unflagging interest pervading every chapter, from the initial to the final; characters and incidents, far
removed from the common-place, challenge our attention, if not
our admiration. It is a tale of the dark and fearful school of Sue
and Reynolds; a picture of life in which the foreground figures
are blackened with crime or shrouded in gloom" (May 24, 1851).
"Strictly speaking, the work is a romance, not a novel. As a
romance it will be generally more acceptable than if it was a
novel" (*Peterson's* on Maria Cummins's *El Fureidis*, a highly rhetorical oriental tale, July 1960). "As a romance, or rather rhap-
sody, this volume can claim some rare attractions. It is strange,
wild, wonderful, and fantastic" (*Godey's* on *The Lone Dove*, November 1850).

Given this general association of the romance, when it was
distinguishable from the novel, with the highly wrought, the
heavily plotted, the ornately rhetorical, and the tremendously
exciting, one has to conclude that the work Hawthorne offered as
a romance rather than a novel—*The House of the Seven Gables*—was
particularly ill suited for the current distinction. And, in fact,
Hawthorne's habit of labeling his works romances called out
reviewer commentary on just this matter, a commentary that
shows the critics saw his definition as idiosyncratic and did not
necessarily accept it as properly descriptive of his practice. "In
the preface to this work . . . Mr. Hawthorne establishes a separation between the demands of the novel and the romance, and
under the privilege of the latter, sets up his claim to a certain
degree of license in the treatment of the characters and incidents
of his coming story. This license, those acquainted with the

writer's previous works will readily understand to be in the direction of the spiritualities of the piece, in favor of a process semi-allegorical, by which an acute analysis may be wrought out and the truth of feeling be minutely elaborated; an apology, in fact, for the preference of character to action" (*Literary World*, April 26, 1851). This review shows that to know what Hawthorne meant by his distinction, you had to know his previous works; it did not mesh with any current distinction.

Knickerbocker for May 1850 called *The Scarlet Letter* a psychological romance, by which it meant to indicate a unique literary product rather than one belonging to a common form. And the *Christian Examiner*, reviewing *The Marble Faun* in May 1860, wrote, "we doubt if Romance be the fit title of the story. . . . Here, where, as we are carried along in the order of external circumstances, we follow still more closely the course of moral struggles and exigencies, and find, in the playing out of the drama, our interest engaged, more than in any outward bearing and action, in the passionate strife, with its catastrophes of evil or issues of good, which marks the temptation and the developing of human spirits, we question whether the addition of 'The Romance of Monte Beni' belongs to the name. . . . The query, however, must not be thought the mere criticism of the title, but as put in the interest of a profound admiration for the thoughtful and serious spirit, and the skillful subtlety in the treatment."

In brief, insofar as Hawthorne used the term romance to signal something to his readers, he seems to have confused them; to the extent that they could make sense of his definition, it struck them as wrong. Readers would expect a romance to contain intensity, passion, excitement, and thrills resulting from ornate rhetorical treatment and from a focus on action. Hawthorne did not deliver these.

The main general discussions of the term romance in this era developed idiosyncratic definitions with no necessary application to the actual practice of fiction writers of the time; the idea of American romance that now controls so much American literary history is equally idiosyncratic and "theoretical." Discussions of the term as though it were historically given, or as though its examples are fixed and known, quickly become arguments for granting romance status to one or another work. These arguments would be beside the point were it not now generally agreed that the most important works of American fiction are romances. This is a position that would have made no sense in 1850.

Historical Novels

Reviewers, especially before 1850, thought of the historical novel as a promising mode for the American novelist but did not suppose that the American historical novel would be essentially different from historical novels more generally. They did not, therefore, discuss American historical novels in terms different from those applied to other historical novels. In the era, an active discussion of the historical novel as a particular subgenre focused on its peculiar formal requirements, both as they were (or were not) satisfied in individual instances and as they distinguished the historical novel from the main variety of modern novel. The only type of historical novel calling for special treatment was the "classical novel," a novel dealing with ancient Greece or Rome and providing particular difficulties because of the remoteness of the subject matter from the knowledge (and perhaps interests) of contemporary readers.

In following the terms of reviewer commentary, it is important to see that the historical novel was thought of as a modern form developing simultaneously with the novel proper, the fiction brought home to everyday life. The *North American*, in a July 1822 review of *The Spy*, spoke of "that commodious structure, the modern historical romance," and a review in the *Christian Examiner* for January 1847 also noted that "the historical novel is a comparatively recent invention." It is again important to note how, in these two instances, the terms novel and romance interchange; it would be false to this discourse to differentiate the historical fiction from the novel proper by defining it as a romance over against a novel. "A new historical romance, and founded on the scenes of Indian warfare which . . . present rich materials to the novelist" (*Harper's*, April 1851).

There was no doubt at all in any reviewer's mind about whether a work at hand was or was not a historical novel, because the distinction was so easy to make. Whereas the main form of novel was set in the present, the historical novel was set in the past and made use of the historical record, to which it had to be faithful. At the same time, it displayed the leading formal principle of the novel: it featured a narrated and *invented* plot. Because the novel proper was an invention in its most important aspect, its plot, and because the "plots" of history could not be invented—because, perhaps, history had no plots—some reviewers thought the historical novel a formal impossibility, a hybrid that betrayed either the form of fiction or the form of history. Most reviewers, however, though separating the historical from the fictional elements in the novel, saw the historical novel as a valid form whose achievement consisted precisely in the successful merging of two different modes, the successful carrying out of two unlike responsibilities.

Thus reviews of historical novels were apt to take one or more of three lines: to discuss the fidelity, or lack of it, to historical fact (the reviewers never thought of written history as substantially different from real history); to discuss the success or failure of the work as a plotted fiction; or to discuss the work's merging or failing to merge these two separate requirements into a unity. To write, as did the *Tribune*, that "the story is carried forward with great skill and in its historical portions with strict adherence to the recorded annals" (April 16, 1841) was to produce praise specific to the historical novel. In Joseph Holt Ingraham's *Lafitte*, "the professor has vigorously adhered to the historical truth of the naval and military proceedings connected with the investment and battle of New Orleans. . . . A beautiful love story is gracefully interwoven" (*Mirror*, June 11, 1836); in *Grayslaer*, "many of the characters and incidents are historical and Mr. Hoffman has connected them skillfully with the fictitious narrative" (*Mirror*, July 11, 1840).

Reviewing Bulwer's *Rienzi*, *Knickerbocker* faulted its history. "Mr. Bulwer has been obliged, for the sake of effect, to do violence to history, and to concentrate in his narrative many events which, in the true records of the times, occupy a much wider space, and are scattered here and there without any connection. . . . Though each individual deflexion from the straight line of historical truth may be small, yet the sum of all is considerable; and the whole . . . is calculated to produce decidedly injurious impressions. . . . These experiments ought not to be tried upon so important a subject as history" (February 1836).

Yet though many historical novels were seen as defective in their fidelity to specific historical incidents, they were more commonly criticized for weakness of plot. Though "many characters, well-known to history, are introduced to our notice, and managed with considerable tact and discretion," still "the domestic incidents, and indeed those parts of the work which are purely fictitious, do not strike us so favorably. . . . It is to be regretted, that a more attractive plot could not have been devised by the authoress, wherewith to interweave the striking events which the records of the times have presented to our hand" (*Knickerbocker* on *The Outlaw*, March 1836). *Graham's* found Cooper's *Mercedes of Castille* invaluable as history but "well-nigh worthless as a novel"; the "necessity of adhering closely to fact in his romance, is the true secret of its want of interest" (January 1841). "We rank Mr. James higher as a historian than a novelist. His romances [note again the synonyms novel and romance] indeed seem to be produced chiefly from his desire to display his historical learning, and his characters are generally little more than puppets set up to show off the effects of his researches" (*Tribune*, August 2, 1842). "Notwithstanding the vividness and value of the work as a curious, elaborate, and varied illustration of history, [Bulwer's *Harold*] is, when viewed as a mere *romance*, one of the most tedious we ever encountered. Indeed, if regarded in this light solely it is inferior in continuity of interest to the flimsiest of Mr. James's tales" (*Literary World*, July 15, 1848).

Failure of balance was a third flaw in historical fiction, as this excerpt from *Knickerbocker* on Simms's *The Partisan* makes evident: "an apparent duplicity of plot strikes us as a prominent defect, dividing, as it does, the interest of the reader between the fictitious and the strictly historical portions of the work" (January 1836). This was, in fact, the most common observed defect of historical fiction. *Graham's* thought Bulwer's *Harold*, though the author's "most successful attempt at writing an historical novel," still "rather an attempt than a performance. . . . Fact and fiction are tied rather than fused together. . . . The work is not homogeneous. At times it appears like history, but after the mind of the reader has settled down to a historical mood, the impression is broken by a violent intrusion of fable, or an introduction of modern sentiment or thought" (September 1848).

The *Literary World*, in a review of Lydia Maria Child's *The*

Rebel, expatiated on the historical form. "The great defect of this, as of most historical novels, is that the historical events which are brought before the reader's attention are not connected with those of a domestic nature to which he is expected to give his attention. . . . To combine these elements, the historical and the domestic interest, by not solving the difficulty by merging the one in the other, and presenting an amplified historical incident in lieu of the imaginative creation of which the novel should consist, is no easy task" (July 27, 1850). The implication of the *Literary World's* rather obscure syntax here is that the historical novelist tended to sacrifice the fictional story to the historical narrative rather than accepting the artistic responsibility of a novelist to make up an original fiction, and thereby "really" wrote history rather than a historical novel. A *Godey's* reviewer disagreed with the *Literary World* on this aspect of Child's book but affirmed the same criterion for judging: the author "has been very successful in connecting an interesting domestic tale with the thrilling political events which preceded the American Revolution" (September 1850). The *Home Journal* said G. P. R. James's "fidelity to historical fact and local scenery is unimpeachable; and the interest of his stories is well-sustained" (September 6, 1851). As late as July 1857, in a decade when the historical novel had apparently dropped out of fashion, the *North American* saw in J. G. Holland's *The Bay Path* proof "that the gifts of the novelist and the historian are not incompatible. The characters of his tale are well conceived and well sustained, and the story . . . is interesting from beginning to end."

The particular historical matter of the novel under review was routinely noted, but only in the case of the "classical novel" did a specific subject seem to imply particular formal or technical demands. "Classical fiction is a dangerous field. . . . The writer must not only be a thorough scholar, but possess that fine power of the imagination, which can withdraw him, bodily, so far into the distance of the antique, as to make him lose all vision of the present with its utterly new forms and customs" (*American Review,* February 1847). To write a good classical novel, the novelist had to be a learned person, far more so than the normal education of the day provided. The audience with learning sufficient to judge the historical faithfulness of the representation would be very small. In that the classical era was unimaginably unlike the nineteenth century, the common ground between the reader and the classical novel was thought to be virtually nonexistent.

"It is a difficult undertaking to produce a fiction the scenes of which are laid in times so long past, while the whole tone of the action, the sentiments, and habits of thought of the characters, and the details of private life, have so little analogy with existing circumstances" (*Literary World*, April 14, 1848). "It is a difficult task to infuse life into times so remote, and when manners and modes of thought were so different from what they are now" (*Peterson's*, February 1858). The very storytelling gifts that the classical novel required to make it live for a contemporary reader were those that the learned classicist probably lacked, since accuracy rather than imagination was his strength. The particular difficulty of the enterprise led reviewers to single out examples of the genre that succeeded. William Ware's *Zenobia* was one that "has taken its place beside the standard fictions which scholars have written to illustrate the periods of classical and oriental civilization. . . . *Zenobia*, from the authenticity of its details, the interest of its narrative, and the singular purity of its style, has been recognized as an entirely successful contribution to this noble department of literature" (*Sartain's*, April 1848).

The Roman Traitor, by Henry William Herbert, was another widely reviewed success. "This novel of Mr. Herbert's is very highly commended by scholars as well as common readers; its classical accuracy being as striking as its story is interesting" (*Sartain's*, January 1848). "A successful specimen of perhaps the most difficult species of fictitious composition, that of a romance founded on fact in the annals of classical antiquity. For accuracy of delineation, splendor of diction, and the dramatic use of historical personages, this novel is not surpassed by any modern production of its kind" (*Harper's*, November 1853). "The truthfulness of this novel to the age it describes, is not less than its merit as a fiction," a *Peterson's* review agreed in the same month; "from first to last the most intense interest is felt by the reader. Few novelists have been successful in their efforts to recall the classic age. . . . But Mr. Herbert, triumphing over every difficulty, has reproduced the days of Cicero as vividly as Scott did those of Feudal times." But one *Southern Literary Messenger* reviewer dismissed the book along with the genre: "it is from no want of dramatic ability that this failure proceeds but from the evident impossibility of interesting us in the men of antiquity by the familiar agency of fiction. We must have something in common with the dramatis personae or we will care nothing about them" (October 1853).

Since the historical novel was formally different from other novels, its effect was also different. A successful historical novel could recreate the past so vividly as to give the reader an authentic experience of a different time and place. "Herein lies the usefulness of this kind of novel," a *Mirror* review explained (July 7, 1839). "People will not read history with sufficient attention to make it familiar, but when the naked truth is clothed in 'a coat of many colors,' all are ready to admire." "Historical novels are not only the most instructive, but the most thrilling" (*Southern Literary Messenger*, December 1843). "We own to a predilection for the historical novel, because, if honestly and capably written, it not only affords intellectual pleasure to the reader, but gives us, as in a mirror, the very spirit of the past" (*Peterson's*, January 1856).

The *Literary World* in a December 25, 1847, review referred to a "deluge of historical romance," but by July 1855 *Putnam's* would observe that historical fiction had gone out of date. After 1836 *Knickerbocker*, which had regularly reviewed historical novels, noticed no more of them, and in the *North American* there is a hiatus between April 1838 and July 1857. The generation of American historical novelists, including Simms, Child, Sedgwick, Cooper, and others, did their major work before the 1840s. Hawthorne was not thought of as a historical novelist. (Of course, his work was considered sui generis, and in any case his historical fictions were almost all written in the short form.) The *Christian Examiner* complained about Hawthorne's "gross and slanderous imputation that the colleague pastor of the First Church in Boston, who preached the Election Sermon the year after the death of Governor Winthrop, was a mean and hypocritical adulterer, and went from the pulpit to the pillory to confess to that character in presence of those who had just been hanging reverently upon his lips. How would this outrageous fiction, which is utterly without foundation, deceive a reader who had no exact knowledge of our history! . . . We cannot admit the license of a novelist to go the length of a vile and infamous imputation upon a Boston minister of a spotless character" (September

1852). Nobody else seemed to think that *The Scarlet Letter* was a historical novel about the Puritans, though many other Puritan novels were labeled and reviewed as such.

American Novels

As the references to French novels in chapter 9 will have shown, American reviewers assumed that nationality entered into the creation of a literary work in a variety of ways mostly beyond the author's control. As products of a particular nation, writers inevitably reflected the attitudes of the society that had acculturated them. In the case of the novel, too, writers were likely to set their fictions in their own time and place; hence the "pictures of life" their works reflected were in fact pictures of their own society. Many examples could be cited in which reviewers grouped novels together by national origin; in doing so they were less interested in analyzing the culture than in identifying, for reader benefit, aspects of the form that might strike them as "foreign," though in the case of French fiction the effort was rather to make certain aspects of the novels *seem* foreign—to distance the reader from an unacceptable morality rather than to close a cultural gap.

The "novel proper" was, to a considerable degree, itself a particular national product, the creation of the British nation. Why, the *North American* asked in July 1827, is "this species of elegant literature so peculiarly suited to English genius?" It answered: "the most ample materials for popular fiction will undoubtedly be found in a country whose political institutions allow an entire freedom of social intercourse, and consequently a perfect display of character; where an equal security of personal and civil rights encourages, in every individual, the entire development of his intellectual and moral energies, in the career best suited to his genius, of ambition or of wealth; and where this entire freedom of selection and action in the commerce of life, has distributed society into a multitude of classes, each independent of the others and set in distinct relief by its own peculiar habits of thought and occupation. . . . Whatever advantages may be presented to the novelist in the condition of the nation, they will all be ineffectual, if the free expression of his own sentiments be controlled by any other power than public opinion." To a very large but hardly surprising degree, reviewers assumed that American culture and British culture were closely related, versions of the same tradition and therefore not calling for the same familiarization that other national novels required; yet, given observable social differences, it was always possible that the "American novel," when it emerged, might turn out to have its own distinct qualities.

An interest in locating and identifying such a class of American novels, conceived as a purely descriptive task, sometimes coincided with but as often ran athwart frequent manifestos demanding the creation of a national literature. This is because nationality, as reviewers conceived of it, was inherently and unconsciously marked in all literary products, and it thus made little sense to ask writers to try to produce what they could not help creating. To "demand" a national literature was "absurd," as the *Home Journal* for June 3, 1854, pointed out. "Whatever is naturally peculiar in our character, views, and modes of life, does and always will exhibit itself without any assistance from us. . . . The complaint of a want of nationality in American literature is borrowed from the ill-founded judgments of English criticism. Even in this, our professed abettors of originality are not original."

The *Home Journal* makes clear that the call for national literature, whether originating in England or in answer to England, was an oddly unoriginal (and hence perhaps unamerican) phenomenon; and it also makes clear that, as a result of its origins, the call for literary nationalism was bound to an idea of literature that was English. Thus, even while reviewers identified the particular characteristics of the French, English, or Italian novel, it was always and only in its differences from the English work that an "American" literature was defined. The most powerful modern statements of the nature of American literature—Lionel Trilling's in "Reality in America," for example, or Richard Chase's in *The American Novel and Its Tradition*—incorporate precisely this same dualism: the American "romance" is distinguished only from the British "novel," not from the literary forms of any other nation.

The call for a national literature, though audible throughout our history, has been louder at some times than others and more likely to find expression in some contexts than others. Although two novelists active in the 1820s had been accepted as worthy representatives of an American literature—Catharine Sedgwick and James Fenimore Cooper—the first wave of American literary nationalism, at its height during the 1820s and 1830s, occurred before the novel emerged as the predominant literary genre, one that could be advanced as the potential vehicle of a nation's best literary efforts. And, in any case, literary nationalist manifestos were always far more common in commencement addresses, Fourth of July orations, and other set patriotic or occasional essays than in practical criticism. Thus, reviews of specific novels do not constitute a rich source of material on literary nationalism even though they are full of references to "American novels," and in turn the issue of literary nationalism is seldom developed with exclusive reference to the novel or novelists. Rather, on this issue theory and practice seem to be operating at a great distance from each other, because though hundreds of American novels were reviewed and identified as American, critics kept calling for truly American novels and bewailing their failure to appear.

The explanation of the suitability of the novel form to English life provided by the *North American* enables us to understand a conundrum that reviewers might face when trying to think, in the abstract, about what an American novel might be. It was not the absence of historical tradition or romantic association that might make the form difficult to produce; after all, the novel was a story of everyday modern life. It was, rather, the absence of the class structure, which gave the British novelist a way of cataloging his individual human beings and relating them one to another. If the novel depended profoundly on the class structure for its effects, then American novels could not, or ought not to be, written unless American society was also divided into classes.

This dilemma is not as acute as it might at first appear, however, and as subsequent American literary history has made it appear. First, it was entirely compatible with patriotism to assert that the United States *did* have a class structure, so long as one made clear that it was neither hereditary nor fixed, but rather one sensitive to individual traits, hospitable to honest ambition, ability, and merit. In fact America might, even more than England, be congenial to stories of "the development of his intellectual and moral energies, in the career best suited to his genius, of ambition or of wealth."

Second, one could perceive in the regions of the nation another

way, analogous to but different from the class structure, of organizing and discriminating customs and individual differences.
One could then claim—and did—that a truly national American
literature would emerge from careful treatment of the regions.
We have seen how the *North American* denied that Charles
Brockden Brown could be said "to have produced an American
novel" because his works did not exhibit "any thing of our native
character and manners," creating rather "those dark monsters of
the imagination, which the will of the master may conjure up
with an equal horror in the shadows of an American forest, or
amidst the gloom of long galleries and vaulted aisles." The essay
then elaborated its idea of the mission of the American novel: to
present "*fac similies* of the peculiarities of the country, and consist
in strong graphic delineations of its bold and beautiful scenery,
and of its men and manners, as they really exist." It approved
accordingly of Sedgwick's *Redwood*, finding it "a conclusive argument, that the writers of works of fiction, of which the scene is
laid in familiar and domestic life, have a rich and varied field
before them in the United States" (April 1825).

In brief, literary critics handled the question whether there
could be an "American novel" by asserting that America was a
better place to write the English novel than England itself, because it possessed those aspects of English culture that enabled
the novel to come into being in a more decisive form than in
England. Since, as we have seen, the historical novel was itself a
special class of novel, the question of the American historical
novel was generally subsumed under the discussion of historical
fiction. Many reviewers, especially before 1840, thought it might
be particularly suited to nationalist literary purposes, for every
nation had a unique history. The *North American* said so in July
1822, in a long review of Cooper's *The Spy*, where it wrote of
looking forward to "the day, when that more commodious structure, the modern historical romance, shall be erected in all its
native elegance and strength on American soil, and of materials
exclusively our own." The 1820s were years when many American historical novels were written, and then reviewers—never
satisfied—complained about a surplus of "Indian novels." As the
form went out of vogue internationally, it lapsed in the United
States as well.

But what *would* be difficult to write in America and could *not* represent national character and culture was the old-fashioned romance. "Not that we would speak disparagingly of the wildest creations of romance, or have it thought that we are less affected than others, by those masterly efforts of a bold imagination, left to luxuriate in its own ideal world," the *North American* critic explained. "But we are not ambitious that scenes so purely imaginary, should be *located* on this side of the Atlantic." In any case it was not clear why anybody, and especially an American, should want to write such a work in modern times. The modern novel was a much more artistic form, as the *Christian Examiner* ironically pointed out: "the historical novel is a comparatively recent invention. . . . The purely imaginative romance greatly needed this resource to diversify its topics, to extend its range, and to give its airy fabrications substantial value. The style of Anne Radcliffe could not last. The age of supernatural machinery passed away . . . and nothing would have been left for many a modern novel-writer but to drivel in nauseating repetitions of an inane sentimentality. For the power of drawing the materials for an absorbing and elevating fiction out of the common and familiar scenes of daily observation is reserved for only a few superior spirits. . . . So that the alternative before a host of romancers has been reduced to this,—the historical romance, or nonsense" (January 1847). In mid-nineteenth-century America the work seen by the *London Leader* as particularly American would not have been accepted as worthy of the up-and-coming nation, and indeed in allotting work reminiscent of the European Dark Ages to the American mind, the British journal was patronizing.

National novels fell, for reviewing purposes, into four categories. First, novels of everyday life in which the particularly American version of the class system—a system adapted to upward (or downward) mobility according to individual talent and ambition—formed the basis for character presentation. Second, regional novels in which the manners and customs of the people, especially as they were controlled by features of the region, were displayed. Third, historical novels. Fourth, feminine novels *only when* the feminine is connected with a purer moral tone—in brief, the domestic novel was thought to have a particular affinity for America. Difficult as it may be to accept, in the early 1850s the two "national" novels were seen to be *Uncle Tom's Cabin* and *The Wide, Wide World;* and the addition of Susan Warner's *Queechy* to the list enabled the *North American* for January 1853 to write "lo and behold, an American literature!" But the reviewing record shows plenty of highly wrought American fiction as well as American examples of every other subgenre that critics recognized. Then as now, the attempt to identify a particularly "American" fiction was crosscut by the desire to make that fiction "superior"; the desire for American novels was subsumed under the campaign for better novels.

Not all journals in the 1850s by any means shared the *North American's* certainty that a national literature had at last emerged. Indeed, only four years previously, in October 1849, a reviewer in that journal had lamented: "we cannot refrain from expressing a regret that we have not a class of novels illustrative of American life and character, which does some justice to both. Novelists we have in perilous abundance. . . . But a series of national novels, illustrative of the national life, the production of men penetrated with an American spirit without being Americanisms, we can hardly plume ourselves on possessing." The most skeptical opinion was expressed in *Putnam's*. "We make it a point to read all the new American novels that come out, with the hope of by-and-by lighting upon one which deserves to be called American. But, the coming novel has not yet appeared; and we almost fear, that, like the American drama, which we have been looking for, it will not come at all. . . . We may always be dependent upon the old world for these luxuries, as we are for olives and claret" (March 1854). "Have we, as yet, besides Uncle Tom, a geniune novel of American life? Has anything like justice yet been done to the peculiarities of the several parts of the nation? Are not the experiences of the emigrant and the settler full of tragic incident, full of pathos, full of stirring adventure, and not without their humorous side?" (May 1856). *Harper's*, too, remarked in May 1856 that "there is, as yet, no American novel."

How did those who felt that no American novels had emerged explain it? *Putnam's* in its May 1856 review decided that the reason was haste: "as the general life of the nation, so the literary life, is hurried." In April 1857 it suggested that the problem was pure bad luck—the emergence of American fiction just happened to occur in a period that saw the rise of remarkable geniuses in England. "The cisatlantic muse was abashed." But if the artist was in part the product of his society, then the emergence of genius (or its failure to emerge) could not be purely fortuitous. *Harper's* (October 1857) maintained that for American artists "the national life is not so much their inspiration as it is the object they would inspire. . . . They have not risen genially out of the national mind. . . . Surrounding influences were hostile rather than sustaining to their genius." The rich field of American life had one great inadequacy—it was hostile to literature.

Here is a rare statement of the idea on which much American literary history now depends. It is well, then, to note that the theory emerged as a means of accounting for the absence of genius among American authors rather than explaining a characteristic American genius in literature. Given the demand—which I have noted earlier—for geniality as an aspect of the greatest literary spirits, the fact that American authors could not "rise genially out of the national mind" meant that there could not be a truly American literature. That is what the *Harper's* reviewer was really saying. This position (no doubt in part adopted because *Harper's* was a major publisher of British books) could not provide much comfort to American authors striving for literary eminence. Later critics, of course, were bored with geniality and were able to find in hostility—a hostility they explained as the legitimate and inevitable response to an uncongenial environment—the source of American literary genius rather than an explanation for its failure to develop.

Nevertheless, the allegation that the nation was hostile to fiction as such is manifestly untrue, however convenient or attractive it has come to seem. The sheer number of novels published and reviewed makes this clear ("novelists we have in perilous abundance"), as do the innumerable references throughout the reviews to the incredible appetite of readers for any and all novels. It has, indeed, been part of my findings that Americans were more attached to novels than to any other literary form; and they were a reading people (as, perhaps, they are no longer). Therefore novelists above all other writers might have been expected to have only the most genial relations with the surrounding mind. Given that so many of the novels reviewed were written by Americans and were American in their subject matter (more than half of the eight hundred or so individual titles in my sample were American in origin), no claim that Americans preferred foreign works can be defended. But why, after all, should the fiction-loving public prefer, as novels, the grim fantasies of *The Scarlet Letter* or *The Blithedale Romance* to the thrilling stories of female triumph written by E. D. E. N. Southworth? Why should they be interested in works that sought to scold, guide, or otherwise patronize them and assert authorial superiority? Why take any special pleasure in works embodying self-conscious decisions to be "national"? Why, on the other hand, did reviewers in the presence of so many American books with American settings continue to insist that there were no novels that "deserved" to be called American? When Hawthorne complained about scribbling women, he was not complaining about absence of novels, but about superfluity—superfluity of what he deemed bad novels. Again, the normative and the descriptive have merged. The kinds of book Americans were producing were not, apparently, the kinds of book critics wanted. But what they wanted, what Hawthorne wanted, and what readers wanted, were three different things.

12

Authors

Reviewers of novels in the American midcentury approached them, as we have repeatedly seen, as individual formal entities controlled by a unitary though complex plot. At the same time, as many quotations in earlier chapters show, they were greatly interested in authorship, constantly relating books to their authors and relating the books by a given author to one another. Their interest was controlled by the concept of the author as a literary practitioner rather than a biographically interesting individual, and it operated between two boundary conditions. At the one extreme was the author's private life, in which reviewers were generally not interested—with the continuing and nontrivial exception of women authors. At the other extreme was the favorite conception of genius, which transcended individual authority and raised the work into a higher realm.

Such a level was attained only rarely, even in the novel form where relative freedom from rules might have been thought to make it more possible than in other literary modes; and reviewers were always on the lookout for it. Again, the notion of genius is applied with the same striking and important exception—the woman author. In both cases these exceptions, though they led in different directions, stemmed from the reviewers' feeling that women ought to write not as individuals, but as exemplars of their sex. Their private lives were scrutinized to see whether they lived womanly lives; the category of genius was denied to them because, writing as women rather than as individuals, they could not attain something that was in its essence the highest expression of individuality.

Here are examples of the continuous reviewer preoccupation with authors. From just a few months of reviewing in *Arthur's Home Magazine*, we find the following: "The author of *The Initials* has produced another work of extraordinary interest" (July 1853); Simms is "at the head of American novelists," and his new work "may be safely pronounced one of Mr. Simms's best efforts, and, being of a lighter and rather more humorous cast than many of his previous novels, will most probably become even more popular" (August 1853); "it is always safe to recommend a novel by Mrs. Gray, since we well know that it illustrates moral principles by examples admirably wrought, and inculcates no lesson but what tends to purify and instruct" (September 1853); "the popularity of the various novels and nouvellettes written by Mrs. Hentz, rests upon a firmer, purer and altogether superior basis to that of many of her contemporaries" (May 1854). The move between author and novel in these and hundreds of other instances is automatic. Each novel is invariably conceived of as a human product created by a singular human being whose familiar presence acts as a signal of the sort of work the reader will find in any given instance. Author, then, after subgenre classification, is the chief way of describing a book, and the corpus of works by a given author becomes a way of describing an author. "The mere announcement of any thing from the sparkling brain of the Bachelor of the *Albany*, is sufficient to raise anticipations of brisk and business-like satire, of felicitous expression, and of good-natured representation of the follies of conventional life" (*Graham's*, July 1849). Granting that every novel was a unique instance of a literary form, reviewers also assumed that all works by one person had real resemblances and could be properly thought of as forming one class.

"A new work of fiction by that excellent domestic writer, Mrs. Ellis, is sure to meet with a cordial welcome in families"; "any work from the pen of Miss Sinclair is sure to be welcomed in America"; "we are among those who recognize in James a sterling historical novelist"; "possessing the same elements of passion, and a certain dramatic force, which have made her books popular" (*Home Journal*, February 8, March 1, September 6, September 20, 1851). "There is no author living who can surpass this man in force and brilliancy of description" (*Peterson's*, July 1845). "Dumas is one of the few French novelists we can recommend";

"a novel of remarkable power and interest, fully equal to the best of Miss Sewell's productions" (*Godey's*, May 1851, October 1855). "No living American author but Hawthorne could have drawn such a character as Clifford" (*Peterson's*, June 1851).

The novel frequently becomes syntactically identical with its author, the one noun substituted for the other. Thus reviewers believed that the totality of the author's work constituted a second, related unity, beyond the unity of form in each novel. The progress and development of that larger unity represented a sort of second story that novels told. "Had this work been put forth anonymously, we should have commended it as a production of considerable merit and more promise. But it is strikingly inferior to the former productions of Dr. Bird, and, measured by his own standard, it is found wanting" (*Mirror*, May 25, 1839). "Never having read any work by this author before, we can hardly judge of it by comparison"; "in the present volume Mrs. Marsh has not been quite as successful as in her former productions generally"; "though exhibiting continually the same genius that shone in *Alton Locke*, this work . . . is, by no means, equal to its predecessor." James's books "are getting to be . . . made to sell. They are always readable, however, and will have numerous admirers"; "presents its author's genius in a new light"; "possesses even more attractiveness and opulence of incidents than is characteristic of preceding works from the same pen" (*Godey's*, November 1848, July 1856, August 1859). The "closure" of this authorial plot does not occur until the career ends, and thus the connection of books with their authors left open the promise of more new novels from the same pen—casting the evolving corpus into the shape of a dramatic serial.

Authors develop reputations, are associated with certain kinds of work, yet change (for better or worse) over time, so that it is important to know who they are, and so that they are part of the novel in a different sense from the narrator's presence discussed in chapter 7. That is, they are there as individual selves as opposed to literary roles. Yet these individual selves are authorial rather than personal selves, defined by the work they produce, not the circumstances of their lives. The relationship between author and novels is entirely circular, wholly self-contained, and purely textual. "*The Glens* sufficiently resembles his former productions to betray the identity of their origin. With greater compression of style, and a more natural development of incident, it exhibits the same passion for dealing with legal evidence, and the same acute and comprehensive analysis of character, which distinguish the other writings of the author. He certainly possesses a rare power of clothing the darker emotions of the soul with a lifelike naturalness, and depicting the excesses of stern and sullen passion in colors that are no less abhorrent than truthful"; "it exhibits her characteristic glow and energy of style, her power of effective grouping, and her facility in applying the forms and colors of the material world to the illustration of a narrative" (*Harper's*, July 1851, August 1858).

The qualities of the author reside in choice of subject, habits of treatment, characteristic tone, and the like. If these characteristics originate in the personal life, that life is not directly present in the work. Indeed, the few comments about the private life (of a *male* author) tend to point out disjunctions between life and writing. For example, this on Dickens: "how any gentleman of five-and-thirty, with a wife and children and a proclivity to dinner-parties and their accompaniments, can sit coolly in his library, month after month, elaborating such horrors, is quite a mystery to us" (*Sartain's*, February 1848). Another comment about the impact of life on art, or the traces of life in art, is this on John Pendleton Kennedy: "it is very plain that Mr. Kennedy has had scant time to study, frame, and perfect the novels, which during this busy life, he has given to the public; and consequently, *Swallow Barn*, which required no labor of this sort, which was but a collection of sketches without a plot . . . is, as a whole, the best of his productions" (*New York Review*, January 1842). The comment explains a weakness rather than analyzes a motif; so do several remarks on Melville as his work radically changed its form (as his authorial story became incoherent)—for example, on *Mardi*: "'vaulting ambition has overleaped itself.' Every page of the book undoubtedly exhibits the man of genius, and facile writer, but exhibits also pedantry and affectations. We are confident that the faults are attributable to the praise . . . that the author's other delightful works, *Typee* and *Omoo*, received, especially on the other side of the Atlantic" (*American Review*, September 1849). Several journals, to be sure, featured columns of literary gossip, but these concerned themselves with the public lives of authors—their comings and goings, the progress of their new novels, and the like.

Having assigned classificatory power to the concept of the author, reviewers were enabled to make connections between works by a single author; they also agreed, however, that distinct authorial identity was not equally possessed by all writers or equally present in all novels. And the reviews show that, where individuality was marked, the novel was thought to be better than where it was not. Here are instances from *Graham's:* Melville's *Mardi* possesses "magical touches which indicate original genius"; "the peculiarities of Cooper's genius are so impressed on the minds of so many thousands of readers, that it is almost an impertinence to mention them anew"; "the sharpest test to which an author can be subjected [is] has he novelty of nature? Is he an absolutely new power in literature?" "brimful of the author's genius"; "contains, with all its faults, enough genius to make a reputation" (June 1849, July 1851, September 1852, October 1852, November 1854). Characteristically, the notion of individuality slides into a notion of genius as a transcendent, transindividual possession of the artist that vindicates art and humankind. "To reveal genius is the highest office of literature" (*Putnam's* on Dickens, March 1855). This kind of genius is a surplus in the work, something beyond the genre's requirements yet not incompatible with it.

The problems of the concept of genius, as we well know, have to do with evaluating a given rule-breaking work: because genius breaks normal rules and operates according to its own, an unruly work may be either an instance of genius or a case of ineptness or presumption. In their own times, Hawthorne was perceived as a real genius and Melville only as aspiring. "The real cause for congratulation in the appearance of an original genius like Hawthorne, is not that he dethroned any established prince in literature, but that he founds a new principality of his own" (*Graham's* on *The Blithedale Romance*, June 1852). In contrast, as the *Literary World* said, reviewing *Mardi*, "originality belongs only to ripe minds, who have a perfect knowledge of their depth and their extent. . . . Pretension to excessive novelty has in this case resulted only in an awkward and singular mélange of grotesque comedy and fantastic grandeur" (August 11, 1849), and the *American Review* saw in *Pierre* only "a morbid craving after originality" (November 1852). Reviewers knew they might err about whether a work was an expression of genius in this transcendent sense. Nevertheless, they operated on the assumption that a really striking genius would declare itself unmistakably through the communication of that sense of power and force that was consistently seen to be at the heart of the reading experience. The genius, then, exceeded requirements while the would-be genius fell short. To go beyond these rules and ask how genius communicated was to ask how language worked and whether human beings were essentially so constructed as to be able to understand each other. The first question remained unanswered and the second unasked: the powers of genius were magical, and if people could not understand each other, authorship was not possible.

We may identify reviewers' candidates for genius rank through the frequency with which they reviewed them and made such reviews an occasion for overviews of their accomplishments. Repeatedly selected were Scott, Cooper, Bulwer, Dickens, Thackeray, Hawthorne, and—usually taken as a group—those pesky "French novelists" including George Sand, Balzac, Eugene Sue, Dumas, and (somewhat less frequently) Victor Hugo. The French novelists presented a serious problem to the reviewer who, wishing to place the highest office of art in its moral tendency, had to acknowledge the genius of a group of irreclaimably immoral authors. George Sand presented a double problem, in that she also raised gender issues in a particularly vivid form. Reviewers devoted considerable space to debate about whether Charlotte Brontë was or was not a genius, and here too the gender issue gave them difficulty.

Female Genius

While reviewers almost never considered the private lives of male authors, they did discuss the lives of women. Throughout the period, journals (including women's magazines) featured essays on women writers, giving biographical information. Such information also appeared in individual reviews, and the womanliness of a piece of writing was a matter for discrimination and praise in a way that manliness was not. "We entertain the profoundest respect for female genius," the *Democratic Review* announced forebodingly, reviewing a reissue of *Pride and Prejudice* in March 1855, "and are well assured that, when confined to its proper sphere, its productions are not only ornamental, but requisite to the completeness of any national literature. We would not see our wives or sisters plunge into the arena of politics or meddle with pursuits unsuited to them; but in the walks of fiction or romance, in song, and in all those branches of intellectual culture where tenderness and sensibility are required, the finer and more delicate mind of woman might greatly aid the full development of human nature. Miss Edgeworth, Miss Porter, Mrs. Sigourney, Mrs. Hemans, and Miss Landon might well be pointed out as exemplars of female genius working steadily in its true direction." The *Democratic Review*'s choice of authors represents a clear effort to impose an identity on women authors, as the term "true" in the phrase "true direction" makes clear. (Yet the willingness of the *Democratic Review* to allow that women might be authors represents an advance over the situation a half-century earlier.)

The category of female author was not symmetrical with that of the male author because there was no such latter category; there were authors and female authors. Female authors were examples of a special case defined in such a way as to put genius out of woman's reach. It need hardly be said that no man would have wished to distinguish himself by achieving female genius. To achieve female genius, to signal oneself as a female writer, was to take on a variant or deviant authorial role, author as woman. Author as woman accepted use and morality as her fictional aims, and she sacrificed greatness and genius. Women authors and women editors and reviewers cooperated in the construction of this special role for women authors. The purpose of this role was to neutralize the threat of the woman author by setting her to work on behalf of true womanhood. Here, for example, is a revealing extract from *Peterson's* by its editor Ann Stephens, a lead article entitled "Literary Ladies" (April 1843):

> Miss Sedgwick and Mrs. Sigourney, Mrs. Child and one or two others, exerted mental wealth to render domestic life lovely, and to persuade their sisters into content with the blessings of their natural [*sic*] condition. Their fiction was full of truthfulness, and the sweet lessons which it gave were calculated to exalt woman in her

own sphere, but never to entice her beyond it. They have taught the ambitious of the sex, in many a beautiful page, and by their own blameless lives, that women may become great, yet remain humble and affectionate, and that the most lofty ideal is not necessarily divorced from the useful. . . . At the time these ladies devoted themselves to literature, they might indeed tremble for the opinion which men would form of them, for at that time a woman who wrote books was considered almost a rival to masculine intellect, and regarded as something strange and unapproachable by her sister women. The division lines which are now so strongly drawn between the masculine and feminine mind, were very little understood in that day, and the idea that a woman of genius could be domestic, cheerful, and unpretending, would have been considered visionary in the extreme.

Observe Stephens's assertion that in the early decades of the nineteenth century would-be women authors had a great deal to fear, that in a context of male dominance their best strategy was to disarm male criticism by disarming themselves, since combat would invariably produce women's defeat. At the same time that the "strong division lines" restrict and structure a female personality, they also enable women writers to come into being. The condition of this enablement is that they will not compete with men. This approach was useful, perhaps necessary, in the earlier decades of the era; its "problem" from a feminist point of view is that many women were afraid to abandon it when the times changed sufficiently to allow for some relaxation of those divisions.

We may think of the woman novelist before, say, 1840 as engaging in a cottage industry that required protection in order to flourish. As early as October 1823 the *North American*, writing on Maria Edgeworth, commented that "an equal degree of merit in a female author, evinces a much greater mental vigor than in a man, and the whole constitution of society is so opposed to the development of the female mind in that degree of maturity and conscious power, which are requisite for a successful writer, that a moderate excellence implies much greater native talent." Said the *Mirror:* "we do not consider it exactly fair to judge of them by the same rigid rules which may be applied to the lucubrations of those who are ironically termed their lords and masters. . . .

Ladies have many difficulties to contend with in coming before
the public, of which male creatures may easily get the better.
Restricted as the former are to a much inferior knowledge of life
and the world, the choice of subjects is much more limited, their
style and expressions must be much more guarded, and their
delineations of the more hidden passions of human nature must,
in many instances, be much more feeble and imperfect. Female
talent, therefore, with a few brilliant exceptions, ought always to
be spoken of comparatively, in reference to itself, and not to that
of men" (September 3, 1842). It does not follow that because
women's experience is restricted, and their knowledge of the
world accordingly limited, their expression "must be much more
guarded." Another criterion has crept in; even if women had
experience and knowledge, the state of their relation to society as
a whole requires them to suppress the expression of it. The threat
of the woman author is balanced by a threat *to* the woman
author.

The bargain being struck here is that women may write as
much as they please providing they define themselves as women
writing when they do so, whether by tricks of style—diffuseness,
gracefulness, delicacy; by choices of subject matter—the domestic, the social, the private; or by tone—pure, lofty, moral, didactic. Where the novel, generally speaking, was defined as a field
for the expression of the individual author, possibly rising to
genius, it was defined in the case of the woman author as a field
for the expression of the sex, in which case genius in the large
sense is out of the question, since the most she can do is lose
herself in gender and hence sacrifice the individuality that is the
foundation of genius.

This bargain permits reviewers over and over to speak of the
"fair authoress" or evaluate the woman writer within the field
only of "lady writers," and it permits most of the field of novel
writing to be left to her in security. " 'Dear delightful woman' is
inking her fingers on both continents in endeavoring the amusement and instruction of novel readers; and by-and-bye the fields
of fiction, in the world of letters, will become crowded with
bonnets, shawls, and green parasols. . . . In revenge for the monopoly in the severer pursuits of literature held by the masculine
mind, womanhood is striving for the monopoly in novel writing.

And if she will allow the world a little of Dickens and Thackeray now and then, we will not oppose the establishment of the monopoly" (*Literary World*, March 9, 1850). Of course the severer pursuits of literature were superior; but what these reviewers were ignoring or forgetting, in "allowing" women this particular corner, was that the novel was the most popular literary form. In effect they were abandoning the novel in toto to women. The enforced sexual differentiation thus worked not only to the obvious disadvantage of women, but to the less obvious detriment of men who were writing for an audience that did not exist.

Thus, where the cult of the author leads in the man's case to the expression of his individuality with the possibility of genius at the end of the road, it leads in a different direction for the woman. For her it leads to the suppression of individuality and the substitution of the expression of her womanhood. This is also precisely what transpires in the criticism of women characters: for where character was everywhere to be individualized, that everywhere did not encompass female characters, who were rather to be "womanized" (see chapter 5). Across an unbridgeable divide we find the highest theoretical expressions of authorship regarding one another: the genius, and the woman. The most bizarre result of this compartmentalization, perhaps, was that in writing as women, female authors were not allowed to say what they knew about their own sex (see the *Mirror*'s comment quoted above), because their knowledge did not accord with the stereotype of the sex they were required to represent.

These generalizations must be qualified, however, because critics were much more rigid in their theoretical pronouncements about authors and authorship than in their reviewing practice. While women were expected to be moral as a matter of course, men were not excused from that requirement on the grounds of their masculinity. The likely feebleness of a woman's work was not exonerated, and women who wrote powerful works were praised; a powerful style and a gripping story were desiderata regardless of the gender of the author. Though virtually no woman writer transcended boundaries to attain genius, women authors were treated as individuals and the nature of each particular genius was isolated and described, usually, without invidious judgment.

Special Cases

Although genius was the hoped-for end of every novelistic venture, it was the special rather than the usual case when it occurred, and on the whole readers did not expect to encounter genius in novels as a matter of course. Those authors who were the subject of repeated essays on account of the extraordinary caliber of their achievement in a genre were not to be taken as defining the genre itself. The novel was more congenial to expressions of genius than some other literary forms, but true genius was rare in it as elsewhere. When a woman author's work called enough attention to itself to be scrutinized for genius in the transcendent sense, however, the terms of the discussion changed; where genius was wholly praised in men, in women it was a controversial possession. In the antebellum era only three women authors were discussed in American magazines as though they were eligible to be thought of as examples of genius: George Sand, Harriet Beecher Stowe, and Charlotte Brontë. In each instance the writing about them was troubled.

George Sand was the most difficult case of all, because she was the only one of these three whose genius could not be debated; because the morality of her private life was problematic to say the least; because it was the intention of her writings to attack the one moral position to which women above all were supposed to be committed, the sanctity of secular marriage; and because her intellectual powers were clearly equal to or greater than those of most men. The *North American* wrote (July 1841), "none but a mind and heart thoroughly diseased could pour forth such effusions, while the impetuosity of manner, the vivid descriptions, the eloquent portraiture of passion, and the richness of style prove, but too evidently, that a noble nature has gone astray" and then added that "the writer is resolute in her determination to unsex herself in the general tone and execution of her works, in the boldness of her theories, and the warmth and freedom of her descriptions." Up until this last point, the review takes the same line toward Sand that it would take toward any gifted but immoral writer; then the sex enters as an additional judgment.

In a similar mode, the *Christian Examiner* (March 1847) ran a long essay devoting more than twenty-two pages to an attack on the morality of her work, only to conclude, "of the literary execution of George Sand's writings, in general, it is not easy to speak in terms of too high commendation. . . . She writes always with beauty, often with singular power. . . . Among the intellectual manifestations of the age she is one of the more remarkable phenomena. . . . She is equal, intellectually, to high endeavors and unusual achievements." Unfortunately, "the strength of her moral principles has not balanced the vigor of her mind," she exemplifies "genius wandering from rectitude," and her false principles result directly from the questionable morality of her life. "For the office of a genuine reformer it is to be feared she has unfitted herself. . . . We naturally require of a Magdalen, that she should be even farther removed, in repugnance, from every trace of the sin forsaken, than another." The fiercest attack on Sand found that "the wastefulness and prostitution of genius is ever a mournful ruin—in woman it is doubly melancholy" and concluded, "we blush for our sex and our species" (*Sartain's*, October 1851). It was signed with a woman's name—Miss Maria J. B. Browne. Sand had broken the unspoken agreement among women that they would write only as women—that is, only as men imagined or expected women to be.

In an earlier review *Sartain's* had acknowledged that "George Sand's books can hardly be noticed like other books" on account of "the acknowledged genius of the author. . . . The talent and even genius, of the writer is most obvious; and there is a certain awe attending the contemplation of genius, as of beauty, which bids us beware with what intent we approach it in the spirit of criticism. But . . ." (November, 1847). And the but triumphed, as it did again in September 1850 when, in an essay on Fredrika Bremer, George Sand's name came up: "the institution of marriage, the roots from which society springs, the groundwork upon which it stands, George Sand, with all the force of her genius and eloquence, seeks to degrade and destroy; while Fredrika Bremer would ennoble, not the institution of marriage only, but she would exalt it into that deeper and holier spiritual union, of which the actual marriage is but the symbol." One sometimes gets the impression that the critics' enthusiasm for the admittedly only modestly talented, though popular, Bremer lay in their ability to present her as an alternative or antithesis to the attractive and even more popular Sand.

"It is too late in the day to discuss the question, whether the writings of the personage variously called Aurore Dupin, Madame Dudevant, and George Sand, shall be introduced to the American people. A name which has excited equal terror and admiration abroad, is fast getting familiar among us. . . . We do not wish to be understood as underrating the talents of the author, or joining in the hasty condemnation of all her writings. She is a woman of great powers of mind, of a philosophical insight in the discrimination of character, of imagination expressed in her acute sympathies, and she conveys all this in a style of pure harmony" (*Literary World*, February 2, 1847). She has a "gifted but erratic muse. . . . It seems astonishing that one who is so much an artist as George Sand, should at times be led into such absurdities; but, after all deductions, we pronounce her the first of French novelists since Balzac died, and Victor Hugo devoted himself to politics" (*Putnam's*, September 1853).

A critic in the *American Review*, considering all the French novelists, began his discussion of Sand by announcing, "it does not please us to speak harshly of any person invested with the sanctity of the female form. But we must plainly state, that we regard her as one who has unsexed herself; who has thrown aside that winning softness and delicacy, which give to the female character its peculiar charm. . . . If, then, the current gossip of her associates is to be credited, George Sand constitutes one of that numerous class, of whom it is said, in strong but homely phrase, that 'they are no better than they should be'; and that assuming occasionally the masculine costume, she also habitually exercises the privileged vices which custom and society have restricted to the sex who wear the pantaloons." The review went on to say both that "we regard her as a gifted, reckless, unprincipled woman of genius" and that "we love and revere the female character too much to accept her either as a fit exponent or advocate of the feelings or sentiments of refined and virtuous women—those intermediate links between the men and the angels who, kept apart and above the contaminating influences to which the ruder sex are exposed, preserve inviolate that purity of heart and feeling, which makes a modest and true-hearted wife the best and highest good attainable below" (March 1846).

This rhetoric is only what a modern feminist might expect to find everywhere, so it is important to note that the *American*

Review's essay is an extreme statement. It does, however, share concerns expressed in milder reviews. Two of these are whether there can be a woman of genius, or whether a woman who is a genius has not lost her character as a woman; and whether there is not a close connection between the freedoms of genius and other kinds of freedoms. Certainly the review makes it seem that a woman of genius is unsexed, hence a biological monstrosity, hence not a genius or a woman either. But at the same time, in her unsexing Sand is associated with "a numerous class" who are "no better than they should be." The woman of genius is associated with a sexual liberty that, the journal admits, is known to quite a number of women, all of whom it is eager to define out of the sex along with Sand in favor of the "refined and virtuous women" who are "intermediate links between the men and the angels" and are produced by being "kept apart and above the contaminating influences to which the ruder sex are exposed." We are in the presence of the Victorian attempt to define the woman without sexual feeling as a representative of her sex and to see the sexed woman (in that horrible Victorian paradox) as one who has unsexed herself. The controlling fear is left unstated: the frightful possibility that Sand *does* speak for women, and in so doing puts the crucial social concept of woman in question.

The sexless woman, the modest and true-hearted wife who is advanced as the true woman, clearly cannot be a genius of any kind; indeed, from her ranks no "fit exponent or advocate" of anything can emerge. Such women would never take expounding or advocacy upon themselves. It follows almost inevitably, then, that a woman of genius will be unsexed and advocate values different from those of the "intermediate link." Thus no women can actually articulate women's values, and the ideal woman must content herself with being silent, or spoken for by men. Indeed, the *American Review*'s essay on George Sand is such a bespeaking. But its speaking, in turn, is put into question by Sand's popularity; for the numerous class that reads her cannot be totally composed of those who are no better than they should be. Certainly reviewers did not imagine they were writing to fallen women! Thus beneath all this rhetoric we sense that reviewers recognized perfectly well that George Sand was a woman and wrote about her as they did because of this recognition.

The same genius and advocacy in a male would occasion commentary and criticism (as it did, for example, in the instances of Eugene Sue and Balzac), but of a different sort. George Sand's peculiarity was to be a genius who was a woman and who wrote the kinds of book she did as a woman, women's books putting into question the very institution whose announced function was to keep women apart from and above life—marriage—in order that a female character be created and society allowed to continue on its orderly and undisturbed way. Because Sand testified against marriage as a woman and on behalf of women, her voice was particularly alarming.

In this context Margaret Fuller's defense of Sand in the *Tribune* was, though admirable, somewhat naive. *Consuelo*, she said, "is entirely successful, in showing how inward purity and honor may preserve a woman from bewilderment and danger, and secure her a genuine independence. Whoever aims at this is still considered by unthinking or prejudiced minds as wishing to despoil the female character of its natural and peculiar loveliness. . . . Miss Bremer, Dumas, and the Northern novelist, Anderson, make women who have a tendency to the intellectual life fail and suffer the penalties of arrogant presumption in the very first steps of a career to which an inward voice calls them in preference to the usual home duties. . . . If the heroines of the novelists we have named ended as they did, it was for want of the purity of ambition and simplicity of character" that Sand's heroines continue to exemplify (June 24, 1846). The purity and simplicity Fuller urged was, if it existed at all, the product of keeping women above and apart from the world, confining her to the "usual home duties," rather than a natural essence. Fuller's hope, for Sand and herself, was that feminism and woman's rights did not threaten the concept of the "female character," but obviously they did. And do. Sand subjected the concept to particular tension because she was, by all standards, a genius. She commanded acceptance as such and therefore raised the possibility that her genius was related to her freedom.

Because Sand was the only woman about whose genius there was no question and at the same time the only woman writer whose life was known to be less than blameless, hers was the most excruciating case of female authorship that reviewers faced in the entire period between 1820 and 1860. Another and perhaps ruder shock, however, was given to their sensibilities by Harriet Beecher Stowe's *Uncle Tom's Cabin*. Though by 1860 Stowe had not produced enough for reviewers to treat her as a genius in the class of Dickens or Thackeray, the one book was considered a work of genius and, though domestic and familial in its ideology, still strikingly in violation of the boundaries of an acceptable woman's literature. It addressed itself to political and social issues, areas supposed to be outside the woman's grasp; and it was unconciliatory and uncompromising—unfeminine, in a word—in its attitudes. After *Uncle Tom's Cabin*, other women authors who dealt with slavery were praised for doing so in the conciliatory spirit that was appropriate to the female mission.

"For Heaven's sake, Mrs. Stowe!" exclaimed the *Literary World* in its first of two reviews (April 24, 1852—see chapter 10 for more on antislavery fiction). "Wife of one clergyman, daughter of another, and sister to half a dozen, respect the cloud of black cloth with which you are surrounded, and if you *will* write of such matters, give us plain unvarnished truth, and strive to advise us in our trouble." Here we note how the writer's personal situation enters as an element of the commentary, and how Stowe vanishes into the cloud of black cloth, not her own skirts but the garments of the *men* of her family, and is asked to keep them in mind as she speaks. *Graham's* in its hostile review of "Black Letters" asserted that "our female agitators have abandoned Bloomers in despair, and are just now bestride a new hobby" (February 1853). As for the *Southern Literary Messenger*, which attacked *Uncle Tom's Cabin* with missionary fervor, it abandoned its usually approving albeit patronizing attitude toward women authors as enlighteners and elevators of the race for something much more savage and cruel. "We know that among other novel doctrines in vogue in the land of Mrs. Stowe's nativity . . . is one which would place women on a footing of political equality with men, and causing her to look beyond the office for which she was created—the high and holy office of matrimony—would engage her in the administration of public affairs. . . . On this ground she may assert her prerogative to teach us how wicked we are ourselves and the Constitution under which we live. But such a claim is in direct conflict with the letter of scripture. . . . '*I suffer not a woman to teach, nor to usurp authority over the man, but to be in silence*'" (October 1852). Two years later, the *Southern Liter-*

ary Messenger approvingly classified *Farmingdale* with *The Wide, Wide World* in a "department of letters eminently calculated to advance the cause of purity and religion. . . . We are quite sure that the sermons preached by these lady writers are of more use than many which are uttered from the pulpit" (July 1854). It seems clear that the causes of purity and religion were no longer living issues to this journal; woman was free to speak so long as she uttered nothing to any important purpose, and to teach so long as she did not presume to teach "us"—the reviewer and those he represented, the adult and dominant males of society.

Even more interesting is the *Southern Literary Messenger*'s second review of *Uncle Tom's Cabin* (December 1852), which began by describing a historical change in the mission of the novel over time. It has "descended from its graceful and airy home, and assumed to itself a more vulgar mission, incompatible with its essence and alien to its original design. Engaging in coarse conflicts of life, and mingling in the fumes and gross odors of political or polemical dissension, it has stained and tainted the robe of ideal purity with which it was of old adorned." Precisely the same image is used for the novel here as the *American Review* used for woman herself. The politicizing of the novel is analogous to the attainment of woman's rights for the woman; extraordinarily, from any conservative man's point of view, these movements were both being carried out by women themselves, something which was plainly inconceivable from the starting point of their thinking, which assumed that the intermediate link between men and the angels was woman's "natural" character, or that society had successfully conformed women to this design. In other words, the women who were doing these things, the Sands and the Stowes, ought not to exist. But they did. In its issue for June 9, 1860, the *New York Ledger* commented in a squib on women's suffrage that "there are 10,000 females in the City of New York, ay twice that number, with whom no modest woman would like to go in collision anywhere, least of all at the polls during the excitement of a hotly contested election. . . . Where is the respectable wife and mother that would choose to go herself, or send her daughters where they would have to mingle with the most degraded of the sex. . . . In the country, where there is more purity and decency than in cities, respectable married women might perhaps approach the polls without danger of con-

tamination or indignity, but not in dense communities . . . mix-
ing up all classes or both sexes at the polls." One gets a sense here
of a mass of women whose existence reviewers were trying not to
acknowledge, whose voices would expose the feminine mys-
tique—expose the existence of this female underclass, as well as
the existence of that secret female in the respectable woman. Any
deviation, on the part of speaking women, from an ideal of the
female voice became the occasion for a generalized gender terror
and called out a gender terrorism.

A third instance, in some ways the most revealing or curious of
these special cases, is that of Charlotte Brontë (sometimes con-
flated with Emily or Anne Brontë since *Wuthering Heights* and
The Tenant of Wildfell Hall were announced as being by the author
of *Jane Eyre*). *Jane Eyre* was reviewed at first as a man's work,
criticized for its masculine coarseness and praised for its extraordinary power and clear evidence of genius. Soon rumors circulated that the author was a woman, at which point the question of
the author's sex became an element of reviewer commentary.
Some maintained that the author was clearly a man, and when
Wuthering Heights, which they took to be even more obviously
masculine in character, appeared, they felt vindicated. Others
compromised by advancing the idea that *Jane Eyre* was the work
of a brother-sister team. Still others, though deciding for a woman author, allowed that in parts it seemed to have been written by
a man. When the author was definitely known to be a woman,
the feminine character of *Jane Eyre* was suddenly perfectly obvious to all. What nobody saw in this sequence of events, however, was that you had to know the gender of the writer before you
could see the book as a feminine product; that, in other words,
reviewers were creating rather than reporting the sexuality of the
text.

In October 1848, for example, the *North American* announced
firmly that "Currer Bell" was a brother-sister team because "the
work bears the marks of more than one mind and one sex. . . .
From the masculine tone of *Jane Eyre*, it might pass altogether as
the composition of a man, were it not for some unconscious
feminine peculiarities, which the strongest-minded woman that
ever aspired after manhood cannot suppress. These peculiarities
refer not only to elaborate descriptions of dress, and the minutiae
of the sick-chamber, but to various superficial refinements of

feeling in regard to the external relations of the sex. It is true that the noblest and best representations of female character have been produced by men; but there are niceties of thought and emotion in a woman's mind which often escape unawares from a female writer. [Note here the contrast between the conscious creation of a female character by a male artist, and the unwitting self-revelation of the female writer.] There are numerous examples of these in *Jane Eyre*. The leading characteristic of the novel, however, and the secret of its charm, is the clear, distinct, decisive style of its representation of character, manners, and scenery; and this continually suggests a male mind." Moreover, "when the admirable Mr. Rochester appears, and the profanity, brutality, and slang of the misanthropic profligate give their torpedo shocks to the nervous system,—and especially when we are favored with more than one scene given to the exhibition of mere animal appetite, and to courtship after the manner of kangaroos and the heroes of Dryden's plays,—we are gallant enough to detect the hand of a gentleman in the composition." (Gentleman!)

But a *Graham's* reviewer, believing Currer Bell to be a woman, had no trouble seeing that Rochester was a woman's creation. "The authoress of *Jane Eyre* has drawn in Rochester an unnatural character, and she has done it from an ignorance of the inward condition of mind which immorality such as his either springs from or produces. The ruffian . . . she knows only verbally, so to speak. . . . The authoress of *Jane Eyre* is not a Byron, but a talented woman, who, in her own sphere of thought and observation, is eminently trustworthy and true, but out of it hardly rises above the conception of a boarding-school Miss in her teens"; the character of Rochester is "romantic humbug" (May 1847). Given the reproaches leveled in the 1840s against Bulwer and Harrison Ainsworth, one cannot see why *Graham's* assumed that only women could or would create romantic humbug; nor do the reviewers consider the possibility that his character was not supposed to be real but was *meant* for the sort of romantic daydream figure that many women enjoy so much (to judge by the popularity of the "gothic romances" of today, works whose heroes women *never* mistake for real men). It is interesting, in any event, that the character of Rochester was taken as brutal but true when the author was thought to be a man, as silly and soft when the author was thought to be a woman. Then, in another odd twist of argument, *Graham's* in a May 1853 review of *Villette* complained about Brontë's portrayal of women, which it saw as a satire on the sex attributable to the woman author's own defective femininity. She is "a strong-minded woman, a hardy, self-relying egotist from the very strength of her individuality, and she has stores of vitriolic contempt and scorn for her weak sisters."

The *Literary World* equivocated in its review of *The Tenant of Wildfell Hall*, beginning its review with the masculine pronoun, allowing the author "a mind of great strength and fervor, but coarse almost to brutality"; there is an "intense vulgarity" in his very fiber that the journal wanted "American readers to recognize . . . while doing just homage to his genius." The reviewer mentioned Currer Bell's genius several times; and then, when considering the male characters, moved to the feminine pronoun: "we shrewdly suspect these books to be written by some gifted and retired woman, whose principal notions of men are derived from other books; or who, taking some walking automaton of her native village for a model, throws in certain touches of rascality, of uncouthness or boisterousness, to make her lay figures animated and, as she thinks, masculine" (August 12, 1848). The interesting point here is that the term "genius" disappears when the writer becomes a woman.

"We hope," a *Sartain's* reviewer said, that *Wuthering Heights* "will be proven to have been written by another hand than that which wrote *Jane Eyre*, but if the authorship *should* be identical, it will at least settle the much-discussed question of sex. No *woman* could write *Wuthering Heights*" (June 1848). Reviewing *Shirley*, *Sartain's* commented that the question of the author's sex "seems to us no more settled than before. We read the first half of the volume with almost a conviction that the writer was a man. There was everywhere manifest a knowledge of affairs, an intimate acquaintance with the outdoor world, such as is certainly very rare among writers of the gentler sex. . . . Yet as we proceed towards the close of the volume, and see the familiar, the truly wonderful acquaintance which the author has with the female character, we are half disposed to doubt the foregone conclusion" (February 1850). Most amusing of all, the *American Review*, absolutely certain of the male authorship of *Wuthering Heights*, criticized the author for his evident ignorance of women: "he dissects to you their characters and finds out motives for them which they never dreamed of. He fancies he understands them perfectly, all the while you are quite sure he is mistaken. . . . He looks upon women as a refined sort of men, and they therefore are unable to give him their confidence" (February 1850). One month later, a critic in the same journal who knew that the author was a woman expatiated on the ignorance of the male character manifest in *Wuthering Heights:* women "see nothing of men in their struggles with the world. Our manners with them are trimmed."

This particular comedy came to an end with the publication, following Charlotte Brontë's death, of her biography, written by Elizabeth Gaskell. But it ended in an ironic fashion, for the mission of the biography—in which it certainly succeeded on this side of the Atlantic—was to define Brontë as a true woman and force a reading of her works that made their womanliness manifest. As the *North American* wrote in October 1857, "those who have been accustomed to regard Currer Bell only as an author who has dared to speak on certain topics with a plainness somewhat unusual among the fashionable lady-writers, and have consequently assailed her for coarseness and immorality, will stand abashed before this record of womanly virtue and tender affection." The coarseness and brutality of the characters no longer rose either from a crude male imagination or from female inexperience, but sprang from the horrible actualities of life in the English moor country as perceived by a deeply sensitive woman. And note the cutting reference to "fashionable lady-writers": the reviewer was using one woman's work to denigrate the achievement of others.

The reviewer responses to Charlotte and Emily Brontë make it seem that they had no real notion of how to tell a male from a female writer, did not know what constituted the very distinction they were certain was innate, inevitable, and—in all other circumstances than the literary—absolutely plain. In fact, the only criterion they could finally think to apply was that of special knowledge: women knew about clothes and sickrooms, men knew about hunting and politics. It is not, then, merely that these books sent out mixed signals, but that the supposed textual differences were in fact the product of prior knowledge and matters outside the text. The woman author in the text was, after all, no real creature but a selection of evidence after the fact.

13

Conclusion

No sooner was the novel invented, it seems, than the review followed. So closely connected have been the form and the commentary on it—both being products of a print culture—that it does not seem extreme to say that the novel has responded to discourse about it almost as much as reviews have responded to the novels they reviewed. In the United States before the Civil War, especially after 1840, there was in existence a broad-ranging and widely circulated discourse about the novel, whose contours I have attempted to describe in this book. It was an ambitious discourse, in the sense that it took as its field the entire corpus of existing novels produced in all European nations. Nobody writing or reading a novel in America in these years could have been ignorant of it, for it appeared, among other places, in those journals whose readership over the decades included millions of literate Americans. It was, moreover, the chief extant discourse about novels, since academic discussion of them, except very rarely on the Lyceum circuit and then only with a very few novelists, did not yet exist. An academic history of fiction had been written in England before 1810, but it treated the novel only in a few concluding paragraphs.

The first step in assessing any long work of fiction was to ask whether it was a novel—which is to say, the question of genre took priority over all other ways a text might be interrogated. The procedure for answering this question was simple: one searched for the presence or absence of a unifying plot. In the absence of such a feature, critics would relegate the work to a marginal or mixed genre, of which the series of loosely connected

sketches was probably the most common. In all but a few instances, these tangential genres were viewed as artistically inferior to the novel; and the likelihood of their success, given the
public appetite for novels, was assumed to be much less than that
of even a crudely executed novel.

The question of membership in the genre satisfied, critics
went on to discuss a variety of formal features of the work at
hand, all following from its status as a novel. Reviewers applied
genre expectations with some latitude, aware that the genre was a
set of rules derived from a body of existing texts, sensitive to the
novel as a historical form changing even as they wrote about it,
and greatly interested in the distinguishing qualities of the individual author's canon. In addition, as novels proliferated over the
years, reviewers developed a lexicon of subgenres. Reviewers
worked mainly with four broad types: domestic fiction, subsuming local color; highly wrought fiction, subsuming urban novels;
the historical novel; and the advocacy novel. The term romance
did not refer to any agreed-on subgenre and was usually employed simply as a synonym for novel. American novels, identifiable by their setting, were singled out for praise by American
reviewers—perhaps they were overpraised—but no subgenre of
the novel was thought characteristic of the nation, nor is a theory
that American novels should be different from other novels beyond their American setting anywhere to be found. The invention of a subgenre called the romance with specifically American fictional properties is a later critical development; it is a
concept alien to the practice and production of the times it is now
used to analyze.

Novels were generally evaluated according to the artistic execution of formal features, the picture of life provided by the
novel, and the interest achieved by the work. Of these three, the
overwhelmingly central one for novel criticism was the matter of
interest. Indeed, I would argue that both formal, artistic excellence and verisimilitude or pictures of life were, during all of this
period, criteria subordinate to that of interest, ultimately viewed
in terms of contribution to or detraction from this final end of the
novel. The unitary plot was viewed simultaneously as a formal
structure by which all parts of the novel were integrated and
through which they were related, and as a psychological structure designed to arouse, sustain, and finally satisfy the reader's

interest. Reviewers described interest as a powerful human experience, involving a greatly heightened and sustained attention, an absorption in the text amounting (as many wrote) to "enchainment" and accompanied at times by an excitement that was almost "painful."

Thus, although at various points I have used the words "pleasure" and "enjoyment" as synonyms for "interest," this last is the important term because it distinguished the *type* of enjoyment or pleasure a reader experienced from a novel. That is, there are all sorts of pleasure and all kinds of enjoyment; that which was characteristic of the novel was the pleasure or enjoyment of a sustained interest. Such human psychological characteristics as sympathy and curiosity were put powerfully into play in the reading of a novel, and so long as the reader was interested, the novel had to be judged a success. The more interesting, too, the more popular. *Uncle Tom's Cabin*, for example, was probably the most interesting novel of the era, for many reasons. The characters were enormously sympathetic or repellent, and their fates were in question from the first page to the last. The adventures that befell them were exciting, life threatening, deeply pathetic, occasionally funny. And while the author speechified shamelessly, she always entered the narrative on her characters' behalf, so that her indignation formally emphasized the emotional responses the story was calling for. And contributory interest was provided by the descriptions of so many regions of the nation and the treatment of a crucial contemporary political issue.

Interest, though not identical to the "willing suspension of disbelief," certainly demanded something like it from readers. This could always be revoked, however, which is why plot achieved its dominant position as the defining formal quality of the novel: because interest derived more from plot than from any other aspect. And it is in terms of relation to plot rather than to an external reality that such matters as "probability" need to be understood. An improbably plotted narrative, or so reviewers thought, was simply not as interesting as a probable one. The public rejection of novels of the supernatural, their interest in stories about ordinary people, seemed to support this contention. The highly wrought novel intensified, but did not abandon, ordinary life.

Reviewers, according to their own account, parted company

with readers in introducing a second criterion: novels should *also* be "pictures of life." Eager to push the novel in the direction of high art as they understood it—and the terms of their understanding were such as to make high art a matter of expressing general human truths—they argued that truth and interest were entirely compatible. But finding pictures of nature in novels involved a distancing from the work that inevitably brought into play a different sort of interest, a meditative or intellectual interest rather than any passionate engagement of reader with text. I do not mean to suggest that the exciting interest was not intellectual. On the contrary, I have tried to show (chapter 4) that the reader's mental faculties were fired up and engrossed by reading a novel; but they were directed toward the construal of plot, not values. Values, rather, were aspects of presentation that enabled a reader to invest sympathy properly, to identify protagonist and antagonist. As an intellectual matter, of course, this is very different from extracting themes or constructing (or deconstructing) a work's value system. But I am not convinced that it is inferior.

Reviewers of the earlier age knew they were looking for a different kind of interest in novels, but they did not recognize that the success of their campaign might split (or further split) the novel-reading audience beyond recuperation, as seems to have happened in our own time. Their crucial choice of a way to make the novel better rises from the essentially didactic nature of literary culture in America and England at the time, a characteristic we continue to exhibit, given that this is the culture that created literary criticism.

The difference between these earlier reviewers and the academic critic now is that the reviewer then thought of the "truth" of the novel as an increment beyond its form, while the critic today asserts that its truth (or falsity, or meaning) inheres in and constitutes its form. Given this difference, the critic then could continue to accept the novel's form as a pleasure-producing entity while carrying out his self-appointed mission of making it something more. The critic now cannot. Now an enchaining interest—an intense pleasure—has vanished as a respectable reason for reading novels. It is only fair to add that, as the novel is part of the culture that discourses about it, the creation of such interest has also mostly vanished as a respectable reason for writing novels. Hence the gap between serious (elite) and frivolous (popular) novels is vast. In critical theory of yesteryear the reader could choose whether or not to be instructed—take or leave the novel's truth while still enjoying its story. Things are much more momentous and serious for the novel reader of today. The good novel, being nothing now but a meaningful (or meaningless) form, cannot produce simple pleasure unless it is misread or read naively. The "good read," all agree, is not a good novel.

As Gerald Graff writes (in *Literature against Itself* [Chicago: University of Chicago Press, 1979], 161), "what chiefly distinguishes the elite forms is precisely that they have something serious to say." But that is not all: they have something to say that is difficult to find, for the assumption is that nothing serious is easy. The work ethic has been attached to what was formerly recreation, and it is difficult to estimate how much this may have come about because novels are the source of real work—paid work—for so many literary academics and hence need to be objects that can be worked on. Elite is now a subgenre and can *only* be read for meaning: "if one is looking for *real* freedom from allegorical or thematic meanings . . . one should go . . . to works that are so innocent of meaning that they do not need to refuse it— dime novels, detective stories, Jacqueline Susann novels, comic books"; these are "entertainments" that "achieve imperviousness to interpretation without effort" (Graff, pp. 160–161). The activity of the reader hypothesized in contemporary reader-response theory, busy constructing and testing meanings; the activity of a traditional Graffian reader, busy extracting the serious truth content of a fiction; the activity of a poststructuralist, busy taking meanings apart—all of these are qualitatively different from the activity of the engaged reader cooperating with the novelist in the game of aims and obstacles that constituted the structural play of the novel's plot, unfolding itself in novel time. Interpretation, always an interesting and important activity to a small group of people, is not what the tremendous success of the novel in the nineteenth century was based upon.

Of course, novel criticism today is fragmented. There remain magazine and newspaper reviews of new fiction that carry on a method of assessment based on formal concerns: plot, characters, setting. My comments above refer to academic criticism, a mode that scarcely existed in the historical era I examine. The genre of academic criticism of current and older novels validates the academic setting; that is, it proves novels are texts that require teaching. It would be embarrassingly frivolous or superficial to set students to writing plot summaries rather than essays on the serious themes of, say, *The Sound and the Fury;* but who says what is and what is not serious? Are we teaching novels or are we using them to teach something else—seriousness?

It is important to recognize, too, that to define elite novels according to whether they have something serious "to say" is to erase genre. Many elite novels are artistically inept, and many popular novels are serious (overly so, some academics would claim). When we read past genre for meaning, we are deprived of the means of assessing an artistic achievement as such. And disallowing genre, meaning- or interpretation-centered criticism cannot investigate the degree to which readers are responding to the formal properties of the work. As a result such criticism assumes about people's reading habits the antiformal bias that it actually manifests itself: assuming that people read fiction for truths and finding no truths in the fiction they read, it concludes that they read for lies. It does not consider that they may read for the interest and pleasure of a reading experience, the fun of reading a novel.

That the populace once read novels of all kinds also serves, I believe, to put into question our view of the specifically *American* situation in antebellum America and thus impinges on our historical (as my comments above impinge on our theoretical) formulations of the novel's story in this country. It is clear to me that the novel's story in this country, where readers are concerned, cannot be confined to the purely native product. In American literary history we seem to have been involving ourselves in the circular enterprise of looking for works that accord with our (highly tendentious) idea of "American" as opposed to something not American (something that is usually a piece of knowledge, a "statement," about our special situation as Americans), devising a history of those works alone, and then acting as though this history were the history of both American literature (literature written by Americans) and literature in America (literature as received by Americans), when "in fact" it is not one or the other. This "history" enables us to imagine Hawthorne and Melville working inside a cultural envelope in which nobody liked and nobody read novels. My study uncovers a different culture, one where their troubles might have derived from their decisions not to write, or their inability to write, novels in an era that would have accepted almost anything if it came in that much-loved form. I would like to think that this book will make it impossible for us any longer to maintain that the literary climate in antebellum America was hostile to fiction.

Bibliographical Note

Books and articles dealing with the "Americanness" of American literature are legion; I think it safe to say that every major general work on our literature as a whole and on our authors incorporates that stance. Books and articles reflecting on the status of the novel as an instrument for producing interpretations are also legion, and the ease with which the approach carries over from a didactic journal like *College English* to an advanced theoretical statement in *Diacritics* indicates, to my mind, the continuity of the critical activity. In the list that follows I note only books and articles with a historical focus on the period I study.

Baym, Nina. *Woman's Fiction: A Guide to Novels by and about Women in America, 1820–1870*. Ithaca, N.Y.: Cornell University Press, 1978.

Bell, Michael Davitt. *Hawthorne and the Historical Romance of New England*. Princeton, N.J.: Princeton University Press, 1971.

Charvat, William. *Literary Publishing in America: 1790–1850*. Philadelphia: University of Pennsylvania Press, 1959.

Charvat, William. *The Profession of Authorship in America, 1800–1870: The Papers of William Charvat*. Edited by Matthew J. Bruccoli. Columbus: Ohio State University Press, 1968. (Charvat discusses the beginnings of professionalism, the conditions of authorship, the relation between literary economics and literary history, and other contextualizing matters that are generally ignored in text-centered and major-author-centered literary histories. While he states emphatically that "we err, as historians, in allowing the taste of the modern reader to nullify the taste of the nineteenth-century reader" and complains about the "persistent neglect of the reader as a force in literature" [p. 290], he also objects to using reviewers as a substitute for readers, believing that the reviewer is not a good guide to reception because he may have been simply puffing and was at best just another reader, so that there is no necessary relation between critical response and reader response [pp. 291–92]. In framing my arguments I have been sensitive to Charvat's objection and have tried to read the reviews for what they tell us directly or by implication about readers whose preferences differed from the reviewer's. The matter of puffery is not so significant, because so long as the reviewer advanced reasons for his praise, criteria and expectations can be inferred.)

Douglas, Ann. *The Feminization of American Culture*. New York: Viking, 1977.

Hart, James D. *The Popular Book*. Berkeley: University of California Press, 1951.

Jones, Howard Mumford. "American Comment on George Sand, 1837–1848." *American Literature* 3(1932):389–407. (Jones takes the reviewer reception to equal the reader reception despite the clear evidence that Sand's popularity was precisely what was calling out the reviewer's commentary. In addition, Jones's extracts stress the Victorian American disapproval in the reviews without noting the constant qualifying acknowledgment of her genuis.)

Martin, Terence. *The Instructed Vision: Scottish Common Sense Philosophy and the Origins of American Fiction*. Bloomington: Indiana University Press, 1961. (Argues for a distinct American fictional genre, the romance, deriving from the would-be fictionist's sense of American hostility to fiction. The evidence is taken chiefly from early antifiction statements in orations, graduation addresses, and the like. An invaluable book for the earliest periods of American literary history but one that does not follow the story into the 1830s and after, when fiction triumphed despite this early hostility.)

Miller, Perry. *The Raven and the Whale: The War of Words and Wits in the Era of Poe and Melville*. New York: Harcourt, Brace and World, 1956. (A melodramatic account of New York City journalistic rivalries with emphasis on American literary nationalism and Melville's career.)

Mills, Nicolaus. *American and English Fiction in the Nineteenth Century: An Antigenre Critique and Comparison*. Bloomington: Indiana University Press, 1973. (Argues persuasively against the parceling out of novel and romance to England and America respectively: "It is impossible to accept as adequate the general assertion that American fiction is distinguishable because it veers 'more freely' than English fiction, 'toward mythic, allegorical, and symbolistic forms'" [p. 17]. Mills's analysis, however, is based on thematic rather than formal concerns, taking fiction as constituted by its meaning: the implications of a historical vision, the treatment of a religious dilemma, and so on.)

Mott, Frank Luther. *A History of American Magazines.* Vol. 1: *1740–1850.* New York: Appleton, 1930. Vol. 2: *1851–1870.* Cambridge: Harvard University Press, 1938. (An invaluable resource for a project of this kind, and useful to all students of American life.)

Mott, Frank Luther. *Golden Multitudes.* New York: Macmillan, 1947.

Petter, Henri. *The Early American Novel.* Columbus: Ohio State University Press, 1971.

Pritchard, John Paul. *Literary Wise Men of Gotham: Criticism in New York, 1815–1860.* Baton Rouge: Louisiana State University Press, 1963. (A study of literary criticism in New York City magazines, designed in part as a corrective to Miller. Chapter 3, pp. 61–82, is entitled "The Art and Practice of Fiction." Pritchard observes that "all reputable fiction was subsumed under the term novel" and that "in discussion it is rarely possible to discover whether the distinction between novel and romance was active in the writer's mind" [pp. 62, 64]. He writes that reviewers, though showing a "preference for profitable pleasure as the end of literature," found that in the novel "the pleasurable ends generally dominated," though there was an increasing stress on profit in the era; he also finds, as a related matter, the novel of character being stressed and increasingly thought of as a higher class of fiction than the novel of pure plot [p. 82]. He identifies and describes individual reviewers.

Reynolds, David S. *Faith in Fiction: The Emergence of Religious Literature in America.* Cambridge: Harvard University Press, 1981.

Smith, Henry Nash. *Democracy and the Novel: Popular Resistance to Classic American Authors.* New York: Oxford University Press, 1978. (An antipopular approach to the dilemmas of "serious" authors in the American tradition.)

Spencer, Benjamin T. *The Quest for Nationality: An American Literary Campaign.* Syracuse, N.Y.: Syracuse University Press, 1957. (Makes clear that the movement peaked in the late 1830s and never centered on the novel. Accepts a distinction between the novel and the romance and observes the role of women authors in fiction, albeit patronizingly: "In their preoccupation with the detail of their own narrow locales, these female writers undoubtedly contributed to an indigenous domestic realism; yet in their general concern for fashion and sentiment per se they also evolved what was frequently called a 'milliner's literature'" [p. 217]. Spencer has a usefully broad sense of the makeup of a nationalist consensus, in contrast to the romance-based theorists, finding groups of novelists including Young Americans, scribbling women, transcendentalists, Knickerbockers, romancers, and incipient realists disagreeing on literary practice but still moving toward "a single objective, a literature consonant with what they believed to be America's peculiar destiny" [p. 218].)

Tebbel, John. *A History of Book Publishing in the United States.* 3 vols. New York: R. R. Bowker, 1972–1978.

Wright, Lyle H. *American Fiction, 1851–1865: A Contribution toward a Bibliography.* San Marino, Calif.: Huntington Library, 1965.

Wright, Lyle H. *American Fiction, 1774–1850: A Contribution toward a Bibliography.* San Marino, Calif.: Huntington Library, 1969.

Index

281

Library of Congress Cataloging in Publication Data

Baym, Nina.
  Novels, readers, and reviewers.

  Bibliography: p.
  Includes index.
  1. American fiction—19th century—History and criticism   2. Criticism—United States—History—19th century.   3. Book reviewing—History—19th century.   4. Books and reading—United States—History—19th century.   I. Title.
PS377.B37   1984   813'.3'09   84-5033
ISBN 0-8014-1709-0 (alk. paper)
ISBN 0-8014-9466-4 (pbk.)